MANCHESTER'S
RADICAL
MAYOR

MANCHESTER'S RADICAL MAYOR

ABEL HEYWOOD

THE MAN WHO BUILT
THE TOWN HALL

JOANNA M. WILLIAMS

Dedicated to Manchester, our much loved city.

First published 2017
Reprinted 2024

The History Press
97 St George's Place,
Cheltenham, Gloucestershire, GL50 3QB
www.thehistorypress.co.uk

British Library Cataloguing in Publication Data.
A catalogue record for this book is available from the British Library.

ISBN 978 0 7509 8408 9

Typesetting and origination by The History Press
Printed by TJ Books Limited, Padstow, Cornwall

1

Contents

About the Author

JOANNA M. WILLIAMS is a native of the Manchester area and studied History at the University of Manchester at undergraduate and postgraduate level. After lecturing for the Department of Extra-Mural Studies, she taught history at Altrincham Grammar School for Girls. Her fascination with the nineteenth century stemmed from her sixth-form teaching, and she has gone on to achieve a lifelong ambition by publishing this, her first biography.

Acknowledgements

I would like to acknowledge the generous and patient help of the staff at The History Press, Manchester Central Library, the People's History Museum, Manchester Art Gallery, John Rylands University of Manchester Library, the National Archives, the University of Reading, University College London, Harris Manchester College, Oxford, and the Middle Temple, London. I am indebted particularly to Andy Haymes and Manchester City Council, Rev. Dr Ann Peart and Cross Street chapel, Manchester and Derrick Murdie at Bowdon parish church. I am also grateful for the support and information provided by Nicholas J. Manning, Sue Nichols, Judith Webb, Pam Dawes and especially Julia Piercy and the Charlesworth family. The kind encouragement of Terry Wyke, Brian Maidment and Martin Hewitt was invaluable, particularly at the start of this project. I would like to thank all those students I taught at Altrincham Grammar School for Girls, who shared and enhanced my enthusiasm for the nineteenth century. I appreciate enormously the vision and generosity of Living Ventures in sponsoring the publication of this biography and wholeheartedly thank Jeremy Roberts for his commitment to the project. And finally, this book would not have been possible without the support of my friends and family, especially Ken.

List of Figures

Abbreviations

CJ   *City Jackdaw*
CRO   Cheshire Record Office
JRUL   John Rylands University Library, Manchester
MC   *Manchester Courier*
MCL   Manchester Central Library
MG   *Manchester Guardian*
MT   *Manchester Times*
NS   *Northern Star*
PMG   *Poor Man's Guardian*

Foreword

Living Ventures is delighted to sponsor the biography of Abel Heywood, creating a new bond with Manchester's rich history. We have already forged strong links with the Victorian city in reinventing and rejuvenating the old Liberal Reform Club as our splendid new restaurant bar, Grand Pacific. Its colonial and ocean themes chime with Manchester's dominant place in global trade in former eras, when its cottons clothed the world, and Britain's huge merchant fleet returned with the products of Empire: tea, sugar, spices, exotic fruits.

The ornate and opulent Reform Club, designed by Salomons, was opened in 1871 to a triumphant fanfare. Earl Granville, Foreign Secretary in Gladstone's great reforming first ministry, was the illustrious speaker at the celebrations. It became the home of the Liberal elite of the city, who had dominated its government. And so it continued, hosting others who have gained their place in history, notably a young Winston Churchill, and David Lloyd George, who was its president on two occasions. It became a popular place for wining and dining not only for its members, but also for others, including the Masons, Manchester High School for Girls and the *Manchester Guardian*. In just one year, no less than twenty-seven tons of meat was consumed, along with 18,000 eggs and thirty-three tons of potatoes! And all this provided by a dedicated staff of fifty-three men and twelve women.

Abel Heywood played his part in the life of the old Club. He was one of the ninety-nine guarantors for its construction, and it became in his later years a 'home from home' where he sat at the 'Corporation table' at the centre of a whirlwind of debate and discussion. A large part of club life was the Billiard Room, with its five huge tables, where exhibition games were played by champions of the day in the inter-war years. Abel was not a devotee of the sport, however, and preferred to participate in the political aspects of club life. And he was feted by the members on several occasions, not least on the opening of the new Town Hall in 1877.

Now Grand Pacific continues the Reform Club's aim of offering excellent hospitality to its guests. The themes of gracious living and travel across the world to far-flung lands, combined with a place for relaxation, conversation and sociability are pursued in a modern context. Service still features significantly in the aims of the establishment, and the original decor is preserved and enhanced. The menus reflect the impact of Empire on Britain's culinary knowledge, combining the traditional with the exotic, in particular symbolised by the colonies' most sought-after and prestigious of fruits, the pineapple. The old Reform Club has come a long way, not least in welcoming women on equal terms with men, but Abel Heywood would find much that is familiar in the ethos and old world charm of Grand Pacific.

Jeremy Roberts
CEO, Living Ventures Group
www.livingventures.com

LIVING VENTURES

Introduction

'Ring out the false, ring in the true.'
(From Alfred, Lord Tennyson's *In Memoriam*, part CVI)

As the twenty-first century citizens of Manchester hurry to and fro, intent on going about their business, they will hear a great bell chime the hour from the imposing tower of the Town Hall. 'Great Abel' weighs over a mighty eight tons; it is the largest of all the bells in the tower, which were named after members of the city council in 1877 when the Town Hall was officially opened as a symbol of Manchester's wealth and greatness in the world. The bell was so-called after Abel Heywood, who was mayor in 1877.

Today, relatively few people have heard of Abel Heywood. Yet he was known in his time as 'the Father of the Corporation' and Manchester would not be the city it is today without his tireless efforts to turn it into a gracious, prosperous and healthy metropolis where its people could live with pride. As a young political radical, he was ahead of his time and espoused ideals which most of us hold without a thought today, but which in the early nineteenth century were considered by many to be revolutionary: an uncensored and accessible press, universal suffrage, free and compulsory education, and an end to poverty and need. Some historians claim that although he started out as a radical, he eventually became a figure of the Liberal establishment as the political and social climate around him evolved. However, he himself would have contested this, and it can certainly be contended that he continued to move ahead of society in its thinking; his early espousal of the cause of political emancipation for the poor and women is a case in point, and his commitment to the interests of the working classes never wavered.

Abel Heywood's biggest claim to fame for the citizens of Manchester, however, is his role in the development of Albert Square and the construction of the 'new' Town Hall (1868–77). In a speech of 1888 he said that he had supervised minutely the construction of the edifice: 'Day by day, I saw this glorious building rise, until every pinnacle was complete…' Indeed, he laid the pinnacle stone of the spire on 4 December 1875 and when the building was opened nearly two years later, he officiated at the ceremony, and was honoured by a procession numbering perhaps 50,000 representing all the trades of the city. The whole experience was clearly a source of huge pride and satisfaction to him, despite the widely noted absence of Queen Victoria at the inauguration.

Yet Abel had roots which were far from the illustrious reputation of his later years; he began his working life at the age of 9, and received an elementary education in Sunday schools. Espousing the virtues of 'self-help', his was the remarkable story of a man who exploited the opportunities of the 'Age of Improvement'; not only did he become an outspoken social crusader, he also forged a career at the heart of local politics, and was a hard-headed and enterprising businessman as a printer, publisher and wholesaler of books and journals, as well as developing a very successful wallpaper business. Abel was remarkable in that he rose to the top of civic society as mayor on two occasions. He even aspired, albeit unsuccessfully, to represent Manchester in Parliament. He was also notable in that he achieved all this it seems without ever losing sight of his working-class origins.

Due to a lack of personal papers, there are episodes in his life which are difficult to interpret, such as his seeming betrayal of his Chartist comrades in 1840.[1] And for reasons which are not fully clear, he seriously upset the veteran radical, Samuel Bamford, who was unusual in expressing a vehement dislike of his former ally. Yet in public Abel was never quiet in the face of what he considered to be injustice; he was regularly on his feet at meetings, regaling his hearers with his views on all manner of current issues, and has even been accused of verbosity and long-windedness. He was certainly often blunt and vehement in his pronouncements, and did not suffer fools gladly. His principles were tempered by a pragmatic realism, and his rejection of any kind of violent protest, at a time when other radicals believed it was unavoidable, earned him respect from members of all social classes.

Although Abel is not commemorated by any statue, but by a much more unassuming bust in the Town Hall, and his grave in Philip's Park Cemetery is low key and plain, he was nevertheless very proud of his achievements. Late in his life, in 1889, the council commissioned a full-length portrait by H.T. Munns which still hangs in the Town Hall. Contemporaries agreed that his significance should not be forgotten, and in 1891 he was given Manchester's ultimate accolade, the Freedom of the City, in recognition of his achievements.

For a window into the fundamental aspirations of Abel Heywood and his contemporaries, there is no better place to turn than to Tennyson's great poem, *In Memoriam*. The choice of quotation inscribed on his bell, 'Ring out the false, ring in the true' provides a glimpse into the best of the spirit of the age and of the man.

In the Shadow of Peterloo: Genesis of a Radical

Manchester, 'Shock City'

Britain in the early nineteenth century was a ferment of economic and social upheaval, and nowhere was this more true than in Manchester, the 'shock city of the industrial revolution', to cite Asa Briggs' dramatic description.[1] His account of Victorian Manchester makes it clear that the city was regarded by contemporaries as unique in its dreadfulness, dirt and disease, and also in its stupendous wealth and cutting-edge technologies; many visitors were enchanted by the wonders of its business, the novelty of huge factories and warehouses, and the marvels of steam power and mass workforces. This was all the more terrifying because Manchester was the centre of an increasing and massive working-class population which flooded into the town in search of employment in the new industries. The small, but growing, middle classes found the immigrants alien and threatening; they were regarded as almost a different species, from the lowest levels of human society.

Those who had the governance of the city, and the country at large, were learning (or some would argue failing to learn) as they went along how to develop a new social and economic system. Manchester had the disadvantage of a local government which was still based on the structures inherited from the Middle Ages; the Lord of the Manor ruled through a Court Leet and Borough Reeve alongside the Parish Vestry, and from 1792 Police Commissioners were elected by only the wealthiest 2.5 per cent of the inhabitants. Such a system was totally inadequate for the task of running a major metropolis.

Despite its material success, Manchester was still renowned for its squalor, smoke and slums. Besides the Cotton Exchange it boasted few buildings of note, apart from the Collegiate Church (thirteenth to fifteenth century), the Portico Library (1806) and the Royal Manchester Institution (1823), notable exceptions in a town of factories throbbing with machinery and smoke-blackened warehouses.

The poverty the workers endured was legendary and grinding even for those in work; under-employment and low pay were common, not to mention unemployment in times of slump. They lived in jerry-built back-to-back hovels, thrown up without any kind of sanitation or regulation by landlords looking to profit from the need of newly arrived workers for cheap accommodation; the very poorest made do with the cellars of such housing, existing without furniture, barely fed and clothed. Not surprisingly, disease was rife. Typhoid, dysentery and most notably tuberculosis were endemic, and from 1831–32 there were also epidemics of cholera. Mortality was horrifyingly high; Edwin Chadwick's investigation, published in 1842, stated that the average working-class life expectancy in the town was seventeen years; 60 per cent of the babies born in Manchester died before they reached the age of 5.

Contemporaries noted with some misgivings how the 'better sort' were moving out to the suburbs as early as the 1830s, and a typical pattern of concentric habitation was established. At the centre were factories, workshops and workers' houses where the density and mortality were high, the most notorious of these being Angel Meadow and Little Ireland near Deansgate. Around this core were the more salubrious areas of lower density and mortality rates, providing housing for the middle class.

Yet even so, in the early nineteenth century Manchester was still surrounded by rural Lancashire, and the inhabitants were within fairly easy reach of the countryside if they had the energy and leisure to get there after their twelve- to sixteen-hour working day. Kersal Moor to the north-west was the site for outings and picnics, not to mention horse-racing, and at times of political upheaval also open-air mass meetings. Moreover, there were open areas even closer to the centre, most notably St Peter's Fields and Granby Row Fields.

Perhaps the French visitor, Alexis de Tocqueville, best summed up the ambivalence of Manchester in 1835: 'The greatest stream of human industry flows out to fertilise the whole world. From this filthy sewer pure gold flows. Here humanity attains its most complete development and its most brutish; here civilisation works its miracles, and civilised man is turned back into savage.'[2]

It is hardly surprising that Manchester in the early 1800s was characterised by serious social and political discontent. This was manifested in the eyes of many contemporaries by the upheavals which followed the end of the Napoleonic Wars, most notably the event on 16 August 1819 which became known as 'The Peterloo Massacre'. The horrifying events of that day are well documented, though the accounts disagree. What seems clear is that a peaceful and unarmed crowd of perhaps 60,000 men, women and children who had gathered not only from Manchester itself but also from the surrounding cotton towns, were attacked by sabre-wielding Yeoman Cavalry. This was on the orders of the magistrates, who had given instructions for the arrest of the chief radical speaker, Henry Hunt, and the dispersal of the meeting. The volunteer Manchester and Cheshire Yeoman Cavalry, led by Tory cotton master Hugh Hornby Birley and comprising factory owners, shopkeepers, merchants and other such 'respectable' citizens, bore much of the responsibility for the death (in the figures of the official report of 1820) of eleven people and the injury of 400. To contemporaries, the events were hugely traumatic;

the 'massacre' coloured the attitudes of radicals in Manchester for the following thirty years or more, and was cited by protesters in the Chartist movement and in the general strike of 1842. Alan Kidd calls this 'arguably the single most important day in Manchester's history'.

Certainly, in the short term there were waves of after-shock in Manchester. The city was tense and mobs attacked property periodically, drawing a violent response from the military; a rioter in New Cross was killed on the evening of the massacre for an attack on a shop whose owner had been a special constable and had paraded a radical flag as a trophy. On 17 August the Exchange remained closed and artillery was prepared for a (falsely) rumoured march on the town by 50,000 armed men from Oldham and Middleton. New Cross continued to be disturbed; on 20 August there was a battle between locals and the cavalry.

Young Abel

It was into this ferment of economic distress and radical upheaval that Abel Heywood came as a little boy of 9 in 1819 when his mother, Betty, brought her four children to Manchester in the hope of finding work. Although Abel does not appear to have made anything in his later life of the wider political significance of the date of his arrival, he certainly knew people who had been present in the crowd in St Peter's Field, notably Samuel Bamford and James Scholefield, and would have heard their stories of the terrible experiences at Peterloo. An example of how this event echoed down the years can be found on Monday 4 November 1839 at the 'Radical Tea Drinking' to commemorate the birthday of Henry Hunt at the Carpenters' Hall in Manchester. Abel was chosen as chairman, and the meeting was introduced by James Wheeler with these words: 'The memory of Henry Hunt should never be forgotten till the blood-stained field of Peterloo be entirely blotted out, or the death of the murdered be revenged. (Loud cheers.)'[3] It seems more than likely that Abel's political views were coloured by the collective memory of the Manchester radicals.

Abel, born on 25 February 1810, was the youngest son of John Heywood, a 'putter-out' for the local weavers, who had five children by his first wife, Margaret, and four surviving by Abel's mother Elizabeth (Betty) Hilton. Abel's twin brother, Samuel, extraordinarily born twenty-five days before him, died at the age of 6. The family lived in what was described in 1860 as 'the pretty village of Prestwich', which lay about three miles out of Manchester. John's early death left his wife struggling to bring up her children. Abel's speech of 1890 to the Liberal Reform Club referred to him as a 'strong democrat' and he claimed that his own 'Liberal' opinions 'came to him from his father'.[4] A few years after her husband's death Betty took her young family to Manchester in the hope of finding employment for them all.[5] They settled in Angel Meadow, one of the worst slum areas of Manchester, where they inhabited a 'single' house – a back-to-back dwelling of the poorest character. Abel said in 1876 that he lived there for four years, 'and at that time not a street or passage, not a place in the whole district where he lived was either paved or sewered'.[6] The area was notorious for crime and vice, and overcrowding and disease were a normal hazard of daily life.

By the time of his arrival in Manchester, young Abel had learned to read and write by attending the village Sunday school. He was presented with a Bible in his seventh year, which he still had in 1860. In 1819, when he probably began to attend the Manchester Bennett Street Sunday School, it was not quite at its peak in terms of attendance, but nevertheless boasted 140 teachers and monitors and 1,906 pupils in a new building completed the year before which was described by the social observer and journalist, Angus Reach, in 1849 as 'a vast, plain building, fully as large as an ordinary sized cotton factory, and exhibiting four long ranges of lofty windows'.[7] The teachers were generally young men and women who had themselves been scholars and were therefore of working-class background; they worked in factories and warehouses in the week. The standards they achieved were not always high, and one ex-pupil later recalled that they were 'very worthy, but illiterate laymen…'

On registering, each child was presented with a tract to remind them of their place in the social order, and of the need to show a suitably grateful attitude:

> it is by the charitable contributions of the Rich – the watchful superindendance [sic] of your Visitors – the unwearied attention of your Teachers – and the spiritual labours of your Ministers – that you have hitherto been supplied with books, with schoolrooms, with instructions.

Many Sunday schools were around this time beginning to expand their hours into weekday evenings, and on some of these occasions to teach a wider curriculum. At Bennett Street they offered in 1817 lessons in writing on Monday evening for 'upwards of 160' scholars, and on Wednesday evenings about 120 children were taught accounts and writing. The balance of the evidence seems to suggest that it was these kinds of classes which Abel attended at Bennett Street. He may also have taken advantage of other facilities offered by the Sunday school; the scholars were allowed, as a privilege, to borrow books, though the subject matter was naturally carefully controlled.

Abel took from his Sunday school experience the tools he needed to continue his education into adult life; he was literate, was committed to self-help, and was noted for his work ethic. It would have been perhaps less pleasing to the founder of the school that he now had, above all, the capacity to think for himself, a characteristic which would lead him into radical politics. Indeed, he left the school in 1825 because of a dispute with the authorities. Joseph Johnson related at length how Abel felt that he was unfairly cheated of a prize and therefore went off in high dudgeon:

I

Prizes had been announced for the discovery of parallel passages in the Old and New Testaments. Abel was quite elated at the discovery of a sentence which he was certain must obtain a prize; to his astonishment, however, another boy in a class higher in the school read out the very passage which he had with so much labour selected! When it came to his turn he could only read what had already been read. Certainly, upon no principle of justice, the prize was awarded to the first boy – his only merit over Abel being that he had the opportunity of first reading the passage. Abel could not brook this act of unfairness, and therefore left the school.

From this account, we gain a glimpse into the character of the young Abel; he was ambitious, driven to win, acutely aware of injustice, and prepared to stand up for what he believed was right in a dramatic and decisive way. He was also clearly a bright and diligent pupil with considerable intellectual ability.

At some point not long after his arrival in Manchester, Abel found employment with a Mr Worthington at his warehouse on High Street, a dealer in smallware and silk, a manufacturer of umbrellas, and father of a future prominent Manchester architect. This employment continued until Abel was in his twentieth year, when his wages had risen to 16s a week; from the age of only 14 he had been made overseer of sixty other boys, making up smallwares, and had shown his ability to manage and organise others.

The Manchester Mechanics' Institution

Abel continued his education from the age of 15 in the newly founded Manchester Mechanics' Institution. Johnson reported that he was most interested in arithmetic and mechanical drawing, and that he was always focused on practical employments – 'dreaming is a luxury in which he never indulges'.[8]

The aims of the Mechanics' Institutions, which were being founded all over Britain, were to educate factory operatives in a way which was considered appropriate by their middle-class benefactors. The middle classes, in their role as directors and honorary members, would associate with the workers in the Institution and spread their values among them, particularly those concerning political economy, the sacrosanct nature of property, and religious commitment. In fact, the membership subscription at £1 per annum was beyond the pockets of many working men. That Abel could afford this, shows that even as a teenager he was doing well, and more significantly he could see the value of investing in his own education.

Abel would have attended Institution lectures in its first home – hired rooms in Cross Street. A new building was opened on Cooper Street on 14 May 1827. Over time, the long series of twelve lectures gave way to shorter series, or even single lectures. The lecturers were impressively well-qualified; they included Fellows of the Royal Society, actors (notably William Macready, who came to give a reading of *Macbeth*), composers, painters and architects, travellers and missionaries, reformers and campaigners, experts on anatomy and public health, and phrenologists. Of interest perhaps especially to Abel, in view of his calling, was the talk of the printer Edward Cowper. Some lecturers were local supporters, such as Samuel Greg who was especially known for his model factory and village at Styal in Cheshire; William Gaskell, husband of the famous author Elizabeth Gaskell, spoke in his capacity as minister of the Unitarian Cross Street chapel; John Dalton, Manchester's most famous scientist, gave five lectures on meteorology and one on atomic theory in 1835–36. It is very likely that Abel also availed himself of the library of the Institution; the number of books issued to members rose quickly and in 1835 had reached twenty-five per member per year. However, any discussion of potentially subversive topics, such as history, politics and religion, was strictly forbidden.

In the later 1820s there was a serious and successful challenge to the management structure of the Institution and to the control of the wealthy. Abel Heywood was one of the leaders of this challenge. In 1824, the management and property of the Institution had been vested in the honorary members, who paid large annual (one guinea) or life subscriptions (ten guineas or more). Clearly, men with such financial means were going to be of the employing class, and despite suggestions from the head of the London Mechanics' Institution, Lord Brougham, that workers should play a part in the government of the Institution, they clung on to power for the sake of 'stability and permanence' and said disparagingly of the ordinary subscribers or members that 'If they came for instruction, they were, of course, incompetent to manage.'

The subscribers tried to have a say in September 1828, in proposals signed by thirty-seven of them, including Abel Heywood and his brother John. They demanded at the resulting meeting that they should be consulted, as the Institution's financial affairs and membership numbers were not prospering. They suggested that ordinary subscribers should be allowed to elect nine of their number each year who would make an annual report, and be able to suggest 'improvements in minor arrangements'. They cited the 'promise' made by the Institution's founder, Benjamin Heywood, in 1824 that 'it is important to its [the Institution's] complete success that the Subscribers should take a part in its management'. A proposal was also included, somewhat randomly, for a class on design to be established 'useful to those connected with Engraving, Printing and Manufactures' – perhaps Abel was already considering printing as a line of business.

Frustrated in their demands, the leaders of the subscriber rebels in February 1829 set up the rival Society for Promoting Useful Instruction or the 'New Mechanics' Institution', with about a hundred members under the leadership of Rowland Detroisier. It was joined by many of those who had signed the proposals of September 1828, among them brothers John and Abel Heywood. This new organisation would be run on co-operative lines by the members, who would each buy five shilling shares and pay an annual subscription of sixteen shillings.

The subscribers would own all the property, and the committee of management, of which half had to be mechanics or artisans, were to be elected annually by all shareholders. For the interim, Detroisier was to be the president, Luke Speight the treasurer, and a provisional committee of eight was appointed, which included one of the Heywood brothers.

Unlike the old Institution, moral and political education was offered and in August 1830 Elijah Dixon, radical and veteran of Peterloo, gave four lectures on 'Co-operation'. The following month it was the turn of middle-class radical and owner of the *Manchester Gazette*, Archibald Prentice, to talk on the improvement of morals and health which the wider provision of infant schools would engender. Then, not surprisingly in view of the feverish campaigning in these years for a reform of the political system, in 1831 and 1832 the New Institution hosted a considerable number of debates on the topic.

The final and most ambitious project of the New Mechanics' Institution, announced by Detroisier on New Year's Eve 1831, was to fund the building of a 'Mechanics Hall of Science', which would be an enormous undertaking specifically for working-class use, to be supported also by middle-class reformers. By 25 February 1832 enthusiasts, including Abel Heywood, had taken up over 800 £1 shares. However, by April 1833, the great project was failing. The attempt to unite working- and middle-class support was undermined when the Great Reform Act of June 1832 gave the vote to middle-class men but not to those below them in the social scale, and divisions over factory reform split middle- and working-class opinion further. Detroisier had left Manchester to live in London, effectively weakening the leadership and success of the New Mechanics' Institution. Fund-raising for the hall stalled, and it was not mentioned again until it was later revived by the Owenites.

Meanwhile, the directors of the old Mechanics' Institution had been forced by the secession to accept change in terms of the subject matter they permitted to be discussed and, even more tellingly, with regard to the constitution and power structure of the body, and by 1834 the members were permitted to elect all the directors. Benjamin Heywood noted that the first board to be elected under the new dispensation was the most 'active and efficient' the Institution had ever had. From the early 1830s there were lectures allowed on such matters as factory reform, co-operation, trades unionism, and education, although some of the middle-class directors objected loudly; they did draw the line at a proposal to let Detroisier speak in August 1831.

As a result of the changes being adopted in the old Institution, and the difficulties of the new Institution, in summer 1835 the latter dissolved itself. Most of the members joined the old Mechanics' Institution, and its membership now grew rapidly to 1,519 by December 1835, although the members were still mostly from the lower middle class and manual workers preferred the cheaper and more socially accessible lyceums.

By 1847, there were no honorary members on the board of directors and the subscribers had complete control of the Institution. Abel himself had achieved the exalted status of honorary member, and continued to subscribe thus regularly thereafter. He gained election as a vice-president of the Institution on 27 February 1855.

The Owenite

The struggle over control of the Mechanics' Institution was the first battle undertaken by Abel Heywood, at the age of 19, in a cause which was wider than his own personal interest, and it was followed by many others throughout his long life. However, for the roots of his sense of social responsibility it is necessary to look at the ideology which he adopted around this time, the teachings of Robert Owen, for Abel has been described as a 'devoted Owenite'.[9] 'Owenism' is associated in the popular mind with the benevolent management of factory workers; in Britain, this is exemplified by the settlement at New Lanark where Owen tried to put his ideas into practice. However, the ideology was far wider and more radical than this, and is seen as an early form of socialism. Owen's radical ideas extended to taxation, co-operation, education, religion, freedom of speech, marriage and divorce; indeed it was a 'theory of social transformation' as expressed in his influential collection of essays, written between 1812 and 1814, tellingly named *A New View of Society*.

The fundamental basis of Owen's theory was that people are formed by their environment, and are not authors of their own fate; as a result he argued that change had to stem from improving the living and working environment, and that education was an integral part of reforming individuals and therefore society, to create a strong community of co-operation and mutual brotherhood and love.

Many of Owen's ideas were reflected in Abel's own views: Abel was a keen supporter of the co-operative movement, and of free, non-denominational and compulsory education; he was described as having 'very peculiar views on religious subjects'; and he was prepared to go to prison in 1832 in the cause of a free press. However, one area on which Abel and Robert Owen parted company was the question of suffrage. The former was a firm believer in universal suffrage, while the latter supported the existing political arrangements, arguing that the vote would not improve the condition of the people.

Owenism had practical consequences. The 1828–29 battle over the management of the Mechanics' Institution was spearheaded by Owenites, like Abel Heywood. In 1831 they set up the Manchester and Salford Association for the Dissemination of Co-operative Knowledge, and supported the establishment of co-operative stores and workshops. Abel joined the co-operative movement in 1828 and visited Rochdale to lecture on it; he sold shares in the London Road co-operative store and acted as the secretary of a co-operative in 1830.

For Owenites, social events were central as they helped to establish community spirit by including the whole family. Abel Heywood is recorded as selling tickets for such events, along with those for many other worthy causes. There were tea parties, bands, choirs, poetry and 'social hymns'; alcohol was not well regarded, as it tended to impede the loving group 'discipline' needed to sustain socialist community life. On Sundays, the community came together in what were referred to as 'lecture meetings' where there was a sermon and social hymns – in other words, an Owenite service.

There were tangible achievements; the Hall of Science built by 1840 at Campfield was an important venue for not only Owenite meetings, but also for other radical groups as the largest meeting hall in Manchester – it held over 3,000 people. It was a significant improvement; before this, the Owenites had often used Batty's Circus in Bridgewater Street, but in March 1837 thirty members fell through the floor during a lecture by Robert Owen!

It is remarkable how far Abel Heywood had travelled by 1830 in his ideas and achievements; it was only just over a decade since he had arrived in Manchester. He summed this up himself in his introduction to a range of self-improvement tracts which he published in the 1830s, relating how he 'was born and bred in poverty', but by dint of his exertions he had raised himself up 'to that state to be enabled to do some little service in the cause of the working people…' Starting out in Angel Meadow with only what little education he could glean in Sunday schools, which in itself was notable for the third son of a poor widow, he had shown ability and application in gaining an education beyond merely the 3Rs, and had acquired prominence locally as a useful and committed member of the Owenite radicals. He had successfully challenged and changed the management of the Mechanics' Institution, cutting his radical teeth and discovering the support of other like-minded young men.

He was probably still resident in Angel Meadow in 1830, although that was soon to change, and he was about to flex his intellectual muscles even more, setting up full time in business, and challenging head on the intransigent government of the day. But with the moral framework of Owenism to support him, he was fully aware that 'knowledge is power'. It is no coincidence that this was the tagline of the radical and illegal publication, the *Poor Man's Guardian*; it was this newspaper which was to bring Abel into direct conflict with the national authorities, resulting in his imprisonment and profoundly affecting his outlook and beliefs.

Free press crusader

Notice. — A. Heywood, newsroom, Oldham-street, begs respectfully to acquaint his friends in Manchester and its vicinity that he is going to remove (on the 6th of January) to more eligible premises, No.28 Oldham-street, next door to the sign of the King, where all Political and other Publications may be had. N.B. The News Room will still continue to be open from 8 in the morning till 10 at night. Admission one penny.[10]

This classified advertisement of 1831 was the first extant notice of Abel's new career as the provider of a newsroom for working men. Around 1829–30, Abel lost his job in Mr Worthington's warehouse, when he in some way displeased his employer, who 'in a fit of choler ordered his discharge'. But by this time Abel had already opened his first newsroom, and had been very successful. Nine months later, in 1830, he was offered the agency of the *Poor Man's Guardian* newspaper published in London by Henry Hetherington. This was especially significant because his agency led to one of the seminal experiences of his life; his imprisonment for selling the unstamped press.

The government did not look kindly on penny reading rooms, fearing as they did a British version of the bloody revolution in France from the disaffected and impoverished elements in British society who apparently read all this radical literature. The secrecy surrounding the distribution from London of Hetherington's and similar publications was elaborate. Many expedients were employed to hide the methods of dispersal from the authorities, with frequent changes of personnel, and the concealment of consignments of papers within shipments of shoes or groceries.[11] The papers were then distributed to retailers by agents such as Abel; in his case to the towns around Manchester.

Illegal almanacs were handled even more circumspectly, and on 30 December 1831 the radical publisher Richard Carlile sent six to Abel which, to get around the law, were printed on cotton cloth, but this was nevertheless on the strict understanding that they would be given to a few friends 'as a suppressed curiosity' and not sold over the counter. It may have been this which inspired Abel himself in 1834 to produce almanacs printed on handkerchiefs, omitting to charge the exorbitant two shillings tax on these publications.

He corresponded on notably friendly terms with some of the most notorious publishers of radical literature. On 16 February 1835 Carlile wrote Abel a long letter about his radical publications, particularly the works of Thomas Paine, and recounting how he had suffered government persecution. Abel was also 'very intimate' with James Watson, 'a gentle, mild-spoken man, fond of and good to children', who published almanacs from the United States; he and his wife were visitors to the Heywood home.[12]

However, in March 1832 it was clear that the government was determined to make an example of Abel for selling the unstamped press. On 8 March he appeared before magistrates Foster and Brierly at the New Bailey Prison in Salford, accused of selling Henry Hetherington's *Poor Man's Guardian*, which was illegal because at the affordable cost of 1*d* it did not pay the 4*d* newspaper stamp tax. During the trial, his counsel, Mr E. Owen, argued that he was to be prosecuted under laws which had been introduced to combat subversion in a time of national crisis after the Napoleonic Wars, but which had by now become a 'dead letter'.

Abel apparently had no warning from the authorities that the sale was illegal, and when he had realised what the consequences might be he had presented himself to the prosecuting lawyer, Mr Casson, and promised he would cease selling forthwith.

This argument may have been slightly disingenuous, for as the prosecution pointed out, the publisher of the illegal paper, Henry Hetherington, was already in prison for producing it, and this would surely not have escaped Abel's notice. Moreover, much later, in 1851, in an interview with a Select Committee on Newspaper Stamps, Abel cast a new light on his actions in 1832, stating 'the publishers plied the Whig Ministry as hard as they could, and published newspapers of all kinds, and at all prices; courting, in fact, prosecutions, for the purpose of breaking through, or compelling the Government to take off the tax'.[13] In court it was stated that 'it was even made a boast of that this [the *Poor Man's Guardian*] had been published, in defiance of the law, to try the power of might against right', and indeed this aspiration was printed on the front page of every *Poor Man's Guardian*.

There is no doubt that Abel was the victim of a government drive to clamp down on the radical press, which was enjoying a boom at this time, with a background of violent agitation for political reform which led to the passage of the Great Reform Act in June 1832. The July 1830 revolution in France had stirred up reform excitement in Manchester which was enhanced further in August when Henry Hunt, radical hero of Peterloo, visited to address a meeting on St Peter's Fields.

It is clear that the authorities wanted to make an example of a vendor, and the prosecution was also pressed forward by other factors; the king himself, William IV, was urging such prosecutions to assure 'the preservation of the Constitution and its Monarchical feature'. He was supported in this by stamped newspapers such as *The Times* and the *Morning Chronicle*, which feared the growth of the radical press. The authorities employed informers to prove the case, and in so doing act as *agents provocateurs*, and in Abel's trial a certain Mr Didsbury had been employed by the Commissioner of Stamps to purchase six different copies of the *Poor Man's Guardian* from him. He was found guilty and was required to pay fines and costs amounting to £48, a very large sum, which was beyond his means. That there may also have been a touch of defiance in his refusal to pay, and a desire to make a point about the iniquity of 'taxes on knowledge', is also possible. Bail was required if he were to be given time to pay, but his sureties were found to be unsatisfactory as one of them could not guarantee that he was worth £20 clear. As a result, Abel was sent to prison for four months, and appeals made thereafter to the Secretary of State were unavailing. Abel was not alone; almost 800 people were imprisoned around this time for violation of the newspaper stamp laws, even though two years later a ruling in the Court of Exchequer stated that the *Poor Man's Guardian* was too insignificant to be defined as a newspaper.

Abel's imprisonment in the name of a free press clearly had a major impact on his outlook and his determination to carry on. His business was maintained by his mother, Betty, and the family, and when he was released he was able to continue to build it up, becoming the best-known retailer of radical papers outside London. By 1851 he was handling an estimated 10 per cent of the country's newspaper trade.

Despite bravado about it later in life, Abel found prison very difficult, although his sentence did not include hard labour, and he quickly found his way into a position of leadership amongst the other prisoners by asking the prison authorities to make him a 'putter-out' for the weavers and other tradesmen in the prison.[14] In 1890 Abel light-heartedly referred to imprisonment as 'a very important event in his life', for it tested his 'ability to live on very short commons'.[15] Indeed, the main hardship was apparently the awful food. While in prison Abel wrote letters to his future wife Ann Pilling.[16] On 13 March 1832, only five days after sentencing, he addressed her father, showing his huge indignation that this was 'the most tyrannical sentence that ever came from the lips of a magistrate'. He feared that the authorities were 'determined to crush me at once', and as proof cited the lack of good food. He admitted that there was a little beef twice a week on Wednesdays and Sundays, but said that otherwise the food 'is not fit for pigs to eat'. In 1890 he mentioned that Joseph Hume took an interest in his case in the House of Commons, and the government sent a medical inspector to see 'if he had satisfactory sustenance'; the inspector disappointingly concluded that 'all he was short of was his liberty'.

On top of this, Abel's letters alluded to the 'miserable beds' which made him feel as though his bones 'had been rolled on the stones'. He was also shocked at the moral character of his fellow inmates, whom he described as 'the most dissolute of men' amongst whom 'the most scandalous discussion is going on the day over', though he did not elaborate on this, probably to spare the finer feelings of Ann, the young lady whom he called 'his sweetheart'. There was also not much in the way of facilities for study and writing (despite the fact that some radical prisoners used prison to gain education and nicknamed it the 'Whig College'), and on this occasion he was writing the letter leaning on his hat!

By the next day, he had acquired a Bible to lean on, and he was swearing that he would never enter prison again: 'When I am free from bolts, locks, and bars, and walls, I hope I shall never go inside again, not even to look at them....' He told Ann, 'You must cheer up. I am very comfortable indeed. I never thought that I could have reconciled myself to my new situation so soon.' He was clearly trying to reassure her that he would emerge unscathed after his sentence – though her fears were justifiable; many men emerged from confinement in such prisons with broken health and spirit. He even managed a joke: 'Ours is a fashionable resort. We have fresh arrivals nearly every day.' But politics were never far from his thoughts as he continued: 'The "Guardian" [*Poor Man's Guardian*] must not be put down. The stronghold of tyranny must be weakened and the liberty of the press flourish triumphant over all.'

There is an incident described at length by Johnson which demonstrates the real horrors of prison and the degree of privation suffered by prisoners. A group of inmates, already 'half-starved', had been punished for some infringement by being denied breakfast. They had drawn lots with the intention that the one on whom the lot fell would be killed and eaten by the others. This was only avoided by the escape of the unfortunate man over a wall into the next yard. Prison was clearly not a place for the faint-hearted.

Indeed, Abel's trials in the Salford New Bailey prison left him traumatised. In later life, he reiterated the experience in several of his recorded speeches about his early career and, as attitudes towards the press changed and the desirability of free speech was accepted, it became something of which he was very proud. Yet at the time it had a marked effect and when he was prosecuted on further occasions, he made sure that the fines were paid; in 1834 he was again fined (£18) for selling the *Poor Man's Guardian* and in 1836 he was twice fined for the sale of almanacs.

In his letter of 17 March to Ann, Abel ended with a sentiment which was one of the hallmarks of his lifelong beliefs and has the ring of his Owenite ideals: 'I hope to see the day when all tyrants and unjust Governments will vanish out of existence before the moral and intellectual strength of the people.' He remembered these ideals later in life, and when, in 1864, he issued a circular announcing the change of name of his business to 'Abel Heywood & Son', he recalled the heady days of 1832: 'My incarceration failed to convince me that I was not engaged in a glorious work in doing my utmost to level the barriers of ignorance and enable the newspaper to become an inmate in the house of every man…'[17]

2

The Chartist: National Notoriety

When Abel emerged from prison in July 1832, welcomed by a torchlight procession of his supporters, he returned to a Britain which was assessing the impact of Grey's Great Reform Act. He was not broken, but in fact ready to launch himself into one of the great movements of the nineteenth century: the cause of electoral reform.

The Great Reform Act of 4 June 1832 was the product on the one hand of widespread, and sometimes violent, national agitation by both the middle and the working classes, and on the other, the response of a fearful Whig government who realised that in order to hold on to power they had to make concessions. For liberals it was a first instalment in what they hoped would become a series of reforms, and for radicals it was the first step towards a vote for every man. The Act included the enfranchisement of middle-class men, and gave industrial cities like Manchester representation in the form of two MPs.

The 1832 election

Since he was in prison from 8 March 1832 for four months, Abel missed all the excitement leading up to the passage of the Act. However, he was released in good time to take a keen interest in the first parliamentary election in Manchester, in December 1832. It is likely that he qualified to be a £10 voter in the general election. It proved a turbulent affair, with jostling for position between the conservative/Tory elite who had hitherto dominated local affairs, the moderate liberals/Whigs who represented the new industrialists, and the middle-class radicals who were largely supported by the unenfranchised working classes as well as the lower middle classes, among whom Abel, as a shopkeeper, can be counted.

Election day on Thursday 12 December 1832 was marked by the ringing of bells to celebrate Manchester's new status as a parliamentary borough. A huge crowd gathered to witness the long formalities, and there was so much heckling from the unenfranchised that only the populist radical candidate, William Cobbett, and his nominators could be distinctly heard. The result of the poll was the election of Philips and Poullett Thomson, both liberals. Apart from 'a small riot' at the Thomson celebration, the election passed off peacefully.

The popular support for Cobbett had obviously been insufficient to ensure his election; the new £10 property qualification had effectively checked the democratic voice. It was surely this kind of experience which convinced radicals like Abel Heywood that nothing short of universal suffrage would ensure the interests of the poor and the triumph of radicalism.

Chartist leader

Although radicals had reluctantly agreed to press for an interim reform measure, they now became quickly aware that Parliament was not going to concede votes for the working classes. The product of their discontent was the formulation in 1838 of the People's Charter in London by a group of skilled tradesmen, led by William Lovett, a cabinet maker, and Francis Place, a tailor. It was supported by large numbers of the working classes, who suffered from a terrible slump from 1837 to 1842, described as 'the grimmest period in the history of the nineteenth century' when the manufacturing population faced 'hunger and destitution'.[1] A sense of resentment built up, and it was in response to this that Feargus O'Connor, Irish lawyer and radical leader, was welcomed in Manchester as Henry Hunt's successor by James Scholefield, the radical minister of the Round House chapel in Every Street, Ancoats.

From the outset, Abel was a supporter of the People's Charter.[2] Brian Maidment is correct when he stresses that 'it is… crucial not to lose a sense of Heywood the radical who maintained a consistent and progressive defence of the need for social dissent to be heard and published'.[3] He had a key role as the biggest wholesaler of radical publications in the North, keeping the flame of the free press burning throughout a period of repression. Yet Abel's part was wider than this: he was a proactive Chartist, involved in the movement's national planning, finances, meetings and lectures, not to mention tempering, and even informing on, the more violent tendencies of the so-called 'physical force' members.

The Manchester Political Union (MPU) was re-formed in April 1838. Abel Heywood took on his first role as a treasurer for this organisation. He was clearly regarded by his peers as a man of personal integrity, of sound organisational skills, and also of tenacity. He was made treasurer of several Chartist funds, but most notably for the National Charter Association (NCA) from its inception at the Griffin Inn, Great Ancoats Street in July 1840 until stepping down in October 1843 when, in one of the many upheavals which characterised the movement, O'Connor himself took on the treasurership.[4]

Manchester became a leading town in the Chartist movement, and Abel Heywood was amongst the movement's chief men; in a speech reported in the *Northern Star* on 22 August 1840, Abel referred to a visit to O'Connor in prison:

Only three weeks since he saw the lion in his den [O'Connor was popularly referred to as 'the Lion of Freedom', notably in a Chartist 'hymn' of 1841] – (enthusiastic cheering) – bearded by the vile Whiglings who misgoverned them – he was the noble and fearless lion crushing the contemptible – what should he call them? – the contemptible beetles. (Laughter.) The spirit of the man was not crushed – (loud cheers) – he was as firmly as ever attached to his principles – as determined as ever to carry the Charter.[5]

In April 1841, O'Connor named Abel as one of his trusted Chartist leaders, and he was apparently O'Connor's business manager around this time. On 21 September 1839 Abel, along with James Scholefield, had stood surety for O'Connor to appear in court at Liverpool. It seems that Abel was O'Connor's saviour on more than one occasion. In an article in his newspaper, the *Northern Star*, O'Connor recorded how Abel had saved him three times when he was imprisoned in York Castle and had no money; Abel 'lent all that was required'.[6] On 27 November 1847, when defending his handling of the ill-fated Land Scheme, O'Connor even cited Abel as one of the people who could attest to his handwriting.

Abel was also a supporter of the numerous Chartist funds: many collections were made in his shop, and he sold tickets for all the advertised Chartist gatherings and publications, as well as selling the unappetisingly named 'Crow and Tyrell's Chartist Breakfast Powder'.[7] Abel was also a generous giver on his own behalf. In the *Northern Star* of 18 February 1843, for instance, Manchester newsvendors were encouraged to donate their profits from sales of the newspaper on 25 February to the Manchester General Defence Fund, for those arrested in the general strike of 1842; the list of donors was headed by Abel Heywood.

He also acted from October 1840 as national treasurer for the Chartist victim fund, helping the families of men imprisoned for their Chartist activities.[8] He assiduously submitted his accounts for all to read in the *Northern Star*, and was quick to write to the editor when he omitted to print them.[9] Abel was fortunate in that he was not later tarred with the brush of scandal surrounding O'Connor's financial mismanagement of the Land Scheme. The *Northern Star* stated that Abel had collected the very large sum of £900 into the scheme by 10 June 1846. Only one of many who collected in funds, he seems to have escaped opprobrium, which perhaps tells us something of the high regard for his integrity amongst the Chartists.

Further evidence of this regard was the frequency with which he was selected to chair Chartist meetings, beginning in November 1839 when the radicals held a 'tea drinking' at the Carpenters' Hall to commemorate the birthday of Henry Hunt. Abel was in the chair, and introduced O'Connor, describing Hunt and other early campaigners as 'the best men that every graced the annals of our country'.[10]

On 1 July 1839, the Chartists had presented the first of three petitions in support of the People's Charter; it was rejected out of hand by a Parliament which regarded the idea of universal suffrage as dangerous and unthinkable. In South Wales this precipitated an insurrection on 4/5 November known as the Newport Rising, which was intended to be part of a general revolt. Joseph Johnson relates that Abel was 'out of town' at this time (though intriguingly not where he was) and his wife, Ann, was woken in the night by a man who 'who told her he had been deputed to assist Mr. Heywood in the general rising of the working classes which was about to take place'. Ann insisted they were mistaken and that 'her husband would assist neither him nor them in such a scheme'.

The Newport Rising was not supported elsewhere and was easily crushed, but the authorities were alarmed, and its leaders were arrested, tried and sentenced to death. In Manchester, on 27 January 1840 a meeting was held at the Olympic Theatre which proposed to ask Queen Victoria for mercy for the condemned men. Abel took the chair, saying significantly, 'They were not there to justify the men of Monmouth, but to petition for mercy. They might depend upon it, that physical force would only bring on physical force against them; and why should their lives be sacrificed?'[11] His strong condemnation of all violence marked him out throughout this period.

Indeed, it was at this time that Home Office documents reveal that he became a police informer with regard to agitation in Bolton on 22 and 23 January 1840, and may have been instrumental in preventing a local rising. As a result, when prosecuted in June 1840 at the instigation of the bishop of Exeter for publishing and selling blasphemous literature, the prosecution was precipitately ended by the mysterious intervention of the Home Secretary, Lord Normanby.[12] The bishop of Exeter was outraged that the Home Secretary had 'ventured to direct the counsel for the prosecution to advise the defendant to plead guilty, in order that he might have an excuse for screening him from justice'. The bishop accused Normanby of 'a corrupt motive', his fear of offending three MPs who had appealed to him on Abel's behalf: Mark Philips and Thomas Potter, MPs for Manchester, and Joseph Brotherton, MP for Salford.

However, Lord Normanby implied that other forces were at work, as he had received information 'from other quarters', and this abandonment by the government of the case leads us to perhaps the murkiest aspect of Abel Heywood's whole career; the question of his relationship with Sir Charles Shaw, government appointed Commissioner of Police for Manchester from 1839 to 1842. The support given to Abel's case by Shaw was probably the most significant factor in his liberation. In the Lords, Home Secretary Normanby alluded to the fact that Shaw had corroborated the claims made by Abel in a memorial against the prosecution, and stated that Shaw's 'representations had great weight with me in the course which I adopted'. He quoted from Shaw's report about the matter, referring to the winter of 1839/40, the period of violent Chartist agitation: 'You are aware of the state of the country at that time; and it is right to say that Heywood materially assisted me in preserving the peace of the town of Manchester at a period of great political excitement and alarm.' In private correspondence Shaw had informed the Home Office that Abel was:

One of the most influential men among the Chartists... I found that though his opinions were "Chartist" that he was a decided enemy to "Physical Force"... & I discovered that at all <u>Private Chartist Meetings</u> he argued against "Physical Force." Finding that his speeches <u>there</u> were in accordance with his words to <u>Me,</u> I thought I might have confidence in him, and I told him that I depended on him not allowing any outbreak to take place without giving me sufficient warning. He promised to give me notice. At great personal risk and the chance of losing his business as a "Chartist Bookseller" he gave me private information of a Rising which was to take place at Bolton during the night of 22nd and 23rd January [1840]... I instantly made arrangements with Colonel Wemyss in command of the troops here, who ordered a Squadron of Cavalry to march on Bolton, while I myself proceeded there. I found a Meeting assembling at Bolton... <u>Armed men were at the Meeting which took place in Bolton that night</u>. I consider that the information given to me by Abel Heywood prevented much serious damage being done, and that the threatened outbreak was prevented by the information.

I understand that Abel Heywood has very peculiar notions on religious subjects. From many enquiries which I have made and from what I myself have seen, no one can prove anything against him as a Man in business, as a Father or Husband, in short that I think him a Respectable Man. However his being able to give me such correct information proves that he must be a man of influence among the Chartists and I believe he does not pretend to deny that he belongs to a Sect called "Socialists [Owenites]."[13]

A letter from Shaw to Edwin Chadwick confirmed on 8 February 1841 that Abel and 'Richardson' were both informers, unbeknownst to each other, and that 'they have both acted as secretaries to Unions [associations] and all sorts of Meetings and <u>they understand</u> [quadruple underlined] the working classes. I get much valuable information on many points.'[14] In the eyes of many Chartists, and indeed of others in Manchester who were strongly opposed to central government interference, Shaw's policing was 'a damnable foreign police system'. Normanby's statement could therefore have been very damaging to Abel's reputation amongst fellow radicals.

Further evidence of Abel's collaboration with the police in Manchester in 1839–40 later began to emerge amongst the Chartists themselves when the pressures of decline led to internecine strife and caused accusations to fly. In 1844, Peter McDouall accused James Wheeler and Abel Heywood of spying. This was followed on 15 February 1845 by a public accusation in the *Northern Star* from James Leach that O'Connor and Heywood were informants who had betrayed the activities of the Manchester Chartists to the government, and so 'in Manchester every step we took was known by the authorities as soon as it was taken'. At this period, Leach was under a cloud, and his evidence was considered shaky. The Chartist council decided to reject the claims and exonerated O'Connor, and by implication those accused with him, including Abel Heywood.

It was probably the case that Abel did not see his actions as a 'betrayal' but as a means of ensuring that any action the Chartists might take would be non-violent, committed as he was to 'moral force' Chartism. But perhaps there were other, subconscious and less noble motives. By the end of the 1830s, with a wife and family to provide for, and the prospect of using the wealth created by his successful business as a springboard into civic power and respectability, it could also be that Abel was using his alliance with Shaw to smooth his own path. It may well have been the case that he believed this was for the greater good; no one would argue with the fact that he thereafter effectively dedicated his life to serving ordinary Mancunians through his role on the council.

Whatever the motive, the issue seems not at all to have besmirched Abel's reputation, and he continued to be invited to speak as a Chartist and was honoured as a pillar of the movement. Apparently, the Chartists accepted their council's judgement of McDouall's and Leach's claims; they seem to have left no stain on Abel's reputation and so far as the sources indicate, he was still viewed as a man of integrity and commitment to the Charter.

The platform was a key part of Chartist activity, and Abel Heywood has rightly been noted as a good speaker by Brian Maidment: 'he did, after all, provide some of the most lasting and thrilling phrases in defence of free speech ever recorded'.[15] Yet perhaps owing to a fear of imprisonment, he did not appear on the platform at public mass meetings, though he did address more enclosed and limited audiences, notably to raise money for the victims fund, though some of these talks were not serious political affairs, but 'phantasmagoria or magic lanthern' lectures at which he would 'shew a great variety of figures, and [pledged] himself to amuse all parties'.[16]

Abel did give at least one serious lecture on the subject of Chartism in the Chartist rooms on Tib Street. He set out his beliefs as they stood on that date in September 1840. He stated that the first principle in man is a God-given equality. His Owenite beliefs emerged under the name of Chartism when he argued that 'man is the creature of education and circumstances'.[17] He went on to claim that the second principle is self-preservation, and posited that laws are passed to allow this by protecting the weak from oppressors. The erudition of his argument is shown by references to the writings of Paine and Burke on the French Revolution. He then went on to put the view that barriers have been erected between man and his Maker – namely kings, parliaments, magistrates, priests and nobility, all of which he tellingly referred to as 'locusts'. He encouraged every man to have a copy of the Charter and to become familiar with it so that they could defend its principles; he decried the contention that working men were too ignorant to vote. Then he went through each point of the Charter, and refuted all the arguments that were put against them. He urged the people to unite to get the Charter enacted, to join the National Association, to read the Charter and books, stating 'knowledge is power, and by union, sobriety, and knowledge, they would obtain the Charter'. He especially recommended the book just published by Lovett and Collins, as the plan they put forward in it would 'insure them their liberty and their Charter at every hazard'.

This last point supports the view of Martin Hewitt that Abel Heywood was a 'Lovettite', favouring as he did peaceful means of campaigning, alongside worker self-improvement through education.[18] He was keen to encourage this approach in others, and it is noted that he mentored young Chartists like William Willis and John Campbell who went on to become sellers of radical literature and prominent in the movement; Campbell was another member of the NCA executive. Abel was also active in raising subscriptions for memorials to role models, most notably Henry Hunt, hero of Peterloo, when on 16 May 1840 as secretary of the Hunt monument committee he appealed for subscribers to attend a meeting at the Radical Association rooms to decide what form the monument should take. Early in 1841, Lovett founded the 'New Move' to encourage a system of national education; Abel urged 'every man to get a copy' of his tract. In this he was going against the O'Connor supporters in Manchester, who regarded this approach as divisive; Abel was prepared to swim against the tide, and even against the great O'Connor.

By the 1840s, Abel's thinking included the acceptance that an alliance with the middle classes was necessary if the Charter was to be achieved. This was a view which many Chartists disputed until 1842, but with the failure of the second petition in that year, and the further rejection by Parliament of the final petition in 1848, many came round to it, and it became the mainstream approach by 1850. As early as 1836 Abel, along with a few others who had risen into the lower middle class such as James Wroe, William Willis and R.J. Richardson, had begun to establish a policy of 'municipal Chartism' in Manchester, by becoming Police Commissioners, which entailed engaging with the middle-class liberals who were struggling to gain dominance over the traditional Tory elite which had hitherto run the town.

However, for many middle-class liberals in Manchester, a burning issue of the early 1840s was Corn Law repeal. After the electoral changes of 1832, an increasing number of voters were of the opinion that grain tariffs, while they might protect landowners, were disadvantageous to the new manufacturing industries. It was argued that they made bread expensive and thus forced employers to pay higher wages and limited the internal market; they also prevented Britain from buying grain abroad and so hampered exports from Britain to potential trading partners. Manchester, as the first industrial city, was at the heart of this agitation and manufacturers like Richard Cobden and John Bright led what became known as 'the Manchester School'; this marked a sea-change in how Britain perceived itself as it moved from an agricultural to an industrial economy.

Most Chartists were of the opinion that the Anti-Corn Law League, founded in January 1839 and based in Newall's Buildings on Market Street, was agitating in the interests of factory owners who wanted only to reduce wages. But Abel took a different view – he believed that cheaper and more plentiful supplies of corn would only benefit the workers, whose staple diet after all was bread. He was instrumental in attempting to unite the two movements of Chartism and Corn Law Repeal and he chaired a series of 'head-to-head' discussions between protagonists from each organisation. The first agitated meeting took place in the Carpenters' Hall on Tuesday 7 July 1840. There was trouble due to the presence of a *Manchester Guardian* reporter named Clarkson who had appeared in court in Liverpool after being subpoenaed to give evidence against Chartists there. Abel Heywood and the *Manchester Courier* reporter Mr Grant tried to get the unfortunate reporter safely out at the end of the meeting, but they were attacked at the top of the stairs. According to the *Manchester Guardian*:

> an attempt was made by a band of ruffians to throw him [Clarkson] over the ban-
> nisters of the stairs, in which case he would most probably have lost his life; but
> the attempt was defeated by the strenuous and praiseworthy exertions or Mr Abel
> Heywood, the chairman of the meeting… and Mr Heywood narrowly escaped
> being himself thrown over the bannisters, in his efforts to protect Mr Clarkson.[19]

Fortunately, Abel was unharmed in the scuffle, and continued to try to put the repeal case despite the hazards.

In an effort to win working-class support, middle-class liberals formed the Complete Suffrage Movement in June 1842. Although it was instituted in the premises of the Brown Street Chartists, it was regarded by many Chartists as a rival, hostile movement, as it also advocated the repeal of the Corn Laws. Very few Chartists were attracted to join, and the only Chartist committee member was Abel Heywood. At its anniversary dinner in 1843 the chairman, Thomas Potter, a prominent middle-class liberal, regretted that 'the operations of that association hitherto had been but limited'. A toast was raised to 'The people, the legitimate source of power.' Abel spoke, 'pressing upon the association the desirability of cul-tivating the confidence of the working classes... by visiting them more generally in their districts'.[20]

The Anti-Corn Law League felt the need to recruit 'minders' against Chartist attacks, and was able to exploit divisions among the working classes to recruit an Anti-Corn Law 'police' who took their part in clashes with the Chartists. These 'police' were recruited from among the Manchester Irish. The Irish nationalist leader, O'Connell, was an enemy of O'Connor and this led many Manchester Irish nation-alists to be hostile to Chartism. The Anti-Corn Law 'police' (called the 'Lambs') rejoiced in names like 'Big Mick' McDonough and John 'prepare to meet your God' Finnegan! They were armed with 'good blackthorn sticks', and were particularly stirred up by rumours that the Chartists were to burn effigies of O'Connell and of the local priest, Father Hearne. On 2 June 1841 an Anti-Corn Law meeting was called in Stevenson Square, Ancoats; the Chartists were encouraged to come and oppose the 'Lambs', and 20,000 apparently turned up. The ensuing violence was, according to the *Northern Star*, tantamount to 'a second Peterloo'.

Nevertheless, Chartists were often sympathetic to Irish aspirations and O'Connor was keen to win over Irish opinion. In October 1841 he announced that 'henceforth he would go for the Repeal of the Irish Union along with the

Charter'; a branch of the MPU was then set up in Manchester's Little Ireland. Abel published a placard for a meeting (one of three planned) the following spring: 'Men of Manchester and Salford, be at your post. F. O'Connor, Esq., will lecture at the Hall of Science, Camp Field, to night, Wednesday, March 9th 1842, on the Repeal of the Legislative Union.' Unfortunately, the gatherings gave rise to scenes of violence and there was some damage to the Hall of Science and O'Connor appealed for funds to be sent to Abel as NCA treasurer: 'A little sent from all to Abel Heywood will crown our glorious victory, and pay for the damage done to the Hall of Science, £20.'[21]

The year 1842 was a turbulent one in the Manchester area as against a background of immense hardship caused by the ongoing slump, the operatives participated en masse in a general strike, sometimes known to history as the 'Plug Plots'. Along with other Owenites, many of whom tried to discourage the workers from striking, Abel was not directly involved with the operatives, but he supported his peers, the shopkeepers, who were also badly hit by the slump. He was nevertheless keen to show that his role as an employer and a businessman had not caused him to lose sympathy with the working classes from which he came. On 28 May 1842, Abel placed a long advertisement in the *Northern Star* for a variety of publications, but ending with a statement of his own integrity as a publisher and employer:

> He wishes it… to be remembered that his Office is not a *knobstick* one, as many others are in the town, but that he employs none but those who belong to the Printer's [sic] Union, and to whom he pays the rate of wages fixed by the working men themselves.[22]

He also used a shopkeepers' meeting on 18 June 1842 to forward the cause of the workers among the shopkeepers when he proposed a resolution that the government should recognise the hardship suffered by both workers and shopkeepers and take action:

> He considered this meeting to be entirely a new feature in the history of public meetings; for who ever heard of a meeting of shopkeepers and tradesmen before?… He was convinced that the shopkeepers were now willing to assist the working classes in obtaining a proper remuneration for their labour; that they would form one united phalanx throughout the empire for that purpose; and then not all the efforts of tories or whigs could prevent their success.

However, there had been a 'rush' of Chartists into the meeting, and they insisted that it be adjourned to Stevenson Square. There a resolution was moved 'That the only means by which the present distress could be relieved… was the enactment of the People's Charter.'[23] On this occasion, Abel had not been able to temper the enthusiasm of the Chartists, however highly they might regard him personally.

The Tory *Manchester Courier* claimed the strikes were incited by the Anti-Corn Law League as well as the Chartists. It stated that the League was using the Chartists and the workers – stirring them up by imposing wage cuts – as a means of threatening the government and thereby forcing them to repeal the Corn Laws. As evidence in support of this thesis, the paper printed the prospectus of the Manchester Complete Suffrage Union, pointing out that its president was John Brooks of the League, and that Chartist Abel Heywood was on the executive committee with League member Elkanah Armitage.

Heywood played his part in attempting to calm the situation, as individual recorded incidents demonstrated. The account of Leon Faucher, a French political journalist who visited Manchester in 1843, was published by Heywood himself. It recorded the story of four men 'sometime in 1841–2' who entered 'a bookseller's' shop with a menacing air:

> "What do you want?" said the master.
> "We are dying of hunger," was the reply.
> "But why do you beg in numbers together?"
> "To get from fear what we cannot get from charity."
> "Why do you not hold public meetings, and make known your distresses?"
> "If you, Mr Heywood, will place yourself at our head, we will go with you for anything – for the destruction of property or aught else!"[24]

Joseph Johnson was similarly keen to stress that in 1842 Abel 'was instrumental in considerably allaying the general irritation'. He recounted how in Thomas Street, Abel:

> obtained the assistance of a working man when he courageously arrested one of the mob; he then procured the assistance of the police, headed by Mr Beswick, the superintendent, when he was enabled to track the footsteps of five of the 'shopbreakers', and arrest them in the act of dividing the spoil.

Yet when the rioters appeared in court, their wives appealed to Abel not to testify against them, and he 'found himself utterly unable to resist the heart appeals of the poor women' and left the court, refusing to speak against the accused, despite threats and cajoling. All the same, there were other witnesses, and the men were transported for life.

On 23 August army reinforcements arrived commanded by Lieutenant-General Sir Thomas Arbuthnot, who had instructions to crush 'the mad insurrection'. He had the local dragoons and police, strengthened by nearly 9,000 special constables, to help him. The scale of the repression which took place after the strike was unprecedented in the nineteenth century; in the north-west alone over 1,500 were put on trial. For now, the government had won the battle, but the war continued and broke out again in 1848, a time of European-wide insurrection and the year of the third petition in support of the People's Charter.

In May 1847, in the midst of renewed hardship, there was a call for a mass meeting in Stevenson Square, Ancoats. Fearing violence in advance of the third petition being prepared for presentation to Parliament, the Chartists denounced the proposal as an attempt by 'the defunct Anti-Corn Law League' to stir up the people 'to a re-enactment of the scenes of 1842'. Abel personally called upon the people not to take part in any such meetings. But matters escalated and on 24 February 1848 there were riots in the New Cross area of Ancoats, and more followed on 8–9 March; crowds attacked the poorhouse, damaged mills and held inflammatory meetings. As time went on 12,000 special constables, mainly from among the shopkeepers and tradesmen, and among them Abel Heywood, were enrolled. The authorities feared that Irish nationalist elements could become involved, and that the riots might be encouraged by the revolution across the Channel in France; and indeed the inspiration of events in Paris became a theme throughout the agitation. On 17 March Chartist leaders, including O'Connor, O'Brien and Leach, attended a St Patrick's Day meeting in the Free Trade Hall, which formally united Chartism and the cause of Irish repeal. The government was extremely alarmed.

There were further meetings, notably of the unemployed on 8 April, and on 9 April a large gathering of about 25,000 people was held in the name of Chartism. The one meeting Abel did attend was on the same day; it was to cement fraternisation between the shopkeepers and the working classes. It seemed to the fearful *Manchester Courier* that 'on all hands arming was going on silently'. However, in the end the violence was contained, despite the gathering of large and threatening crowds and the use of violent words.

Defender of the free press

Although his participation in the Chartist movement was wide-ranging, it was primarily as an advocate and provider of radical literature that Abel made perhaps his most significant contribution to the Chartist cause. He was dedicated to the principle of free speech, and not only spoke out on the subject, but also continued to be hounded by the authorities for acting on his beliefs. On Tuesday 3 December 1839 he chaired a meeting in the Corn Exchange focused on protecting 'mental liberty', with resolutions protesting at the victimisation, particularly by the clergy of the Church of England, of those expressing opinions. The meeting ended with those on the platform, including Abel himself, forming a committee to expose persecution and raise funds to fight it.

Of course, Abel had become a man of means by the late 1830s largely due to his role as a distributor of the radical press, and in particular of the Chartist *Northern Star*. He was a huge supporter of the newspaper and in August 1840, at a celebration held in the Hall of Science to welcome Peter McDouall and John Collins on their release from prison, he proposed a toast to the *Northern Star*. He praised the work and commitment of its editor, William Hill, and also that of 'the noble and dauntless proprietor of the Star [O'Connor]' and continued:

> Would to God they had a Northern Star in every town in the kingdom! Would to God that every town could write on the pillars of their churches "A Northern Star to be obtained here." The very existence of such papers would be a guarantee that the Charter would be obtained.[25]

His sincerity was confirmed on 6 October 1842, when Abel entered into a bond for the large sum of £400 to guarantee the court appearance of William Hill at Liverpool on the following Monday.[26]

Abel sold a large number of other newspapers, books and journals of a radical nature. In 1839 he sold 40,000 newspapers, pamphlets and books each week. Although not in support of armed force, as a hard-headed businessman he was prepared to sell literature about it, and an advertisement in the *Manchester Times* on 19 October 1847 cited his agency of a new book on the Newport Rising of 1839, *A Night with the Chartists, Frost, Williams and Jones* which was billed as 'A narrative of thrilling interest connected with the Monmouthshire insurrection.'

Abel's prosecution in 1840 was but one example of the risks he ran in the cause of freedom of expression. The attack on him was launched by a committee set up to hunt out 'Socialists or Owenites'. They described him as 'the principal printer and publisher of the blasphemous, profane and immoral publications issuing from this Town…' The prosecution was sparked by Abel's publication of a series of penny pamphlets by Charles Junius Haslam, called *Letters to the Clergy of All Denominations*, written in incendiary tone:

> What wretched stuff the Bible is, to be sure! What a random idiot its author must have been! I would advise the human race to burn every Bible they have got. Such a book is actually a disgrace to ourang-outangs [*sic*], much less to men.

Home Office records of March 1840 show that three government agents were employed to further establish Abel's guilt when they purchased 'socialist' pamphlets in his shop, including works by Tom Paine, *Moral Physiology*, a tract on birth control, and Clarke's *Critical Review*.[27] Without warning Abel was indicted and an officer was brought from Bury to bring him in for trial because 'our own officers could not be trusted with such a mission'. At 10.30 p.m., despite his protests, he was arrested and locked up in the Town Hall cells.

A meeting was held in the Hall of Science on Wednesday 20 May to show support for him, attended by over 1,400 persons. The upshot was a resolution 'that the meeting considered the prosecution against Mr Heywood as unjust, and pledged itself to support him to the best of their ability'. One method they used was the time-honoured practice of sticking up placards all over the town, headed 'Persecution for opinion's sake'.[28] Another was to press for the prosecution of other, 'respectable', conservative booksellers who had also sold illicit literature – in this case, Shelley's *Poetical Works*.

Abel also acted in his own defence, and memorialised the Home Secretary with the signed support of over a hundred manufacturers and shopkeepers. He wrote to the *Manchester Guardian* reiterating his claims that he had ceased publication of Haslam when he realised the nature of the pamphlets, and ended with a refusal to answer 'all the petty attacks of malice and vituperation' to which he had been subjected. Joseph Johnson stressed that Abel desperately wished to avoid having again to serve a prison sentence, which could have been two years. Abel was also said not to be 'in good health and… required more delicate food than Prison allowance'.

Meanwhile he appeared on 1 June 1840 at the sessions house in Salford New Bailey. Although he maintained throughout that he had been unaware that the publication was of a blasphemous nature, at the instigation of the Crown he reluctantly agreed to change his plea to guilty. The counsel for the prosecution, Dr Browne, stated that he was instructed by the government not to press for judgement against the defendant, but to consent to his discharge on his entering into recognisances for good behaviour, which was duly done for the sum of £300.[29] Abel had been saved only by his connection with Police Commissioner Shaw. An unknowing public celebrated his release, and Shaw privately explained to MP Mark Philips that he hoped Abel's release would dampen down defiant support for 'Socialists' in Manchester.

After 1848, Chartism went into a rapid decline. On 28 June 1849, Abel chaired and addressed a meeting of only about 500 Chartists at the Corn Exchange. In the end, Abel Heywood and James Scholefield led most of the NCA members to form the Manchester branch of the Parliamentary and Financial Reform Society in September 1851, accepting something less than manhood suffrage for the time being. A minority in the NCA, led by Julian Harney and Ernest Jones, wanted to keep to the Charter; with their slogan of 'the Charter and something more' they took with them around forty others to form 'The Manchester branch of the NCA' with premises on Deansgate.

With the final decline of Chartism as a movement, Abel turned his attention to other means of attaining parliamentary reform, and it was at this point that he accepted the presidency of the Manhood Suffrage Association in 1858, and then the candidacy for election as a Member of Parliament for Manchester in 1859. The last great Chartist occasion saw Abel in a prominent light, reflecting the significant role he had played in the movement's heyday; on 30 January 1869, with Elijah Dixon, Elkanah Armitage, Jacob Bright and Thomas Potter, Abel was a pallbearer at the funeral of his old Chartist comrade, Ernest Jones. The funeral demonstrated how extensive were the inroads into middle-class opinion the suffrage campaigns of the 1830s, '40s and '50s had made. The working classes turned out in great numbers, and the temperance United Kingdom Alliance and representatives of the working-class Reform League joined the funeral procession, which was led by 'four old Chartists' (described as 'Peterloo veterans')'. But the middle classes also came to pay their respects to this radical campaigner for universal suffrage. The 1868 election committee of the Liberal candidates Bazley, Bright and Jones were present, as were representatives from the middle-class Reform Union. With the passage of the Second Reform Act of 1867, the gap had at last been tentatively bridged between middle- and working-class radicals in the struggle for working-class votes.

3

The Businessman

Abel Heywood's achievements were informed by the philosophy of Samuel Smiles, expressed in *Self Help*, a book which found a place in his shop and enjoyed strong middle-class approval. As a husband and father with a growing family to feed, the route through which he chose to make a living was business. By the 1840s it had apparently dawned on him that he could no longer afford to be the hot-headed radical, but needed to establish himself as a respectable businessman.

Newspaper wholesaler, printer and publisher

Beginning with his penny newsroom, Abel had extended his interests into selling the products of the radical press, notably the *Poor Man's Guardian*, becoming a major wholesaler for the Manchester region by the late 1840s. The shop, starting out at 28 Oldham Street on 31 December 1831, by 1841 had settled at its final destination, 56–60 Oldham Street. He had become a publisher, and in 1847 he branched out into wallpaper manufacture. He also seems briefly to have been running a retail establishment specialising in patent medicines at 52 Market Street. By the end of his life, despite the claims of his grandson George Basil in 1932 that he had let the business go due to his civic and political commitments, he had the wherewithal to leave £24,682 as personalty in his will, as well as his businesses, shares, land in New Zealand and a fine house in the affluent suburb of Bowdon in Cheshire.

Nevertheless, the road to wealth had been a bumpy one. Johnson recorded that there were some dead-ends in Abel's business career; he tried to start a new newspaper on two occasions, but failed. In 1849 the *Manchester Spectator* was to be a 'Record of Politics, Opinions, Literature, Events, and Local Intelligence, and the Advocate of Political and Social Progress.' At 3½d it was not aimed at the very poor, though it would have been accessible to the better-off worker, or his newsroom. It was suspended in 1851, but publication was resumed in 1856 at the reduced price of 1*d*, when it 'attained for about two years a considerable circulation', but in the end it again ceased publication.

In the book trade too, things could get very tough; at the meeting of shopkeepers on 18 June 1842, when many tradesmen explained their economic difficulties, Abel told listeners that:

> He had always employed eight printers till within the last few weeks, when he
> had employed only one... Recently a man owing him £45 had run away to
> America, and on the same day another, owing him £35, had gone off in like
> manner – £80 in one day. (Hear, hear.)[1]

It is not known how many employees he had overall, but to keep eight printers going he would need a considerable amount of publishing business. If they were all paid the £129 a year he mentioned for one printer, that would mean a wages bill for printers alone of over £1,000.

Nevertheless, Abel's business survived and went on to considerable success once the crisis was over, branching out eventually into premises at the back of Oldham Street in Lever Street, Stevenson Square, where the printing works were situated, and 47 and 49 Spear Street, which housed the paper warehouse and news department. It was an extensive concern and, in a city full of desperately poor people, a temptation to crime. The *Manchester Courier* on 6 May 1848 reported that robbers had broken in by removing slates from the roof, so accessing the printing office in the attic storey. On this occasion, one of several, the thieves stole about 5*s* in copper from the locked 'money drawer' in the shop, along with a silver watch.

Sometimes theft came from within. On 10 August 1887 the Manchester Police Court heard the case against Thomas Rampley, a cashier in the employ of Abel Heywood & Son for nineteen years, who was imprisoned for four months for stealing various sums from the company, including one as large as £40. The thefts had taken place only in the last year, which Abel junior, who was by now a partner in the business, said he believed had been occasioned by the man taking to betting, and it may be that the sentence was more lenient than it might have been due to the recent nature of Rampley's fall from grace.

Fire was also a frequent hazard. For instance, in 1863 Abel's premises on Oldham Street were damaged in a blaze. The prompt attendance of the fire brigade with hose carts was effective, perhaps expedited by the fact that Abel was mayor at this time, but the damage to Abel's shop and the tobacco manufacturer's premises next door amounted to £200, covered by his insurance in the Leeds and Yorkshire, West of England and Scottish Union for £5,000.

The nature of Abel's stock may to a degree be ascertained from the classified advertisements placed in the press, which were admittedly only a selection. In the early 1830s the single most prolific category in the *Poor Man's Guardian* was radical literature such as the works of Thomas Paine. Alongside this were political works focusing on the ballot and the workings of government and its oppression of the people, with a volume on trade unionism and another on 'the Factory System'. Perhaps the most radical offering alongside these was the journal *Republican*, which prided itself on being described by *The Times* as 'a malignant sheet, the most furious of the furious' and focused on dangerous topics like 'Who is William Guelph, commonly called William the Fourth?' Surprisingly, considering Abel's dedication to non-violence, he did advertise 'Defensive Instructions for the People' which instructed on techniques of street and house fighting. Less surprising was his stock of history books, engravings of the Peterloo massacre, tomes on co-operation and Irish repeal, and a lecture by Detroisier on the projected Manchester Hall of Science. There were also early indications of support for the rights of women; a portrait of Mary Wollstonecraft, a volume named *Moral Physiology* which was on the taboo subject of birth control and a book of lectures by the American Frances (Fanny) Wright. To add to the mix there was also Shelley's *Queen Mab*, the blasphemous work which was believed to have helped Abel escape punishment in 1840. To top it off, Abel also sold 'Hunt's Matchless Blacking' in either liquid or paste form; a typical use of political radicalism in the interests of commerce.

In the *Northern Star* in the later 1830s there was a similar spread of topics, although here Chartism and Owenism made overt appearances on several occasions, and there was more focus on discrediting organised religion. It was in the later 1830s that Abel also began to advertise in the *Manchester Times* and the *Manchester Guardian*, and interestingly here he featured educational works and literature – including the Lancashire dialect works for which he later became famous as a publisher – and tomes on science. It seems that he selected his audience carefully, tailoring his advertisements according to the newspaper and its readership.

Overwhelmingly in the 1840s, the biggest category in the *Northern Star* was radical and Chartist literature. Next came education, and other works included religion and temperance, Corn Law repeal and middle- and working-class rapprochement, factory reform, O'Connor's land plan, Ireland and history. In March 1846, there were advertisements for a number of cut-price pamphlets Abel had bought from the frequently impecunious O'Connor, stating that '[he was] anxious to clear them off as soon as possible'. Making an appearance was an area which would increase considerably in the next decade: works on medicine, and cures such as 'Hoskin's tooth-ache specific'.

By contrast, the advertisements in the *Manchester Times* and the *Manchester Guardian* of the 1840s were dominated by works of history, self-improvement, literature and poetry (some in Lancashire dialect) and religion, with some volumes on political economy, education and maps, as well as almanacs of a non-controversial nature. Here too medical products were entering the arena with 'Bostock's Botanic Purifying Pills' and 'Frank's Specific solution of Copaiba to cure urinary ailments'. There was a commercial tendency to advertise books suitable for special occasions, in particular Christmas presents. Abel was also developing a profitable line in stationery, such as scrapbooks, blotters, ledgers and the like, along with Stephens pens. A minor concession was made to those middle-class readers who were interested in the plight of the working classes; in both papers Abel advertised plans for model workers' cottages, and there were a few books on socialism.

By way of similarly informing an interested group within the middle classes, in 1849 the journalist Angus Reach visited Manchester and wrote a series of articles on the industrial poor which were published in the *London Morning Chronicle*. He made a point of visiting Abel Heywood in his shop, in particular 'to ascertain the species of cheap literature... most favoured by the poorer reading classes'. He described him as 'one of the most active and enterprising citizens of Manchester'.[2]

Brian Maidment argues that Reach saw Abel's shop as a trope for the surrounding society. The 'ambiguous energy' of urban industrial culture, the chaotic life of the streets was reflected in the apparent contrasts, disorganisation and exuberance of the bookshop: 'Masses of penny novels and comic song and recitation books are jumbled with sectarian pamphlets and democratic essays... Altogether the literary chaos is very significant of the restless and all devouring literary appetite which it supplies.' Maidment further points out that the information gleaned by Reach was very much on Abel's terms, and it is his version of the business that we read.[3] He ensured that his visitor noted that 'Educational books abound in every variety'. Among all this were the works of Puritan divines, scriptural commentaries, and lots of music ('Little Warblers').

Abel made sure that the reporter understood that, although 'the foremost place' was occupied by novels 'utterly beneath criticism' which were 'weekly instalments of trash' with 'objectionable features', he was 'compelled' to sell them because they did so well. Indeed, the list of titles with which he furnished Reach was annotated 'Average 6,000 weekly sale. All this mass of literary garbage is issued by Lloyd of London, in penny numbers.' In other words, Abel wanted to distance himself from the 'garbage' which he sold to make good profits.

Next Abel supplied a list of penny weekly journals which he distributed throughout Lancashire; the most popular by far, at 22,000 copies a week, was *Barker's People*, followed by the *London Journal* at 9,000 copies. Interestingly, *Barker's* was noted by Reach to be 'political and democratic', whereas most of those listed were 'social and instructive'; testimony to the political excitement and ferment generated around this time by Chartists and other reformers. Bearing in mind that Abel had been in court in 1840 because of his sale of 'blasphemy', it is interesting that Reach found 'nothing more fatal to Christianity than abuse of the Bishop of Manchester'. Reach continued with a reassuring assessment that 'the Lancashire mind is essentially a believing... one. Fanaticism rather than scepticism is the extreme into which it is most likely to hurry.'

Pursuing his agenda of demonstrating improvement, Reach moved on to 'the better class of publications', of which the best seller was the *Family Economist*, with a sale of 5,000 a month at a cost of 1*d*. Surprisingly perhaps, Dickens's cheap double-columned editions did not sell so well and Abel recorded them at only 250 a week.

Reach's account of the business was probably highly selective. It is notable that there was no mention of the almanac trade, but we know that Heywood, since the early 1830s, had been a leading distributor. Although he supported Charles Knight of the Society for the Diffusion of Useful Knowledge in his campaign to encourage worthy and dour types of almanac, notably the SDUK's own *National Almanac*, he continued to be a large-scale seller of the more scurrilous, superstitious and disreputable ones. *Paddy's Watch* and *Old Moore's* were among those which found a place on his shelves, though these were sometimes concealed in discreet and genteel covers to avoid offence to respectable customers.

Abel was interviewed about his business again on 30 May 1851, this time by the Parliamentary Select Committee on Newspaper Stamps, which included Richard Cobden. As a leading distributor, Abel was an obvious choice; moreover, on 20 February 1850 he had chaired a public meeting in the Mechanics' Institution to agitate for repeal of the 'taxes on knowledge'. The committee's remit was to investigate whether the residual 1*d* tax on newspapers, which was by now rarely enforced, could be abolished without damaging the moral progress of the working classes. They were clearly set up to find evidence to support such a move; Abel told them what they wanted to hear. So great was the willingness of government to tolerate such literature that would earlier have been suppressed that Maidment notes there was 'almost a purring complicity between the... Committee... and Heywood himself'. Essentially, the committee reflected back to him 'as social policy, opinions which he had held consistently and publicly for many years'.

Abel explained that he was the principal publisher in Manchester of small and weekly unstamped publications which he supplied to the towns around Manchester to a radius of twenty miles, and that his business was 'principally wholesale'. For the Select Committee Abel's stock fell effectively into three moral categories: the worthy or 'unexceptionable', the 'pernicious' and the extreme radical. He was keen to show that his stock was varied and balanced by differences of view in its content. Maidment points out that although this is partly due to his rejection of the idea of censorship, and his faith that most readers would choose edifying literature over 'trash', it was also in line with his business awareness that there was a lot of money to be made out of all types of publication, particularly the 'trash'. He was asked to estimate the overall figure of his circulation; in 1849 it had been 80,000, which he thought had grown in the intervening eighteen months. He agreed with the committee that this meant 10 per cent of all cheap publications were sold through him: 'Therefore, you have probably the largest experience of anyone in the kingdom in the sale of those publications? – I think so; the trade say so.'

The most worthy of the publications can be exemplified by the *Family Herald*, a penny publication of which Abel sold 9,000 a week out of a total 14,000 sold in Manchester and its surrounding region, its circulation with Abel having grown by a third in the preceding year. According to Abel himself, this was a journal:

Principally made up of light reading, and there is a peculiar feature about the *Family Herald* which is not possessed by the others [the *London Journal* and

Reynolds's Miscellany, which also sold well], it addresses itself to the fairer sex in
a great measure, and to that perhaps may be attributed its very large circulation.

And, germane to the preoccupations of the committee, 'the tone of morality in
these publications is quite unexceptionable; I take home the *Family Herald*, and
read it with a great deal of pleasure, and it is read by every member of my family'.
Interestingly the circulation of the very political *Barker's People*, so popular in 1849,
had fallen from 7,000 to 1,000 in Manchester; Abel attributed this to the fact that
'Mr Barker has gone to America, and his peculiar style of writing is not to be met
with', but perhaps it also reflected the decline of Chartism and interest in politics.

Abel argued that there were far fewer really bad publications than in previous
times, and that those that were published often sooner or later went out of business.
Nevertheless, the novels published by Edward Lloyd, which had been so deprecated
by Reach, were still very popular, dealing as they did in 'bloody murders and all
other crimes which it is possible for the imagination to invent'.

However, there was one publication which exercised the committee considerably due to its 'pernicious' nature and its worrying popularity in some quarters;
this was the *[Mysteries of the] Court of London*. Published by Reynolds, it recounted
tales set in the Georgian era about the seedy underbelly of London, though, as
Abel said, 'whether it is true or false, it is not for me to say'. He continued, 'it is not
in reality an indecent publication, because I do not believe that any words appear
that are vulgar; but certainly the language is of a most exciting kind, and directed
to excite the passions of its readers'.

As well as playing down, to some extent, the indecency of the work, Abel also
tried to reassure the committee that it was of limited appeal, its circulation in the
whole Manchester area being only 1,500. However, later in the interview he made
the worrying admission that 'A great many females buy the "Court of London".'
But then, immediately, perhaps having realised that he had undermined his own
arguments for allowing people to self-censor, in that the vulnerable 'fairer sex'
seemed to be in need of a firmer hand, he attempted to divert the point by adding
colourfully 'and young men; a sort of spreeing young men; young men who go to
taverns, and put cigars in their mouths in a flourishing way'. He concluded on this
matter that the sales were down by two-thirds because sales of good publications
were rising and those of bad ones falling. But, he admitted finally, 'I believe that it
would be almost impossible to put down the "Court of London;" I believe that
you could not educate people so that there could not be found 10,000, 15,000 or
20,000 of people in this country disposed to buy it.'

Abel's sale of extreme radical literature was a focus of some interest on the
committee's part, and he was keen to show how it was no longer to be feared. The
Chartist Julian Harney produced the *Red Republican* which took 'extreme views
in politics', but such had been the unpopularity of a publication with so radical
a name that he had had to change it to the *Friend of the People*. Its circulation
in Manchester was still only 250 a week. Similarly extreme was Robert Owen's

Journal, advocating 'socialism', which might have worried the committee since, as Abel admitted, 'Manchester was considered a stronghold of socialism, and to a certain extent, the views of a great number of the working classes were in favour of socialist principles.' Again he dismissed the *Journal's* importance with its small circulation of no more than 250 in Manchester and its neighbourhood.

After discussion of the individual publications, the committee was interested in eliciting Abel's opinion on the key question of the impact of removing the stamp duty on newspapers, with particular concern about the reading morality of the working classes. They were of course fully aware that he would be in favour of such a move and, as their remit was indeed to find evidence to support it, they fed him leading questions, many of which required a simple 'yes' from him, such as:

> Chairman: This extensive sale of publications shows that there is a taste and a desire amongst the working classes of those districts to which you have referred for reading, for mental improvement, does it not? – Yes, it does.
>
> And it shows that there is a want of cheap literature amongst those people, does it not? – Yes.

Maidment points out the crucial remark: 'Heywood went on… to agree, without noticeable triumph, to Cobden's assertion that "they [the working classes of Lancashire] may be safely let to discriminate between the good and bad newspapers".'

There were extensive discussions about unfair competition from the London papers in Manchester, owing to the stamp tax levied on the local papers, from which the London ones transported by post were free. Abel furnished complex explanations of the costs of transport to Lancashire by the London and North Western Railway. He said that he considered that local papers were much better than London ones. 'In a town like Manchester, though a large one, the readers know the editor and all the parties connected with a paper, and as their characters are free from stain, have considerable influence over their readers.'

The committee was also keen to discuss with Abel what happened in 1832 with regard to the *Poor Man's Guardian*, and what had been the impact of the subsequent reduction in the stamp duty. Abel responded rather pointedly that 750 people were prosecuted and imprisoned, and that he had never been compensated for what was afterwards pronounced an illegal imprisonment. Apparently, there had been no prosecutions in recent years, because publishers had ceased publication rather than face the courts.

Discussions about repealing the stamp duty continued, and on 4 January 1853 the Manchester Association for Promoting the Repeal of the Taxes on Knowledge, of which Abel was a committee member, held a meeting at Newall's Buildings which resolved to call a public meeting to lobby Parliament and raise a subscription in Manchester. The tax was finally abolished in 1855, helped on its way no doubt by the useful ammunition provided by Abel in his Select Committee interview.

By the 1850s the pattern of Abel Heywood's classified advertising had considerably changed. With the disappearance of the *Northern Star* and other radical publications, Abel's focus was now on the *Manchester Guardian* and the *Manchester Times*, along with the addition of the *Manchester Courier*. In view of the fact that these were all 'respectable' papers, it is unsurprising that Abel's selection reflected the tastes of more middle-class readers. However, the advertising also seems to have been specific to each publication.

In the *Manchester Guardian* the focus was strongly towards medical works, including one on homeopathy. But by far the most frequent such advertisements were for a small group of works about 'Manhood; the causes of its premature decline...' which dealt with the dreadful consequences of 'rash indulgence of their passions' by 'the gay and thoughtless', and suggested 'plain directions for its [manhood's] restoration' complete with anatomical drawings and 'explaining the various functions, secretions and structures of the reproductive organs in health and disease'.[4] Why *Guardian* readers in particular were treated to a veritable bombardment of such advertisements remains somewhat of a mystery. Nevertheless, the paper continued to carry publicity on works of literature, including those of local writers like Edwin Waugh, some of them in dialect. The Manchester Art Treasures Exhibition was celebrated in 1857 with publications and guides, and for the romantically inclined there were advertisements for valentines, even as early as November! Abel also used the *Manchester Guardian* to broadcast news of other publications – the *Daily Guardian*, *Tait's Edinburgh Magazine*, the American *Farmer and Mechanic*, the *Family Economist*, the *Constitutional Journal* and his own *Manchester Spectator* were all advertised here.

The readers of the liberal *Manchester Times* were treated to advertisements on works of history and education, including matter thought suitable for whole family consumption. Abel targeted this audience in particular for children's literature, including *Pleasant Tales for Little People* and *Easy and Interesting Histories for Very Little Folks*. There was also room for satire in the form of *The Great Exhibition of the Idleness of all Nations* in 1851.

Readers of the Tory *Manchester Courier* were apparently not thought to be much interested in history or children's books, but more so in religion and in naval and military history. Abel also publicised his agency for Dickens's journal, *All the Year Round*, the *Cotton Supply Reporter* and the *Cornhill Magazine*. Interestingly though, it was here that Samuel Bamford's *Passages in the Life of a Radical* appeared; for some of the middle classes the veteran radical had become the acceptable face of working-class reform.

Indeed, a unique glimpse into the day-to-day world of Abel's publishing business is provided in the later 1850s and early '60s through the arguably jaundiced view of Samuel Bamford. In 1858 he returned from London and aspired to make a living by reissuing books first published in the 1840s which at that time had gained him national recognition. The editors of his diaries for 1858–61 note that he was a difficult character, with an unfailing self-belief, quick to perceive slights and insults. Nevertheless, his career and commitment had earned him the respect of a wide circle of reformers.[5]

The first publisher to whom Bamford turned on his arrival was Abel Heywood; he entrusted him with the reprinting of his *Passages in the Life of a Radical*. However, by this time Abel had ceased publishing radical literature, as there was no assured market for it with the decline of the Chartist movement. Bamford seems to have been oblivious of this commercial shift, expecting the same sort of interest from Abel as he would have had in the 1830s and '40s. He was to be sadly disappointed.

Their relationship was certainly on the decline by Wednesday 8 September when Bamford's diary recorded that they fell out over the issue of whether their contract should be stamped. 'This omission to get the agreement stamped is a breach of the understanding there was betwixt us, and I don't like it; I trusted to Heywood in confidence that he would rigidly adhere to what was agreed upon and understood by both of us.'[6] From a prickly interview, things went from bad to worse as is clear from the entry for Thursday 7 October: 'Took in my acc[oun]t with Heywood, who paid, and was seemingly in a sullen and distant mood: which mood, if he knew how exceedingly indifferent I felt about either himself or his airs, he would scarcely take the trouble to exhibit.'[7] It seems as if Abel was beginning to find his venerable customer somewhat tiresome to deal with.

This spilled over into other areas; on Tuesday 7 December 1858 the radical Manhood Suffrage Association held a meeting, which Heywood as president chaired. Bamford suggested amendments which were somewhat confused, aimed at supporting John Bright's arguments that ratepayer suffrage was a more realistic aim, but also keeping manhood suffrage as an ultimate goal. He claimed Abel refused out of hand to accept his amendments; this was not the sort of slight Bamford would tolerate.

The war of attrition went on when Abel's 1859 parliamentary candidacy was discussed between Bamford and his friend Belfield:

Some animated conversation about Bazley, Turner, and Heywood [the three Liberal candidates in the parliamentary election], the latter huffed, and spoken of slightingly. I did my best to render him justice, without placing him on a par with the other gentlemen, which indeed I could not do with truth.[8]

A backhanded compliment if ever there was one!

Despite all the ill-feeling on Bamford's part, Abel did apparently sell him copies of his book at discounted rates, which Bamford then sold on at a profit. It was clear to everyone that he was in desperate straits, and Abel was willing to help out to some extent. This did not appease Bamford, however, and on 5 May he was even more offensive about Abel:

I called at Abel Heywoods for the books, 8 copies, and paid £1.7.0 for them, the shab-rag not allowing me full trade discount of 25 copies for 24, because I do not, I cannot indeed afford, to take and pay for, the whole 24 at once. And I am

I

determined never to take a book out of his shop on credit. He is a shab-rag, a Jew [*sic*], and has latterly become quite a snob. I dispise such characters…[9]

Eventually, on 25 March 1860 Bamford was approached to sit on a committee for a testimonial for Abel Heywood. His reaction was perhaps predictable, for by now Abel could do no good in his eyes. 'Was informed by a letter that I had been unanimously chosen one of the committee to act on "the Heywood Testimonial", a proceeding I never authorised; an honour I never desired; and an office I shall never fulfil.'[10]

By July 1861 it was three years since Abel had purchased the copyright of *Passages in the Life of a Radical*, and Bamford steeled himself to ask how many he had left. The terse nature of the exchange indicates that both men had little time for each other; Abel clearly felt that he had done enough for Bamford, and was disappointed in the sales of his book. Bamford continued to libel Abel, suggesting on 16 November that he was downright dishonest:

> Cassells, I see is quoting freely from My Life as a Radical, in his cheap History of England. These quotations, in which my book is honestly acknowledged as an authority, should be the means of selling a large number of copies; half of the edition I should think, yet I scarcely expect that "Abel Anything", the honour-able Alderman will acknowledge to having sold a dozen extra copies; we shall see how he moves.[11]

The story of Abel's relationship with Bamford at this period is instructive; it gives us a uniquely hostile slant on Abel as a person, and if Bamford is to be believed it shows us that he was not always sympathetic towards people who had fallen on hard times. Abel's abrasive manner and hard-headed approach to business produced a bitter reaction in the veteran reformer.

Paper and wallpaper

The wallpaper branch of Abel's business, Heywood, Higginbottom and Smith, was started in 1847 when 'the manufacture of paper-hangings was comparatively in its infancy'.[12] New machinery had been devised for 'paper staining and making paperhangings' by 'two ingenious and industrious working men' who sought Abel's 'pecuniary assistance'. The process as it developed used machine-printing, with an endless roll of paper, printing rollers and steam power. It was reported that the company used as many as fourteen cylinders, and that 'each colour is made to fall precisely in its proper place'. They were able to produce the hangings 'at prices unprecedentedly low' and won a medal at the 1851 London Great Exhibition.

On 28 October 1858 Abel, listed as a paper maker and stainer, took out a patent, sealed on 2 April 1859, on 'improvements in machinery or apparatus for suspending paper and woven fabrics to be dried'.[13] The firm continued to expand its marketing and win prizes; in 1862 it was awarded a further medal at the London International Exhibition.

Indeed by 1860 Johnson claimed 'their trade has become enormous'. The firm was paying over £20,000 in paper duties and making three million pieces of 'paper-hangings' annually. They owned a paper-staining works and paper mills at Hyde Road in Gorton, and Woodley in Arden near Stockport 'in which two machines are constantly at work, and a third is in course of construction'. There were branches in London and Glasgow, and representatives were 'in all parts of the world; their paper-hangings being as well known in the United States as they are in England'. Apparently, the paper maker T.B. Crompton tried to buy into the business with an unsolicited offer of £10,000, but was declined by Abel, 'his own resources being at the time amply sufficient for the development of his business'. However, in the early 1860s the whole business, with a capital of £250,000 was disposed of to a company of shareholders, with Heywood its chair of directors.

Abel's prominence in this branch of business was demonstrated at the conference of paper makers, held in Manchester Town Hall in January 1864, at which he presided. It was agreed to petition Parliament on the free export of rags for paper making, especially in the light of the recent removal of taxes on foreign paper.

By the 1860s, Abel was also participating in the activities of the very middle-class Manchester Chamber of Commerce. His continuing interest in international exhibitions was demonstrated there at a meeting called by the mayor and the president of the chamber to consider the Paris Exhibition of 1867. Heywood, Higginbottom and Smith's stand at the 1880 Melbourne Exhibition showed that the secret of their success was to keep up with fashion and to continue to be innovative. They showed 'Decorations in the Japanese style' which were then all the rage. In addition, they had examples of imitation wood, 'with Dado, Filling, Border, and Centre Piece', which they had invented some years before.

Running such a business was not easy, however, and managing staff in other towns and even countries could be challenging. The company seems to have dealt leniently with the transgressions of an employee in their London branch. John May, a 'country traveller', was brought before the Lord Mayor at the Mansion House charged with embezzling £200 from the company. In April 1870 he had set out for a three-month trip, but had never returned. The company's London manager, Mr Shorrock, therefore brought the case against him. However, there had been negotiations for the accused to repay the sums owed. The company also said that 'it would be better for him to serve them than obtain other employment'. Perhaps they had fears that he would take custom with him, or divulge company secrets? However, the Lord Mayor was not prepared to countenance any bargain between the parties. It is not known what became of the offender.[14]

Other employees sought to assert their own interests through union activity. On the afternoon of Monday 14 March 1870 a strike took place at Heywood, Higginbottom and Smith's paper mill in Hyde Road, Manchester. This was reported in the press when a young man, Henry Wood, was accused of intimidating and beating up a fellow worker, John Tipping, because the latter had not joined the strike. The court sentenced Wood to fourteen days in prison.[15]

Work for employees in manufacturing was often hazardous in other ways too, particularly in an age before 'health and safety', and Heywood, Higginbottom and Smith experienced at least one tragedy. In 1868 a teenager named Catherine Moore died as a result of an accident at their paper works at Woodley, when she fell into a pan of boiling liquid. The coroner found that it was an accidental death.

A further challenge to be negotiated was the changing law relating to child labour in factories. In 1872 the Manchester Police Court heard how the company had illegally employed two boys under 13 years for full-time work. The inspector of factories, Mr King, found that one of the boys had been working full time for five months 'without once attending school'. The company admitted its guilt. This was certainly a blot on the record of a company whose chair of directors was an avowed champion of education for all.[16]

New ventures

As early as the 1850s, Abel began to branch out into new areas of manufacture and trading, and to take on directorships in insurance companies and speculative banking enterprises. His interest in these ventures included financial gain to himself, though on exactly what terms is not known.

Joseph Johnson related how Abel joined a weaving company which was unsuccessful, and this may have been the partnership which was dissolved early in 1853 between Henry Fletcher, Richard Woolley, Joseph Sutton and Abel Heywood; in the notice they were described as 'power-loom cloth manufacturers'. On 23 April 1853 the *Manchester Guardian* carried an advertisement for the sale or letting by Abel Heywood of a mill in Beswick Street, off Bradford Street 'lately used for weaving purposes' with fittings for 300 looms and a steam engine of sixteen horse-power. This must surely have been the bitter end of the enterprise.

In the area of financial matters, Abel made an early appearance in 1852 as one of the directors of the newly established Lancashire Rent Guarantee Company, which was set up to help landlords secure receipt of their rents by ensuring that they were honestly collected, and offering to manage properties.

It seems that his elevation to the mayoralty in 1862–63 opened more doors to him in various enterprises; when his directorship was listed in advertisements for investors, he was frequently described as 'ex-Mayor'. And his ex-officio appointment as a magistrate, in which position he continued thereafter, would have added to his reputation of moral and financial probity as well as demonstrating and enhancing his influence. For instance, from 1864 Abel chaired the directors in the City and County Assurance Company Limited, and joined the committee of the Manchester Guardian Society for the Protection of Trade, a body which used its funds to help members who were owed debts.

Beyond this, in a completely new arena, by 1865 Abel was also a promoter and director of the Clayton Plate and Bar Iron Company Limited, set up to manu-facture steam boiler plates, which were claimed to be in short supply. On the notice offering the shares, it stated that Abel was an alderman, and most notably a director of the Alliance Bank, and therefore the sort of respectable man whom shareholders could trust. It also explained at length the plan and concept behind the new business, and that it was to be run partially on co-operative lines, with the workers receiving a share of the profits. By combining entrepreneurship and co-operation, it was hoped to create a new kind of working environment in which all had a stake in success; a concept still operating today in modern 'partnerships'.

Not content with insurance and metal works, Abel's eye lighted also on the shipping industry in the form of the Manchester Shipping Offices and Packing Company Limited, a new company aiming to 'meet the great and increasing demand that now exists for the rapid and prompt dispatch of good to foreign markets'. Abel was top of the list of directors. Its headquarters was on the new Albert Square, where the Albert Memorial was even then in process of erection, and 'near the proposed site of the intended New Town hall'.[17]

Perhaps his most striking venture was into the banking sector. This also had a commercial use; it was the Alliance Bank of London and Liverpool Limited (founded in 1862) which served both the Clayton Iron Company and the Shipping Offices and Packing Company. Despite financial problems in 1866, it was agreed at the annual general meeting that bank directors would be paid £5,000 per annum 'until further ordered'. This was clearly a lucrative venture for all concerned, even in a difficult financial climate. However, perhaps the storms of 1866 were not as innocuous as the report suggested, as the business was broken up in 1869, and it seems likely that Abel did not continue to receive the sums for which he had hoped as a director from this concern.

It was apparently on the back of this directorship that Abel joined what sounds like a far more speculative London-based venture – the Mexican Bank Limited. In the list of directors, not only was he noted as ex-mayor of Manchester, but also as director of the Alliance Bank, which was backing the Mexican Bank. The remuneration of the directors was left to the shareholders; much would hang on the success of the venture. The signs were promising and on 17 February 1864 it was reported that the issue had been oversubscribed almost ten-fold. In the event, this was the start of modern banking in Mexico, and the Bank of London, Mexico and South America continued well into the twentieth century. Although it is not known how this affected Abel's personal finances, it may be speculated that over the years he did better out of this bank than out of the Alliance Bank.

Having found what appeared a lucrative seam, Abel took on a third directorship, this time in the Warrant Banking Company Limited. The Warrant Bank was formed to fill a niche; it provided credit for importers who could not or did not want to sell their goods immediately. The directors were not to receive remuneration until the shareholders had been paid 5 per cent by way of dividend, and thereafter the directors would receive a healthy 20 per cent of the net profits.

What seems clear is that an increasing proportion of Abel's income was coming from sources other than his publishing and stationery business or his wallpaper enterprise. This should not be a surprise; he had ever been an astute businessman. Moreover, it may reflect the fact that the vast amount of time he was devoting to public business was causing him somewhat to neglect his printing and publishing concern and that he needed to seek greater income elsewhere. On the other hand, perhaps new enterprises were also having their effect on his commitment to the old company, and were a factor in its eventual decline.

Abel Heywood & Son

With the arrival of two sons, Abel (1840) and George Washington (1842), the possibility of passing on the company became a realistic hope; from 1864 the publishing business was called 'Abel Heywood & Son'. Abel junior apparently took on the bookselling business, whereas his brother George Washington was for a time employed in the wallpaper part of the empire, to judge by the census entries in 1861. However, later on George Washington devoted himself rather to a career in the law.

On 13 November 1880, when he was 70 years old, Abel established a partnership with his elder son. The premises on Spear Street, acquired at least as early as 1858, by 1883 provided a warehouse and cellar 'in which my partnership business is carried on', and where Abel junior also ran 'the business of a printer on his own account'.[18] We can perhaps see evidence of the interests of Abel junior reflected in the stock advertised in the 1880s and early '90s. The *Penny Guides* to towns and regions in Britain, for which Abel Heywood & Son was famous, took off in a big way in these decades and the range of other publications offered was extended to include Bradshaw's and Sim's railway guides. There was a growth in local literary products and those in the Lancashire dialect by the Manchester Literary Club, of which Abel junior was a member, and there was a large volume of literature for the theatre, such as plays, recitations, musicals and manuals of advice for amateur productions.

However, there were still some volumes advertised which would have been to Abel senior's taste; works on financial reform were stocked, and after each general election there was *Heywood's House of Commons* which recorded the statistics and composition of the new Parliament. National politics also continued to be reflected by occasional advertisements on current foreign issues. Technical books were produced about cotton manufacture, steam boilers and the Manchester Ship Canal project. The business still sold educational books, items on temperance, religious literature and notably published *Bennett Street Memorials* which was a memoir of Abel's old school.[19]

Abel senior continued to take an active part in running the business on Oldham Street until the last years of his life. It may well be that his involvement became a problem for the younger generation; Abel junior's son, George Basil, clearly thought that his grandfather had tried to keep too many balls in the air. 'He was an indefatigable worker but did not appreciate the necessity of delegating any of his responsibilities, and he was so busy with the work of the Manchester Corporation, that his business suffered, and his competitors prospered.'[20]

Once the battle for a free press was won, perhaps the crusader in Abel found more reward in public service, rather than in the making of profits through business. Indeed, he suggested this himself in a speech to the Liberal Manchester Reform Club in 1877, when he stated that 'a man in an active business cannot give 34 years away [the length of time his participation on the Paving Committee had lasted up to that point] from his business without having sacrificed a fortune if he had any business worth following'.[21]

The business suffered a blow towards the end of Abel's life when a serious fire broke out on 12 May 1887. The fire brigade attended, but the two upper floors were already ablaze. After about an hour and a half the fire was 'subdued', but there had been considerable damage. The result was a fire sale later that month, which included about sixty tons of paper, cards, envelopes and forms which were water-damaged.

Further difficulties were presented by two reported court cases. Although neither of them were as serious as they might have been, they are symptomatic of the challenges faced. In 1879 a Richard Owen was accused of selling obscene publications, such as *Town Talk, London Life* and *Quiz*. As a way of defending himself Owen claimed that hundreds of thousands of copies had already been sold in Manchester by 'the Messrs. Heywood'. The police had inspected the premises, but 'had found none of the objectionable prints there'.[22] A decade later Charles Leonard, an unemployed compositor who was an ex-employee, had published a libel against Abel Heywood senior and junior. This consisted of 'some immoral and most filthy and indecent verses in print, round the margin of which, in the prisoner's handwriting, was a statement to the effect that these verses had been printed by Mr. Alderman Heywood'. When Leonard appeared in May 1889 he pleaded guilty to libel and was sentenced to a month in prison, without hard labour.

The business continued into the twentieth century. Towards the end of its independent existence, before being taken over by W.H. Smith & Son, in 1964 a commemorative twenty-eight-foot long, six-foot tall mural showing the history of Abel Heywood & Son was painted on the wall of the new canteen at the Lever Street building known as the White House. The first image was of Abel Heywood himself holding the *Poor Man's Guardian*, and it continued with the newsroom, a bare-footed newsboy and a horse-drawn delivery van, and the White House; it ended with a group of children poring over books, as an image of the future.

It was a vision of which Abel himself would have been proud, reflecting his aspirations to inspire learning and to promote the education of ordinary people. Abel's motivation in business was not to make money or to enjoy a lavish lifestyle per se. He had started out as a crusader in the interests of a free press, and at the end of his life his speeches show that he was at least as proud of this as of his more tangible achievements. His business ability and drive did bring him wealth, gained in a wide range of enterprises, and by the end of his life he was a highly respectable and respected figure in Manchester. But his ultimate aspiration was that his life should benefit the class from which he sprang through education, good living standards, political rights and civil freedoms. His business was the foundation of his efforts in these causes, but from the start there had been a greater focus, and this found an expression in his involvement in radical politics.

4

The Radical Liberal (1840–64)

As a committed campaigner and proponent of a free press, Abel was a well-respected member of the Chartist movement. However, his willingness to seek alliance with the middle-class liberals of Manchester sometimes put him at odds with his radical comrades. His roles in the campaign for the repeal of the Corn Laws and as a leader of the shopkeepers in the town demonstrate that he was a man of independent mind, who was not afraid to state his opinions even when he was a lone voice amongst his lower-class political friends. He gained acceptance among middle-class liberals and his commitment as a member of the Manchester Council went hand in hand with his rise up the social scale as he became an alderman in 1853, and then twice mayor in 1862–63 and 1876–77. What is more, his political stance began to appear less radical as both the Chartists and the government shifted their ground. By the end of the 1850s, on the one hand it was a mainstream Chartist policy to join forces with the more liberal middle classes to gain universal suffrage, and on the other hand, the establishment was now focused on incorporating, tolerating and thus neutralising radical ideas, rather than suppressing them. This gave Abel the latitude to continue as a social campaigner without falling foul of the law, and his later description of himself as a 'radical liberal' was substantiated by the breadth and number of social and economic causes of a liberal hue which he espoused from the 1840s and '50s.

Corn Law repealer and shopkeepers' leader

It has already been seen that Abel Heywood was keen to build bridges between the working and the middle classes with regard to the issue of Corn Law repeal. Much earlier than most other members of the working classes Abel perceived that repeal did not have to be an employers' ruse to lower the wages of operatives, but that it could be a vehicle for the elevation of the living standards of the workers not only by making bread cheaper, but also creating bigger domestic and foreign markets and therefore more work in Britain. This argument was especially telling at times of hardship, particularly after 1845, and the focus of his immediate campaign was to persuade the authorities to open the ports to allow in foreign corn and thus lower the price of bread. This was an angle on which he could appeal to the workers, without seeming to be siding with their employers in the Anti-Corn Law League.

Abel likewise demonstrated his leadership qualities at a meeting of the shopkeepers in the Town Hall on 21 June 1842. The purpose of the meeting was to use examples to illustrate to the government the distress from which the shopkeepers were suffering. Abel's resolution was to the effect that the government should be aware that while trade was declining, taxes had become unaffordable.

It seems that many Chartists had gathered both inside and outside the hall, and when they heard that Abel had also proposed a resolution linking support for the Charter to tariff repeal, they shouted three cheers for O'Connor. This caused trouble in the hall, and 'Mr Heywood got upon the table amidst the greatest confusion, and it was some time before he could get a hearing, the people were so much afraid of being jewed [*sic*] by the middle class.' Abel then made one of his stirring appeals: 'Men of Manchester, have not I sprung from your ranks? Nay, am I not one of yourselves? My greatest happiness would be to be instrumental in ameliorating your condition, and when I cease to hold these opinions may I cease to live.' He then went on to show them how an alliance with the middle classes, which they had said they wanted, was within reach. He was cheered 'for several minutes' when he stated that this was what O'Connor would have desired. In the end, the resolution for the Charter and the repeal of restrictions on trade was passed.[1]

The following month a shopkeepers' deputation which included Heywood was sent to London to speak to the government. Abel related to the Earl of Ripon that one shopkeeper had refused to donate towards the expenses of the deputation, but had said he would subscribe to a deputation to shoot the prime minister, Sir Robert Peel. This caused alarm bells to ring, as there was talk of plots against the prime minister's life around this time.

The Tory *Manchester Courier* gleefully took advantage of Abel's admission to try to discredit him, as well as the shopkeepers and the Anti-Corn Law League. On 30 July 1842 the paper recounted details which showed 'the diabolical spirit that animates the disappointed members of the League' and called on Abel to make known the man's identity because 'concealment is scarce a less atrocious crime than that attaching to the bloodthirsty wretch himself'. The writer even suggested that perhaps Abel made up the story as a 'rhetorical flourish' and finished that 'it is at least an edifying specimen of the animus which lurks beneath the ostentatious professions of sympathy for the distressed poor, so industriously put forth by the foiled and defeated factions of the League'.

Despite his dismissal of the shopkeeper's words as not 'seriously intended', Abel explained that he had related what had been said to exemplify the point that 'discontent among the people was becoming more widely disseminated… even until it had reached a class [shopkeepers] which invariably has supported and assisted in preserving the peace of the country'. He added that, to his regret, he had heard working men in extreme hardship say much worse things about Sir Robert Peel. The MP Busfield Ferrand claimed that this was part of an Anti-Corn Law League conspiracy to intimidate the government, but Abel defended the Anti-Corn Law League, saying that they had no more to do with what was said 'than the inhabitants of Kamschatka have to do with the Manchester charter'.

The *Manchester Courier*, which was still predictably hostile, had to have the last word. By now it was claiming that Heywood had in the original meeting in July 1842 'told a cock-and-bull story of some ruffians drawing lots to shoot the premier'. Thus was the story rolling out of control, and what had been almost a throwaway remark was eighteen months later being spun into a full-blown assassination plot.[2]

On 6 December 1845 several newspapers carried Abel's letter of appeal to the prime minister, Sir Robert Peel, to open the ports. This was the result of a public meeting of the Manchester working classes, which he chaired and addressed in the Town Hall on 2 December. He admitted that hitherto there had been no unity of thought on the topic of Corn Law repeal, but 'I deem it my duty to inform you, that this is the first time during the last eight years that a public meeting of the working men of this town have unanimously agreed to memorialise or petition either her majesty's government or parliament for the entire abolition of all food restrictions.'[3] His satisfaction at this development, for which he had worked hard, was manifest. He was sensible of the impact of prices on the poor, those who lived 'from hand to mouth', and he cited the rise in the price of a loaf from 5*d* to 8*d* in the preceding six weeks, going on to discuss also potato prices.

He also explained how this was having an effect on the sales of manufacturers, so emphasising that all social groups were affected, and stressing the necessity for the government to listen to the workers' petition and take action. Throughout a series of meetings on opening the ports, Abel was consistently keen to stress that it was the workers who were most affected by food prices, and therefore their opinions were crucial; he clearly perceived that the minute this seemed like a movement for the interests of the employers, the workers would revert to a hostile stance on Corn Law repeal.

The Corn Laws were finally repealed on 15 May 1846. Even then the ports continued to be closed, and an indignant meeting was held on 15 January 1847, expressing disbelief that in response to two deputations Prime Minister Lord John Russell still said he did not consider the hardship yet to be sufficiently extreme. The meeting at the Town Hall was so heavily attended that it had to be split into two – one in the building and one in the street outside. Abel chaired the second and, marking himself out as a radical in an interesting breach of received laissez-faire liberal opinion at the time, averred: 'It was almost impossible that private charity could do anything to remove the evil, and he thought it was therefore the bounden duty of the government to see that the people did not starve.'[4]

In the troubled year of 1848, on 10 April, there was a well-attended public meeting in the Corn Exchange, called at the request of over 500 shopkeepers and householders to consider how they, enrolled as special constables, should approach their duties 'towards their fellow men who are striving to obtain the People's Charter' as well as to express opinion 'on the critical state of the times'.[5] There were fears that some of the shopkeepers and others enrolled would be heavy-handed in their approach, which could provoke a violent reaction. Abel, himself a special constable, was 'called by acclamation to the chair'. Other speakers included R.J. Richardson, John Watts and James Cooper, radical reformers and Chartists, but it was Abel who was the leading figure of authority.

Although he had firmly established himself in the lower ranks of the middle class as a leader of the shopkeepers, at this meeting Abel was eager to assert his common interest with and belief in the working classes. He used the opportunity to put the case for 'moral force' in the struggle to gain political rights, pointing out that a resort to physical violence 'armed the parties with the strongest argument against their rights being granted'. Abel, identifying himself as 'one who had sprung from the working classes', proceeded to proclaim his faith in their good sense and character. He went on to dismiss the alarmists who filled the town and cried that some revolution was about to occur, but said that the special constable's role was to protect any property which was in danger, not to prevent the people from expressing their views and peaceably demanding their rights.

When the government finally acted and opened the ports, celebratory banquets were held by the middle classes. At one such on 20 October 1852, Abel was one of thirty men on the executive committee; he was moving up the League hierarchy and now appeared alongside names like middle-class leaders Sir Elkanah Armitage, Thomas Worthington and Thomas Bazley.

Social campaigner

Abel demonstrated a lifelong commitment to improving the moral and physical welfare of the working classes from which he sprang. But as a believer in the gospel of 'self-help' he was keen to encourage efforts from the grass-roots, of which an early example in Manchester was the co-operative movement.

Abel had been committed to this movement since 1828, but with the fading of Chartism his participation burgeoned. In September 1850, chairing a co-operative meeting, he reviewed developments in optimistic vein. His perception that the movement could raise the economic, moral and intellectual level of the working classes, meant that it would be acceptable to the wealthy because it was meeting them on their own terms. By 1861, the Manchester and Salford Co-operative Society was described by the Tory *Manchester Courier* as 'this flourishing company', and when it held its annual meeting and tea party in the Corn Exchange in January Abel presided over the thousand and more participants. He pointed out that by co-operating working men were able to become 'capitalists and traders equally with capitalists and traders amongst other classes'. Indeed, they were 'establishing themselves as the friends of order', which had been the unachieved object of every 'enlightened statesman' for the last thirty years.[6] Co-operation, in other words, was the means by which the working classes could be brought into the social fabric and made respectable.

When the Manchester Co-operative Spinning and Manufacturing Company was set up by the shareholders' purchase of a mill at Newton Heath, Abel accepted the post of chairman of the board of directors. At the inaugural tea in the mill itself Abel voiced the ambition that the co-operative should be able to compete on equal terms with the largest manufacturers in the kingdom. He 'dwelt at some length' on the success of the Rochdale Equitable Pioneers Company as a model to encourage them on. In a revealing phrase in 1863, Abel said 'co-operation realised the dream of his life'. He saw in it the empowerment of the working man through diligence and moral rectitude.[7]

But co-operative ventures relied on a degree of education among their participants. Education was therefore also an early priority in Abel's career as a social campaigner. He regarded it as crucial for self-advancement, and had only to look at his own career for evidence of this. His interest fell into three main aspects: mechanics' institutions and lyceums, a national education system for children, and public libraries, museums and art galleries.

From the start he was a keen evangelist for mechanics' institutions; as well as continuing to support the Manchester Institution, he appeared from the 1840s onwards at annual meetings of the Miles Platting Institution, of which he was the chairman. He supported a broad role for these bodies at the inaugural meeting of the new Longsight Mechanics' Institution in March 1859, when he proposed a resolution that not only should it provide 'direct and specific instruction in its classes', but that it should also afford facilities for discussion on social and political science and make provision for women, though only in terms of 'domestic economy and kindred subjects'. He moreover hoped there would be scope for such 'healthy recreation and amusement as are not… inimical to the moral welfare of the people'.

He regarded such bodies as a means of enhancing career prospects; at the Ancoats Lyceum Christmas party in 1850 he encouraged young men to become members: 'For his own part, and he knew that many employers had a similar feeling, he should much more highly esteem any young man in his service if he were a member of such an institution, than if he were not.'[8]

However, the point was raised in 1849 that the mechanics' institutions and lyceums could not fully succeed as 'colleges for the people' unless there was an effective system of primary education. Abel was aware of the weight of this argument and from its inception supported the Lancashire Public School Association, chairing a meeting at the People's Institute in April 1849 at which support was declared for a universal system of secular education. When the organisation adopted a new name, the National Public School Association, Abel was on the executive.

The proposed Manchester and Salford Education Bill, which appeared before Parliament in 1852 introduced by Joseph Brotherton, MP for Salford, provoked much interest in and outside the Manchester Council. Abel was called upon to chair a meeting in the Athenaeum convened by some working men. Several objections were expressed: that the system to be established would be funded by ratepayers, but that they would have no control over it; that religious teaching by the established Church of England in the schools would exclude large numbers of children who were of different denominations or religions; that the bill was introduced as a private member's bill with no real consultation with those living in the borough or with the Corporation; that it did not help the ragged or the factory schools, or for that matter the night schools for adults. Although there were dissenting voices, the resolution upheld these objections, and Abel ended the meeting by averring that Lord John Russell, the prime minister, of whom he had a very high opinion, would not allow the bill to pass in its present form.

Using his influence in the council and public meetings, Abel continued to preach the line of the NPSA, and in his own radical liberal journal, the *Manchester Spectator*, he advertised a feature entitled 'Popular Education – What Can Be Done?' By 1859 he was hopeful that 'within a very few years the primary education of the people would be taken [into] a national system'.[9] Meanwhile he supported a variety of approaches towards the education of the masses. Most obviously, he was frequently to be found patronising schools for poor children, supporting the Hewitt Street and Gorton Ragged Schools.

He also regarded the provision of libraries as a key element of the education of the masses. By the early 1850s this was coming to fruition with the acquisition by the Corporation of the Hall of Science in Campfield for the provision of a public library. Abel, on the book sub-committee, was prominent on the platform at a well-attended meeting of perhaps 2,000 working men and some of their wives at the Hall of Science, now being called the Free Library, on 25 February 1851. Abel praised the mayor, John Potter, for his work in purchasing the building for the purpose, which he later described as 'the brightest gem in the diadem on his forehead'.[10] He appealed to the working classes to contribute beyond the £1,000 which was hoped of them, and also to give books towards the formation of the 'proposed vast library'.[11]

Yet he believed that the libraries should not impinge on the principles of self-help. When he presided over the Harpurhey Mechanics' Institution annual soiree early in 1864, he expressed regret that subscriptions to the Institution had decreased partly due to the competition from a free branch library:

> For, when a library established at the public expense tended to destroy the vitality of an independent institution like this, he thought that to some extent it was injurious rather than beneficial. It was much better for people to obtain at their own cost, and by their own energy, that instruction which mechanics institutions provided.[12]

The Free Library provided lectures, and a meeting on 2 December 1852 touched all the bases for Abel when Dr Vaughan gave a well-attended talk on 'Books relating to History'. The standard of understanding expected of the working-class audiences who packed these talks was remarkable; a lecture on 'Poetry and Fiction' by Professor Scott, Principal of Owens College, in February 1852 made enormous demands on listeners. It is notable that Abel, who attended many such lectures, often exhibited broad and erudite knowledge.

But successful education was predicated on decent living standards, and so Abel also took a great interest in the physical conditions in which the poor lived. By October 1854 he had become a leading campaigner for the Manchester and Salford Sanitary Association as chairman of the Ardwick and London Road branch, which was well-attended by members of the working classes. In a typically blunt statement Abel opened the meeting with remarks highly offensive to modern sensibilities, but at the time unexceptionable: 'The chairman, in opening the proceedings, explained the meaning of the word "sanitary," which simply implied "washing a blackeymoor [sic] white," or removing dirt and filth, and making places clean.'

He later pointed out that Manchester had largely avoided the visitations of the cholera from which other cities had suffered, and he attributed this mainly to the paving and sewering of the streets, by his own council Paving and Sewering Committee. He went on to explain how the Sanitary Association, by means of house-to-house visiting, pamphleting and consultation 'with all parties', had taken the work on to a more effective and detailed level. But he ended with a reminder that the work was not finished; overcrowding remained a major issue, and he cited Angel Meadow, where the Board of Guardians reported there were still up to fourteen people living in a single room.[13] The work of the association also included a series of lectures for the working classes such as that given on 19 December 1854 on 'Sanitary laws in their bearing on education' at which Abel presided. His London Road branch was noted as being particularly active, and had offered a three-guinea prize for the best essay by a working man on 'The domestic position which a working man's wife ought to hold, and the evils, social, moral, and physical, which result from her employment in factories.' It would have been a step too far to ask the working man's wife what she thought about the matter!

With the growth of the industrial city, open spaces became built up for the housing needed for workers, and it began to dawn on those in charge that some form of public park was essential for health, recreation and leisure activities. It was also widely agreed that parks had a role in public morality by offering an alternative to the pub, regulated by the values of the respectable and well-off.

On 8 August 1844 a ticketed meeting was held in the Town Hall to appoint Manchester's high-flying parks committee, led by the mayor. The radical R.J. Richardson suggested that there were no members who were familiar with the desires and needs of the working classes, who were after all the objects of this philanthropy. He proposed the inclusion of Abel Heywood and James Scholefield, but failed to persuade the committee. It was nevertheless considered fitting to enlist the financial support of the workers and Abel was appointed as treasurer to collect in the funds.

Following on from this, Abel chaired a 'very numerous' meeting of the working classes in the Free Trade Hall which aimed to promote measures to establish public parks in Manchester. By September 1846, Queen's Park and Philips Park had been opened. Abel took an interest in the minutiae of the parks' organisation and rules, expressing a view against allowing preaching in the parks, as it could lead to trouble, as it had apparently done in St Ann's Square. In August 1857 he voiced his concern, in colourful and now unacceptable language, about the toilets in Philips Park: 'Alderman Heywood complained of the discreditable sanitary arrangements at Philips Park, which were more fitted for Hottentots than the inhabitants of a civilised city. – (Hear, hear.)'[14]

However, once the desirability of parks was established in the minds of the wealthy, Abel seemed content to 'take a back seat' on the issue, only sallying forth when he perceived that the freedoms of the poor might be infringed by an overly controlling Corporation. This was the case, for instance, with regard to the acceptance or otherwise of bands playing in the parks on the Sabbath; Abel nailed his colours to the mast in support of this 'innocent recreation of the people' in 1856.[15] This time, he was on the losing side and the religious lobby won the battle, but the general principle of the benefits of public parks was well established by the 1860s.

It was all very well to establish parks for the recreation and health of the workers, but many of them were working long hours, six days a week, and had little time in which to enjoy them. Abel therefore espoused the 'Ten Hours Movement' and in the council expressed the hope that Lord John Russell would be influenced in its favour when he visited Manchester in 1850. With the exception of James Scholefield, he was apparently supported by very few others in the council, many of whom were factory owners worried about the impact of the legislation, but going out on a limb was nothing new for Abel.

The main event of the year 1850 in Manchester was indeed the visit in April of Prime Minister Russell. The stir surrounding this involved Abel in two capacities, and thus symbolised his continuing efforts to be a bridge between the middle and the working classes. On the third day of the visit at midday Russell attended at the Town Hall, where he was received by the mayor and council, amongst whom Abel was numbered. Abel appeared again at a second meeting in the evening, consisting mostly of factory operatives. The intention of the latter was to prepare an address to the prime minister thanking him for passing the Ten Hours Act, and entreating him to back also a proposed new bill to prevent factory owners using a loophole to avoid its effects. Abel ended his address with the adjuration: 'Let his lordship treat the working men as so much human nature, instead of as mere machines, and he (Mr Heywood) felt satisfied that the confidence of the people would remain steadfast in his lordship…' Although the Factory Act of 1850 only cut the hours of women and young people aged 13 to 18 to ten and a half per day, ultimately the agitation did succeed in achieving effective ten-hour day legislation in 1856.

Abel was never directly involved in the trade union movement, but he did on occasion show support for workers who were in dispute with their employers. During a trade dispute in 1852, when the union of the Amalgamated Society of Engineers reduced the payments to workers on strike from fifteen to ten shillings, many workers were forced to return to work. This was alarming to those in other trades, and Abel chaired a meeting at the Corn Exchange which included speakers from the joiners, the spinners and the bookbinders. He argued that the employers' terms would harm not only the workers but also the employers themselves and he 'hoped that working men who had a latent spark of liberty left in them would never sign it'. The meeting resolved to find funds to help the strikers, because 'the independence of the operatives of this country is threatened by the proceedings of the employers in the iron trades'.[16]

Abel likewise supported shopworkers campaigning for shorter hours, such as the female milliners and dressmakers, who were campaigning for a Saturday afternoon holiday and a twelve-hour day in 1851. He seconded a resolution to appeal to the wealthy ladies of Manchester to use their influence over the proprietors of dressmaking and millinery establishments, to give their orders with consideration, and to curtail late shopping and the transaction of business on Saturdays.

When thousands went on strike in Preston the workers of Manchester held a meeting chaired by Abel Heywood to raise funds to support them. He hoped that the meeting might bring 'belligerent parties' closer together and believed that 'a large proportion of the crime of this country was in a great measure to be attributed to the want of sympathy on the part of the rich towards the poor'; indeed, he said that 'the truth of this statement he had sealed with his life'.[17]

Abel also acted as an arbiter. In 1857 the building trade was experiencing industrial unrest in the form of a seven-week strike over working hours. It was agreed that Abel would act for the workers, and Alderman Bancroft for the masters. At a meeting at the latter's office in St Ann's Square, and therefore on the territory of the employers, two workmen represented the men, being perhaps somewhat overwhelmed to find that the employers were represented by no fewer than five of Manchester's more influential citizens. In the event, having narrowed down the difference between their two positions, 'the arbitrators recommended the men to resume work at the hours proposed by the masters' and assent was given to abide by this decision. We do not know whether the workers were content with the settlement Abel negotiated for them.

But overall industrial conflict did not sit comfortably with Abel Heywood, and he found the self-help philosophy of land and building societies more to his liking. He was keen that those who could should be encouraged to invest in property, and so add to their security. The notice for the Manchester Villa and Cottage Association Limited which was published in the *Manchester Courier* on 21 November 1863 explained the role of such societies; to provide homes it would select:

I

the most eligible plots of land in the suburbs of Manchester and Salford. Semi-detached houses and cottages, of such size and rental as are best suited to the neighbourhood will then be erected thereon… they will be much more substantial and better built than is usual for property of the kind indicated, and in most cases they will be sold separately for parties to live in themselves.[18]

On 23 October 1847 the Working Men's Benefit Building Society advertised an affordable option of £50 shares with a subscription of 4s a month. Abel chaired the first meeting on 6 November 1847 as one of its 'promoters'. The Manchester and Northern Counties Freehold Land Society also received Abel's support, and there is concrete evidence of its activities from 1851, when they bought four acres in Sale Moor which they named 'The Freetown Estate'. On 19 May around 100 people went by train from Oxford Road to visit the site for a ceremonial handing over to the new owners. In 1852 Abel was a trustee of the British Freehold Land Society, which held its first, crowded general meeting in March 1852, when Abel, having been unanimously elected as chairman, took the opportunity to explain the features of the society and then to exhort its potential beneficiaries to commit:

Working men were now beginning to understand an important truth, that if they would rise in life, they must themselves be the builders of their own fortune and realise the truth of the sagacious Franklin, – "God helps them who help themselves."[19]

And so a lifetime's support was established; he continued to chair the annual meetings of the Queen's Building Society until February 1893, when he wrote to say he could not attend through illness.

Abel was eager to help the poor avoid pauperism and sought alternative solutions. He was active in raising money, especially in times of hardship. The most well-known group to suffer in the first part of the nineteenth century were the handloom weavers, and in 1846 it was feared that their extreme distress would lead to famine and crime, and therefore a public subscription was launched. At the request of the weavers themselves Heywood was chosen to act as treasurer.

He was a strong opponent of the Poor Law as imposed by the Amendment Act of 1834, which the poor believed was intended to punish poverty by forcing the destitute into prison-like workhouses. The stated aim was to make life more unpleasant than the supposed alternative of working in the lowest paid job. When the factory campaigner Richard Oastler was imprisoned for debt having opposed the Poor Law, Abel was appointed to a committee set up to raise money in Lancashire, Cheshire and Derbyshire in his support.

It was also around this time that Abel started a campaign within and outside the council regarding the treatment of the bodies of deceased paupers which were used for scientific purposes and were buried 'after dissection in Walker's Croft without the burial service being read, which he said was an outrage upon the public decency'.[20] The records of the Poor Law Commissioners show that he was also pursuing this matter at a national level. After a meeting with a Dr Turner from the Commission, on 12 August 1845 the Commissioners drafted a letter to him, assuring him that no further interments would take place without a proper service, and another letter giving instructions accordingly to the Honourable C.S. Clements, Assistant Commissioner.

Meanwhile, Abel had to deal with his electors who complained at the high level of the poor rate. The voices became louder in times of hardship, and in 1846 the council was criticised by a public meeting which had met to oppose the imposition of a rate of five shillings in the pound. Heywood and two colleagues from the council attended the meeting and it was forcibly brought home to them that there was great strength of feeling on the issue.[21]

Perhaps such experiences convinced Abel to stand for election as one of the Manchester Poor Law Guardians in 1853. He had already been campaigning since 1848 to improve the treatment of paupers by drawing up a petition for the abolition of stone-breaking and oakum-picking, both common occupations imposed on the 'able-bodied' in the workhouse. Once on the board, he lost no time in proposing a motion for ascertaining the age and previous employment of those able-bodied poor receiving relief, with a view to providing work, and so relieving the ratepayers. However, as older hands had in fact told him, he found that fifty supposedly able-bodied men in the workhouse were in fact not so, and could only discover one who could be so described. The rest were 'wholly unfit' for work. After this debacle, which he followed up with suggestions that there had been underhand dealings in the election of Guardians, to which the others responded with accusations that he was in the control of anti-Poor Law campaigners, Abel found himself isolated on the board; the rest of the Guardians did not trust him or his motives.[22]

Early in the new year Abel participated in deliberations as to how to deal with Relieving Officer Joseph Clarke, who had been accused of violence against female paupers. Abel stated that he had often attended Clarke's relief board and found him to be able, but he pointed out that his violent conduct could not be ignored. In the same meeting, the Guardians supported a resolution proposed by Mr Hodgson and seconded by Heywood that a number of men in receipt of outdoor relief – that is, not living inside the workhouse – could be put to street cleaning in Manchester for the Corporation, if the latter so desired.

With his particular interest in education and as a Poor Law Guardian Abel attended the annual examination of the children at the Swinton Schools, which educated 750 pauper children. Ratepayers were concerned at the expense, which was said to have 'reached an amount that is inconsistent with the class of children for whom the schools were designed'.[23] The ethos of the school was summed up by a slogan prominently displayed: 'Train up a child in the way he should go.' The *Manchester Courier* claimed that 'they all seemed very happy and very healthy'.[24]

But further frustration came in February when Abel found himself a lone voice in objecting to the board's method of dealing with a proposed bill in Parliament which would do away with the law which settled paupers in their place of origin; Manchester was likely to lose out financially if the bill became law. The board decided to send a deputation to London to meet the President of the Poor Law Board, but Abel claimed that the expense would not be worthwhile. He was a lone voice and was thwarted. Soon after April 1854 Abel had given up his role as a Poor Law Guardian. Although his explanation was the pressure of his work on the council, he may well have felt that there was little that he could achieve as a Guardian; having alienated them, the vested interests were too strong, even for him.

It was widely believed, and with some justification, that a major factor in destitution was excessive consumption of alcohol. Accordingly, in the 1850s Abel was developing some sympathy with the ideals of temperance. In the summer of 1852 there was a move in the council to petition for a ban on the sale of alcohol on Sundays. Abel, however, on this occasion defended licensed premises selling alcohol, who had not had 'a single complaint preferred by the police', and 'he believed that such an interference with the habits of the people as the memorial contemplated would be the means of creating greater evils than those which existed at present'. He also maintained that Parliament would not pass any such Act. The council agreed, and rejected the proposal. When he stood for re-election in Collegiate ward in October he had to defend this position, and cited figures showing that alternative activities would have to be found for 40,000 adults if each of the 2,000 public houses were visited by twenty of them.

Abel was clearly not an anti-alcohol zealot. He attended the annual dinners of the Licensed Victuallers on several occasions, such as on 21 October 1853 when he praised them because 'they conducted their houses in a manner so satisfactory as not to be equalled by the licensed victuallers in any other part of the country'. He explained that the number of beer-sellers, disreputable rivals to the licensed victuallers, had doubled since 1843.[25]

Abel finally became a teetotaller in about 1855, although his friends said that 'of all men [he] had the least necessity for such an act'. It was claimed that he was thinking especially of the example he was setting for his growing sons. His commitment was manifested in his disappearance from the licensed victuallers' dinners and his appearance at temperance meetings. He was stocking the *Alliance Weekly News* in his shop by 14 February 1856, and presided when the United Kingdom Alliance met in the Free Trade Hall in April 1857, to show support for the total suppression of the 'liquor traffic'. Ironically, he reiterated the figures first used at the victuallers' dinner about beerhouses, elaborating that there were now 2,041 in the city. This meeting was overwhelmingly working class; a sign that Abel was in step with ordinary people in his view.

However, he was not in favour of imposing his own beliefs on others, and wished rather to persuade his community against alcohol rather than to impose bans. In 1852 he had said the temperance lobby 'must go on endeavouring to reform the habits of the people... It was a waste of time to suppose that the habits of the people could be reformed by acts of parliament.'[26] This view did not change, as was demonstrated in his speeches in the election campaign of 1865, by which time he was a dedicated member of the United Kingdom Alliance.

Temperance was picking up pace, and Abel's involvement became more prominent when he became vice-president of the Manchester and Salford Temperance League, and took the chair when celebrated temperance campaigner John Gough from the United States lectured to 'a monster audience' in the Free Trade Hall. Reflecting his belief that the young were particularly at risk from the dangers of alcohol, in 1858 Abel promised £5 worth of books to young persons in Ancoats who would sign the (teetotal) pledge, attend the weekly meeting in Mather Street Temperance Hall, and keep their word till Christmas. Strikingly, 200 'youths and girls under 16 years of age' complied.[27] In September 1864 Abel presided at a huge meeting in the Free Trade Hall of the Lancashire and Cheshire Band of Hope Union, an organisation aimed at dissuading the young from partaking in alcohol. In the light of the statistics quoted by other speakers, for example that in the Edinburgh Industrial School 85 per cent of the children had been begging or in ragged schools due to 'intemperance', Abel showed his optimistic expectations of the temperance movement:

> It was most gratifying to him to find that there were between 6,000 and 7,000 persons before him, and that every individual was a protest against the system of drinking. (Cheers.) He saw before him material which, if properly directed and instructed, would in the course of a few years work a complete change in the social system.[28]

Foreign affairs

Abel did not limit his radical liberalism to domestic affairs, but took an active interest in liberal *causes célèbres* across Europe. He was much exercised by upheavals in Hungary, especially espousing the cause of Lajos Kossuth, the nationalist leader fighting to free his country from the Austrian Empire. When news of fighting in Hungary between the nationalists and the Russians, supporting Austria, was reported in the British press in 1849, he chaired a meeting of over 1,000 working people held at the Hall of Science in Manchester 'to sympathise with the brave patriots of Hungary in their glorious resistance to oppression'. In true liberal style, he was keen that the government should support the Hungarians, not by going to war, but by diplomatic means; thus would Britain avoid 'increasing the national debt', but achieve 'a great and important object'. The meeting passed resolutions accordingly, and a memorial on the subject was also to be sent to the Queen.

Nearly two years later Kossuth was reported 'imprisoned' in Turkey and Abel, with over 400 others, signed a requisition in Manchester requesting the mayor to call a meeting to petition the government to secure his 'liberation'.[29] The mayor agreed to a meeting in the Town Hall at 11 a.m. on 16 July 1851. However,

Kossuth's supporters apparently wanted a gathering in the Free Trade Hall in the evening, so that it would be accessible to as large a number as possible, and were disappointed in the mayor's response. So strong was Abel's annoyance that, when the mayor, Sir John Potter, retired in November, he took the unusual step of using the occasion to criticise him because he had refused to accede to the requisition. Abel argued even more extremely that public feeling about Kossuth's visit in the same year was stronger than the feeling manifested about that of the Queen. This did not go down well in the council.

Kossuth, described by the *Manchester Times* as 'perhaps the most remarkable political character in Europe', visited again in 1856 and in January 1857 spoke in the Free Trade Hall to working men on the political state of continental Europe. When the speech had concluded, Abel successfully proposed a resolution stating a strong objection to an alliance between Britain and Austria.

Since the Russian army had been instrumental in the removal of Kossuth from power in Hungary, such events fed into the strong support manifested for the government in the war with Russia, centred on the Crimea, in the mid-1850s. Abel was invited by the speaker Mr D. Urquhart, former MP for Stafford, to chair a rowdy and argumentative meeting in the Corn Exchange in which Urquhart argued that the real enemy was France. Abel agreed to do so as long as it was recognised that he had really come to learn and was not the representative of Mr Urquhart or anyone else at the meeting.[30] Urquhart was supported by several 'strangers to Manchester' who, apparently, 'were nearly all distinguished by tremendous moustaches'.[31]

Although a high-powered liberal conference was held in Manchester to oppose the war against Russia in 1853, Abel took a more conventional stance. Rather than focus on the difficulties of interpreting foreign policy the patriots of Manchester decided less controversially to set up a fund to raise money to help the widows and orphans of soldiers killed in the fighting. Abel's idea of raising funds within the Collegiate ward gained the support of the mayor and it became a successful model for other wards.

The deprivations of the ordinary soldiers fighting in the Crimea did not go unnoticed. In the new year, the working classes held a meeting in the People's Institute on Heyrod Street in Ancoats to discuss 'reform of parliament and of our military system', advertised on placards headed with the liberal slogan 'Peace, retrenchment, and reform!' It was clear that in the popular mind the slaughter of the war was linked to the inequalities of the political system. As chairman of the meeting Abel spoke of the need for continued petitioning of Parliament for reform of the suffrage system, including the ballot. He then went on to state his views on the war, and that 'he believed in the possibility of its necessity'. He was not in favour of 'peace at any price'. What he did object to, however, was that 'our brave soldiers in the Crimea had been compelled to submit to "all sorts of degradation" which many believed might have been avoided, if those who had the management of the war had known how to wield the power they had in their hands. – (Loud cheers.)' After some confusion, the meeting ultimately accepted a resolution in support of the war against Russia and its prosecution with the utmost vigour, but also advocating retrenchment and reform of foreign policy in favour of better relations with other countries, and a remodelling of the army. All this was to be achieved by a reformed Parliament which was a true representation of the people by means of universal male suffrage, the ballot and three-year terms for parliaments.[32]

By 1860, Italian nationalism had replaced Hungarian as the favoured international cause of British liberals. A meeting convened by circular expressed sympathy with General Giuseppe Garibaldi 'in his present struggle for freedom in Sicily'. Heywood led a deputation to present a requisition with 825 signatures of firms and individuals of all political parties to the mayor, 'it having been felt that in a question affecting the interests of humanity, all local politics should be merged', unsuccessfully requesting that he call a meeting of the inhabitants of Manchester. A subscription was launched instead.[33] Abel was a prominent member of the deputation which met the general in London, but excited hopes of a visit in April 1864 were dashed by a letter which stated that 'for many reasons' the hero was unable to visit Manchester.

Although most of the discussion of foreign affairs was highly worthy and serious, there was occasionally space for some Victorian levity as evidenced by a letter to the editor of the *Manchester Guardian* on 4 December 1858. Rajah Brooke had settled Sarawak in what is now Malaysia; it was proposed that it should be governed on 'Manchester principles', and 'Mercator Junior' therefore added his own suggestions for the personnel who might take up the reins of power in the settlement. It was to be an independent republic based on manhood suffrage; the president would be George Wilson, leader of the Anti-Corn Law League. In his cabinet a place was to be found for Abel Heywood as Minister of Justice, perhaps recognising his ubiquitous crusading zeal against injustice.

Although in the 1840s and '50s Abel's activities often focused on local social and economic issues, it was clear that national political aspirations were central to his understanding of working-class improvement. By the end of the 1850s his hero, Lord John Russell, was also campaigning for an extension of the suffrage, and the time was perhaps ripe for Abel to join in the struggle at a national level. In 1859, therefore, he allowed himself to be proposed as a Liberal candidate for Manchester. However, that a man of his origins found himself in a position where this might even be considered was only possible because of his evolution as a member of the middle class and his substantial record of public service as a member of the Manchester Council.

5

Police Commissioner, Town Councillor and Alderman (1836–62)

Abel Heywood's rapprochement with the middle classes commenced at the time of extreme strife which tore Manchester apart in the late 1830s and early '40s over how the town should be governed. It was controlled by a traditional Tory elite of landowners and wealthy families, loyal to the Church of England and the aristocratic constitution. This was challenged by a key group of radical liberal industrialists, including Unitarians Archibald Prentice and Thomas and Richard Potter. Manchester's medieval manorial system which prevailed up to the early 1840s in their view, was totally unsuited to the administration of a town which was growing rapidly into a great metropolis, with an industrial and mercantile economy which was quite new and unique in the world. They courted the increasingly articulate shopkeepers and artisans for their campaign.

'Incorporate Your Borough!'

In October 1836 Heywood, qualifying as the occupier of a shop worth at least £28, was elected to the Police Commission for number 5 district, Collegiate Church ward. He immediately joined the ranks of those responsible for 'cleansing, lighting, watching, and regulating'. This was the start of a career in local politics which was a key focus of his life right up to his death in 1893. It was also another way in which he engaged with the middle class by forming strategic alliances with those radical liberals who were in contention with the Tory elite for civic power. As a Chartist on the Commission, moreover, he was not alone in the 1830s; Paul Pickering has described how the *Northern Star* urged upon members of the movement that they should gain influence in local politics, which he avers amounted to 'a policy of municipal Chartism'.[1]

The involvement from 1837 of Richard Cobden, later a leading light of the anti-Corn Law campaign, was significant; he coined the phrase 'Incorporate Your Borough' in a pamphlet produced in 1837–38 in response to the 1835 Municipal Corporations Act which allowed large towns to set up chartered corporations and thus modernise their systems of government. He showed the town's liberals a way to promote their power, and a way to win over the 'shopocracy' by offering them a supposedly better deal than they could get from the Tory elite.

Cobden found the working class hostile; they did not trust middle-class radical liberals or the Whig party, and joined with the Tory opposition to denounce Cobden as 'a mere spouter to gain applause'. James Wroe, Chartist and Police Commissioner, condemned the campaign; such a proposal by the 'base, bloody and brutal Whigs' was associated in the minds of the poor with other measures they had introduced, in particular with the hated Poor Law Amendment Act of 1834.

But Cobden appealed more successfully to the shopkeepers, people like Abel, and succeeded in awakening them to their present status and its indignities:

> It has always been a maxim, at the election of municipal officers, that no retailer was eligible to fill the office of borough reeve or constable!... The tone which has so long prevailed in the government of the town has naturally enough pervaded all our public institutions, and even entered into the private arrangements of social life...
>
> But in the city of London, where you will find no manor court-leet diffusing its town of feudal insolence or slavish servility, there is a corporation renowned for its liberal character; and more than a moiety of its common councilmen, and several of its aldermen, are shopkeepers.[2]

On 2 February 1838, Abel Heywood's name appeared in a list of around 1,000 leypayers (ratepayers) who signed a requisition for a public meeting on 9 February with the purpose of petitioning the Queen to grant a charter of incorporation. The meeting was attended by nearly 2,000 people and lasted for four and a half hours, with most leypayers standing throughout to hear Cobden, Prentice and others speak. The opposition also had their say, with radicals like James Wroe and Elijah Dixon speaking out against Cobden. It must have been a fine line for Abel to walk, bearing in mind that he was a Chartist comrade of men such as these, but was on the other side of the argument when it came to the incorporation debate.

The Charter of Incorporation was finally granted on 23 October 1838, and Manchester was to have a mayor, sixteen aldermen and forty-eight councillors, representing fifteen wards; the first election was to be held on 14 December 1838. Yet the agents of the old dispensation were as obstructive as they could be. The new council, to which Abel was elected, had to meet in the York Hotel in King Street as, despite repeated requests, the Police Commissioners refused to give them access to the Town Hall. There was further wrangling about finance; the old agencies were still collecting the rates and refused to hand them over to the council. The new town government was seriously financially embarrassed, and at one point there was a danger of policing breaking down entirely. In view of the concurrent popular unrest – the growth of Chartism in particular – central government stepped in to take control of the police, and appointed Sir Charles Shaw as Chief Commissioner over a special new force financed by a new levy.

Ultimately, the Charter of Incorporation was pronounced valid on 22 February 1841 by a court ruling, strengthened by the Borough Incorporation Act of August 1842. Thus were the old agencies finally defeated and the reign of the liberal middle class began in Manchester. Cobden attributed the success of the incorporators to the 'shopocracy'; in the new dispensation they were to play an increasingly dominant role. These were men like Abel Heywood, who, as a member of the new Corporation, attended all fifty-five of the meetings of the Nuisance Committee between October 1841 and October 1842. The Tory elite boycotted the municipal elections and ultimately left themselves emasculated until the later nineteenth century.

The council was dominated from 1842 until 1890 by the lower middle-class liberals; men such as Abel had the opportunity to rise in the world of civic power, and it was a chance he seized with both hands. In the 1830s and '40s he was perhaps predictably pugnacious in discussions, featuring frequently in news reports, and usually challenging the more established and powerful members of the Police Commission and its successor, the council. He was especially keen to defend the interests of the ratepayers (his electors) and also those of the poor, against privilege, inefficiency and tradition. We may surmise that his efforts met with success as far as his constituents were concerned, since he was invariably re-elected every three years as a councillor for Collegiate Church ward until his elevation to alderman in 1853.

Police commissioner (1836–43)

The press covered an animated discussion in the Police Commission meeting on Wednesday 28 November 1838 concerning the cleansing of streets and pavements in the town. This was the occasion of Abel's first recorded contribution to the government of Manchester, when he supported a motion to recommend the Nuisance Committee to strictly enforce the law, and thereby to clean the pavements as well as the streets. The motion was rejected; it was not the most notable of beginnings!

By the time of the meeting of 14 October 1840 Abel was getting into his stride. He was concerned with the partiality of the Nuisance Committee in prosecuting some people but not others for displaying goods for sale on the pavements. He took his duties seriously and had attended a meeting where those affected told their stories and aired their grievances.

On several occasions, Abel attempted to defend the interests of the ratepayers, many of whom were people such as himself – shopkeepers and small businessmen – against inefficiency and lax financial management. For instance, on 24 February 1841 he unsuccessfully opposed increases in salaries for officials, arguing that 'if the hours were the same, there was no ground for an increase; it would not be just to the leypayers'.[3] By October, Abel was again arguing strongly against increasing salaries because of 'very great distress' amongst the shopkeepers.

However, the chief concern by the end of the year was the transition of authority from Police Commission to Corporation, and how committees nominated under the old regime would fare. During this discussion, G.N. Winder proposed that Abel Heywood and James Hampson be elected to the Finance and General Purposes Committee in place of Mr Gasquoine and Mr Garnett, who rarely attended, but this was defeated fifty-one to thirty-five. Perhaps the commissioners felt that moving Abel to this committee would have stirred up too much of a hornets' nest, in view of his constant attempts in favour of 'retrenchment'.

At last, on 13 April 1842, Abel found himself in agreement – in a rare case of unanimity – with his fellow commissioners, when they all supported a resolution to the government against the introduction of the new-fangled income tax. He argued strongly that, contrary to government claims, it was bound to damage the interests of the poor because of a knock-on effect from its harm to the interests of those who employed them.

Abel clearly perceived control of the Finance Committee as an important part of his mission on the Commission, and when he was re-elected in October 1842 he challenged the fitness of one member, Mr Mayson, who had only been present at twenty out of twenty-eight meetings. He proposed Thomas Wheatley to replace him, but was narrowly defeated by the casting vote of the Borough Reeve. It was perhaps fitting in the view of some of the gentlemen present that Abel was again appointed with twenty others 'as a nuisance committee'! He lived up to the title towards the close of the discussions when he spoke in favour of a very thorny topic, the amalgamation of the Police Commission with the new Town Council. The subject was stonewalled by other commissioners. They would have been well aware of Abel's enthusiasm for the new dispensation, as he had already unsuccessfully put himself forward to be elected to the Town Council for Oxford ward.

On 23 June 1843 the Police Commissioners met as a body for the last time. At the end of the meeting, they handed the chairmanship over to Sir Thomas Potter and a motion thanking him for 'his courtesy, impartiality, and general conduct in the chair' was 'cordially' seconded by Heywood 'as one of the extreme section'. The commissioners and the Corporation were to dine together after the meeting, presumably to show that the transition was amicable.[4]

Town councillor (1843–53)

In the following November, when new Corporation committees were appointed, Abel moved from the Committee for Nuisance to those for Improvement, and Paving and Soughing. In 1876 he revealed that his commitment to the latter originated in his formative years, when he had lived in the unpaved and unsewered streets of Angel Meadow, and on appointment his first duty had been to go into that district, when he 'determined not to rest satisfied until the whole had been paved, sewered, and otherwise improved'.[5]

As chairman of the Paving and Soughing Committee, Abel frequently participated in discussions about the state of the city streets. In April 1846 he supported a pilot scheme for scavenging to clean the streets as 'it was a crying sin that in a town like Manchester such a mass of dirt in the streets, and so much night-soil should be allowed to accumulate without anything being done…'.[6] Abel's work on the committee took centre-stage at the council meeting of 22 September 1847, allowing a glimpse into the workings of that body. He was responding to a request for an investigation about the cost of paving the streets of Manchester. The committee had clearly researched what was done elsewhere, and all the different stones available for paving, comparing the costs not only of paving the actual streets but also for flagging and edging the footpaths. Opposition was silenced and the proceedings of the committee were approved by a large majority.

At the start of 1848 the committee presented a major summary of its work since it was formed in 1842. Abel had been a member throughout, and chaired the committee from at least October 1845, and the report therefore reflected significant achievement in his council career. The statistics showed that between 1830 and 1844 on average twenty-four streets had been paved each year; between 1845 and 1847 this had risen to fifty-eight. Almost fifteen miles had been paved in the period, which equated to 246 streets.

This was accompanied by fourteen miles of sewers, and much was made of the invention by the engineer, Mr Francis, of an egg-shaped fire-brick tube which had been adopted by the committee as a more effective sewer. The same gentleman had also developed a cheaper and more effective 'stench trap', and suggested laying the sewers in longer, two-foot lengths. Abel, as chair of the committee, was clearly very proud of these innovative developments, in which he said Manchester was leading the way. Improvement was a matter of trial and error in the novel situation of huge industrial cities, and to facilitate development Abel's committee also took over supervision of the highways in 1851.

Late in 1844 the council was in discussion as to how to respond to the important Borough Police Act, passed by Parliament to enable Manchester to deal with 'nuisances and other offences within the borough'. The General Purposes Committee had recommended that existing committees be given the powers to enforce the Act, and the establishment of a new committee made up of members of the Improvement, Nuisance and Paving and Soughing Committees to improve the conditions of the 'poorer classes in many districts'. It is no surprise that Abel was named as a member of this new Buildings and Sanitary Regulations Committee. He took his duties characteristically seriously and in January 1850 he and other councillors attended a meeting of cottage owners who feared that the council was about to ban the use of cellar dwellings, the worst kind of housing, without compensation to landlords. Abel's thoughts on the issue reflected the complexity of the situation, particularly for a councillor trying to help the poorest citizens while also protecting the interests of the ratepayers and electors. He expressed a desire to get rid of such dwellings, being also in favour of compensation for the owners. Then he reassured them that there was currently no move to ban the cellars in Manchester (though it had been suggested in Salford). By March 1853 there was, however, a bill before Parliament which included clauses on cellar dwellings. Abel equivocated in the council meeting, expressing his former opposition in general to the dwellings, but also claiming that some of them were of an acceptable condition and that the law would ban these too. His conclusion was that it was too tricky an area to legislate successfully!

Despite this failure to commit, Abel continued to assert the provisions of the Police Act with regard to substandard housing in general. At the council meeting of 15 December 1852 he raised the issue of twelve houses built in Rochdale Road with no privy or ashpit, as the Act required. He reminded his hearers that thirty years previously, he himself had inhabited a 'single' house without privy or ashpit 'and he was naturally prompted to use his utmost exertions to rid the town as far as possible of a state of things, which pressed most heavily upon the working classes'. In the end, after lengthy discussion, the council agreed to take legal advice on the case in question, frustratingly shelving the issue further; Abel's annoyance can only be surmised.[7]

Another issue which must have been close to Abel's heart was the construction of a borough gaol to replace the use of the New Bailey, shown to be woefully inadequate for the number of prisoners housed there. He believed that the time for action was right because, due to the current economic circumstances, there was likely to be a lot of poverty and 'unless some steps were taken to prevent it, there would be in all probability a great increase of crime'. Interestingly, his points were not humanitarian, but rather intended to appeal to the propertied in terms of efficacy in fighting lawlessness; they were perhaps tempered by the need to convince his audience, who had spent a lot of time discussing the cost of the venture. He was interested not only in the financing and establishment of the new prison, but also in the treatment of prisoners. He expressed disquiet at the use of a treadwheel and remarked at a dinner that it was 'their duty to adopt such practices as would be instrumental in producing a reformation in the party who committed crime'.[8]

Standing for re-election in 1846 at the end of his term, Abel had the opportunity to hear the views of his electors at a ward meeting, which gave many telling insights into the grass-roots working of the system and the preoccupations of the Manchester ratepayers. Reassuringly, 'Mr Heywood was loudly cheered on rising to address the assembly.' Abel addressed an issue of great controversy – the five-shilling rate. He praised the institution of the Ratepayers' Association as a body set up to oversee the interests of the ratepayers and to demand explanations of council conduct. However, he contended that the body had been used 'for the purpose of foully blackening his character'. It seems that in the elections for the new council, there was a campaign against him purporting to be authorised by the Ratepayers' Association, saying that he had supported the five-shilling rate, and indeed implying that if he were elected there would be a ten-shilling rate within a year! When Abel affirmed that he had voted for an increase in the town clerk's salary, there were cries of 'Shame' and hisses heard. But he argued that this had been in return for the town clerk no longer having private interests connected to his public duties. He had thoroughly investigated the pros and cons of the pay rise, deciding that the town clerk was worth the money, particularly as he had 'conducted through parliament the various bills which had been applied for during the last three years.- (Applause.)' and had saved the town more than the amount of his salary.

The meeting continued in the same vein; it amounted to a rigorous grilling of the way Abel had voted on various matters, usually to do with spending ratepayers' money. Finally, when a proposal was made and seconded to nominate him for re-election, another candidate was also put forward – John Middleton. A show of hands supported Abel.[9] In the event, Abel came a close second in the poll, and was thus re-elected with Matthew Thackray.[10]

One aspect of the career of a municipal councillor, which Abel seemed disinclined to shirk, was attendance at banquets, and on Friday 21 September 1849 such an occasion took place to honour the Lord Mayor of London who was the guest of John Potter, the Mayor of Manchester. Abel took his place on the first of the five cross tables – one of the two furthest away from the guest of honour, perhaps reflecting his relatively lowly status in such company. The splendid bill of fare consisted of six courses, accompanied by six wines, including champagne. The event was enhanced by musical entertainment which interspersed the speeches of the chief hosts and their honoured guests. His presence at such a grand occasion must surely have confirmed to Abel, now aged 39, that he had arrived in the upper echelons of Manchester municipal society.

However, he met with a setback in the council. When he stood for alderman on 9 November 1850, he received only eight votes, coming last by a long way. It seems likely that his long-term role as a mover and shaker, and a blunt critic of his fellow councillors on occasion, were part of the reason for this failure. But the events of the meeting on 9 November may have been equally significant. Dating back to the early years of the Corporation, they illustrate Abel's desire for the council to be run in a way which was transparent and above reproach.

In 1846 Abel had campaigned for council meetings to be open to the public. He argued that it would be especially worthwhile to open up the proceedings of the committees, where there were 'more fantastic tricks played' than in the general council because the latter were observed by the press reporters. Opening up would ensure their probity and responsibility to the public.

In December 1844 he had also begun to pursue an interest in rationalising Corporation salaries, resisting a rise in salary for Mr Martin, clerk to several of the borough committees, because he did not think it was merited by the capabilities of the young man. He also 'objected to the piecemeal and dovetailing advance of salaries' and proposed a more regular system of salary review. This seems to have been ignored as Abel was still agitating for it in 1848, now with more concrete proposals for a book to record the duties, hours and salary of every servant of the Corporation. This time he was thwarted by the mayor's casting vote.[11] Meanwhile, in August 1847, he had given notice of a motion intended to check vested interests with regard to employees of the council. He proposed, 'That it is inexpedient for the servants of the corporation to engage in any other business or trade, either directly or indirectly, whilst in the employ of the council.'[12]

Now in 1850, when Mr Alderman William Neild proposed the re-election for a third term of John Potter, the outgoing mayor, objections to his standing again had been raised on grounds of 'principle' by Councillors Clark and Heywood. Both protested that they had nothing but respect for Mr Potter personally. But Abel claimed that there was a 'compact' formed, which he termed 'the tea party', which was not interested in the public good, but in 'individual aggrandisement' or 'raising'. In his usual blunt way, he pointed out that 'This was neither honourable nor wise on the part of such councillors' and went on to develop his theme: 'it was a matter of deep regret to him to think that any individual would so far give up the exercise of his mind to another, as that he should be held in a kind of slavery to party'. His audience was not entirely hostile and the speech was punctuated by some calls of 'hear, hear'.

However, John Middleton, who had been Abel's opponent in the 1847 council election, accused Abel himself of creating the split of which he spoke. Neild in vain tried to conciliate and persuade him not to vote against the nomination. In the end, according to the *Manchester Guardian* there were three 'noes' out of apparently fifty-two councillors present. In this account, Abel was out on a limb.[13]

But the *Manchester Times* challenged this interpretation on 16 November, claiming that nearly thirty councillors were induced to 'give a reluctant and passive acquiescence'. The article ended sarcastically with the opinion that Potter had been chosen because he gave 'the best dinners'.[14] A letter to the *Manchester Courier* by 'Veritas' seemed to attribute Abel's discovery of a clique in the council to the fact that he was 'disappointed of an aldermanic dignity'. The writer was correct perhaps in his view that 'the small numbers who voted for the speaker's [Abel's] exaltation in municipal honours shows that he is by no means popular'. Or it could be that it was impolitic to show open support for a man who had so strongly opposed the ruling group in the council, and that Abel's attempt to build up a following for himself was less successful than he had hoped.[15]

When almost a decade later the same issue arose over the re-election to the mayoralty of Ivie Mackie in November 1859, Abel was again to be found in opposition. On 8 October the *Manchester Guardian* reported that fifty-one councillors had signed a memorial to request Mackie to allow himself to be elected mayor for a third term; it was followed by another signed by eleven other councillors against the re-election. They explained that this was a matter of principle because such re-elections had the effect of 'limiting the number of those who can possibly attain the mayoralty and so tending to prevent many of those who are eligible from undertaking the arduous duties of a councillor' and therefore would act to the detriment of the council itself. By this time Abel had attained the dignity of alderman, and was therefore himself eligible for the mayoralty, and it may be that there was also a personal motive to his public-spirited campaign. In a letter to the *Manchester Guardian* two days later, Abel denied rumours of a climbdown, saying in his usual pugnacious way: 'I trust the people of Manchester entertain a better opinion of us than to suppose we could doff our principles, as some men do their coats, making a show to evaporate in smoke.' In the event, Abel proposed as mayor his colleague on the Paving Committee, Thomas Goadsby. This was the first occasion on which the election of a Manchester mayor had gone to a division; Mackie received forty-one votes and Goadsby sixteen.

While in both of these elections Abel claimed to be acting purely out of principle and defending the integrity of the council, what is inescapable is that he was a determined opponent who may also have had some ulterior motive, perhaps in terms of his own career in the council hierarchy. In 1850 he was keen to become an alderman, and although he failed miserably to gain the support he needed for election, only three years later he did attain that position. Building on that, by 1859 he may have been preparing the ground for a bid for the mayoralty itself; and indeed he was elected mayor for the first time in 1862.

The 1850s saw numerous other controversial issues in which Abel chose to involve himself; the subject of council robes was hotly debated in 1851 on the occasion of Queen Victoria's visit. Those who wanted to adopt special robes intended to show their gravitas and the importance of their town. However, a considerable number of councillors, headed by Heywood, objected to this decision as a misuse of ratepayers' money. They also feared a return to the corrupt practices of the old days of the Police Commission. Abel was equally against the idea that the mayor should have a chain and badge of office: 'The Mayor of Manchester [he said] stood as high as any other mayor in the country, and needed not any ornament. Things not valuable were gilded, but the Mayor of Manchester needed not such a process.'[16]

It may be that his stance was taken as anti-royalist in some quarters, as by September he was eager to demonstrate his support of the royal visit, and willing to go along with even an indefinite sum being voted by the council to fund the occasion. Indeed, he was a member of the special committee deputed to arrange it. It seems that the question of the robes remained unresolved and therefore some of the council took it upon themselves to buy their robes. Those who did not, whose number included Abel, defended themselves against accusations of disloyalty, saying it was a matter of taste. When the Queen visited the Manchester Art Treasures Exhibition in 1857, Abel again appeared without special robes.

Many of the values expressed by Heywood were commensurate with what became 'Gladstonian Liberalism' and it is no surprise that he showed admiration for William Gladstone on the occasion of his visit to Manchester when Chancellor of the Exchequer in 1853. Abel was voluble in seconding a motion to present an address to Gladstone, praising especially his abolition of duties, notably on soap and advertisements. Abel was also keen to sow a seed on his own account, suggesting the Chancellor 'must remove the paper duty… and that he (Mr. Heywood) had no doubt would be one of the objects which the right honourable gentleman would contemplate removing… (Applause.)'

Despite his admiration for Gladstone, when 'the great robe question' was again raised in 1853 by the town clerk, Abel would no more wear a robe for the Chancellor's visit that he would for Queen Victoria. He objected that robes were 'part of the paraphernalia of the old corrupt corporations, and if adopted would lead to a corruption of this'. The Corporation had not robed for the visit in 1850 of Lord John Russell, he said, and 'If it was made a rule that all members present should wear robes… he should be obliged to stay away.'[17]

In the aftermath of Queen Victoria's visit in 1851, Abel, delighted with the reception given to the Queen by the working classes of Manchester, was keen to reinforce the idea that the people could be trusted to behave responsibly. At the council meeting following the visit, he turned this into a political point as 'he hoped… that when it was necessary to give a further extension of political power to the working classes, the members of the council would be prepared at all events to say, that on the day when loyalty was called for they were not behind any class of her Majesty's subjects'.[18]

Abel must have found it particularly pleasing to be able to contrast the sober and responsible attitude of the poor with the rowdyism of a group of wealthy 'gentle-men'; at the next meeting he referred to an incident on the night of the Queen's visit at the Market Street corner of Spring Gardens. A 'number of parties in a cart' had violently assaulted the police, but it was said that the matter had been hushed up due to the social status of the offending parties. Official knowledge of the event was denied, but the point was telling.[19]

Another matter of strong interest to Heywood, the issue of the 1852 Manchester and Salford Education Bill, was a topic of heated discussion inside and outside the council. Abel 'expressed his opinion that by this bill the public generally would be called upon to pay for the propagation of religious opinions of which they entirely disapproved… the local bill would exclude from its benefits the Jews, the Unitarians, the Quakers, and even some of the High Churchmen themselves.' The bill was debated for six hours in the council, and was rejected because it would 'usurp the most important functions of the council, operate oppressively on the ratepayers, invade the rights of conscience, and interfere with the sacred duties of parents'.[20]

As the time approached for the election of aldermen in October 1853, Abel made a spirited presentation of the achievements of his Highways, Paving and Sewering Committee. He was able to go so far as to claim that there:

> was not a single street formed within the township of Manchester but what had good and effective sewerage… and they attributed a great deal of the health of that district, which, as a member of the Board of Guardians, he had to relieve,

which was bounded by the River Irk, and comprised Angel Meadow, the inhabitants of which, he believed, were never in better health; he attributed this to the fact that there was scarcely a street within the walls of that neighbourhood which had not a good pavement over its surface and a sewer underneath.

The council was apparently impressed, and the statement was allowed to pass without challenge.[21]

Alderman (1853 onwards)

On 9 November 1853, after the election of Benjamin Nicholls as mayor, Abel was elected alderman for Exchange ward in the place of Alderman Hopkins, though he quickly swapped with Alderman Bancroft to become the alderman for Collegiate ward, his old constituency. Not everyone was delighted at Abel's elevation. The *Manchester Courier* thundered against his success, especially as it was at the expense of Thomas Hopkins. The Tory paper referred to the 'tea-party' faction of Abel Heywood, also known as 'the Caucus', who had made it their business to oust Hopkins, despite what the paper considered to be the latter's excellent public service in deputations to the Westminster government.

A correspondent to the *Manchester Courier* of 26 November known as 'Mentor' seems to have had the last word on this affair. He reminded readers that three years ago, Heywood 'when disappointed of aldermanic honours, bitterly complained of the influence of the tea party, which he styles "a council within a council, a party of individuals banded together for their own aggrandizement."This year he supports this tea party, and his inconsistency is rewarded by his being raised to the dignity of alderman.'[22] The implication was that Abel managed to ally himself with the powerful 'tea-party', and the support of the group resulted in his elevation to the dignity of alderman. It seems that he had learned to play the political game more effectively.

On occasion council discussions were illuminating with regard to the day-to-day lives of Manchester citizens, and Abel frequently interested himself in the minutiae of such matters. One discussion took place in February 1854 as they considered overcrowding on horse-drawn omnibuses in the city. The topic was introduced by Abel, himself a passenger, probably in the commute from his home in Ardwick, in a proposal that the buses should be managed by the Hackney Coach Committee. 'He regretted the tendency that had been manifested to interfere with their management in respect to overcrowding. He had frequently ridden in them when they had contained four or five persons more than could sit down, and yet had never felt any inconvenience from it.'[23]

Again, in June 1855, it emerged that the gas lamps in the streets were not usually lit when there was a full moon. This had become an issue in Whit week, when, despite the moonlight, the sky clouded over and gave rise to a dangerous situation where the streets were peopled with disreputable characters of evil intent. Abel, as so often, had something to say on this topic, and he focused on the Sunday scholars returning late by train from their Whit outings; they had had to pass through 'the utterly dark streets, causing great uneasiness and inconvenience to their parents. He thought the subject ought not to be laughed over; but that some arrangement should be made with the gas committee to light every night...'[24]

But there were many other, more weighty matters, which were seen as a challenge to local power and the liberal principle of *laissez faire*. Early in 1856 there was serious consternation in the council over a government bill to take the police under Home Office control. Abel was totally against the bill because it undermined the Municipal Corporations Act and admitted the principle that the central government should interfere in policing. His overriding concern was that the bill would deprive them of 'one of their noblest privileges as Englishmen – that of self-government'.[25]

In August 1856 religion underpinned a major debate as to the suitability or otherwise of bands entertaining the poor in the parks on Sundays. Abel entered the fray in defence of the freedoms of the working classes. In a meeting which lasted over seven hours, the council debated at length the various memorials presented by religious leaders and others that they should prohibit such entertainment as damaging to the spiritual and moral character of the people, and particularly of the young. Abel proposed his own amendment that, since the people listening to the offending bands were exceedingly well-behaved, the council should refrain from interference in the current situation. He reminded the councillors that he had already presented a memorial signed unforced by 15,000 working men, whereas there were only 11,309 signatories for the religious lobby. He alluded to the fact that the aristocracy were known to break the Sabbath ('that was a delicate point') and so intimated that there was one rule for the rich and another for the poor.

Typically, Abel had been to investigate for himself: 'There were working men with their wives and families, and their "perambulators"; large numbers appeared to be enjoying themselves to the greatest possible extent...' But despite his best efforts, the bands were in the end forbidden and the religious lobby were victorious.[26]

Abel was still keen to root out any kind of corrupt mismanagement, although he was sometimes accused of selfish motives. In the spring and summer of 1857 a serious question arose with regard to work supervised by the city surveyor, George Shorland, in carrying Hulme Street over the River Medlock by means of arches and a tunnel. Changes had been made to the plans, resulting in the lowering of the arches, but this had created a flood from backed up water in the river. For dereliction of duty, Shorland was to be dismissed and legal proceedings were considered against him and the contractor, Mr Wright. At the Manchester Council meeting of 16 September 1857 Abel defended Shorland as he had 'served them [the council] well for upwards of 25 years'. He put the blame squarely on Mr Randall, the chairman of the Chorlton-on-Medlock committee, who had 'sneaked away' and 'behaved in this transaction the part of a base man'.[27]

The *Manchester Courier* of 26 September aired its views on the matter, suggesting that the Improvement Committee, of which Abel was a member, must have been aware of the alteration, and that some of them must have sanctioned it. The paper felt it was a pity that the prosecution did not go ahead, as it would have led to a clarification of the whole murky affair. The implication was that Abel's accusations against Randall were a smokescreen to divert attention from the failings of the Improvement Committee.

In 1858 a major debate erupted in the council on the topic of a site for a new Post Office, a building of high importance in a commercial centre. In the end it was said to have taken up more council time than any other subject to date. Abel featured prominently in the discussions, determinedly favouring or opposing the various choices proposed. By 3 March 1858 the proposal was to use a site known as Bancroft Street, which incorporated the Town Yard, an area used by several council departments, including the Watch Committee in the guise of the fire service, storing their machinery and stabling their horses. The area was likewise the depot for Abel's Highways, Paving and Sewering Committee.

The convolutions of this debate, which revolved around four sites and involved several deputations to London for meetings with the Postmaster General and the Chancellor of the Exchequer, were the subject of ward meetings and were reported in great detail in the local press. Abel was at the heart of the action, demonstrating a detailed grasp of all the costings and features of each site. The agenda which seems to have underpinned his arguments was an apparent desire to steer the choice away from the Town Yard on Bancroft Street.

This leads to the question of what game Abel may have been playing in this affair. The clue may lie in his statement that the Town Yard should be used for some important public building, as in fact this became the site for the new Manchester Town Hall, which was Abel's most high profile project in the 1860s and '70s. As early as 1852 he had commented that the council chamber in the old Town Hall on King Street was unsuitable: 'Mr Councillor Heywood called the attention of the members to the defective state of the ventilation of the council chamber. At the last meeting of the council himself and Mr Councillor Goadsby caught severe colds, from which they were suffering still.'[28]

Furthermore, at a meeting of the Collegiate ward electors on 3 October 1854 there had been speculation on a supposed discussion within the council as to the construction of a new Town Hall. Had Abel already earmarked the Town Yard as a suitable site for a municipal palace that was as yet only a twinkle in his eye? What seems likely is that, had he not led this campaign, Manchester today would have had a post office instead of a splendid Town Hall on the site.

Abel's opposition to Mayor Mackie's proposal in 1859 to use part of the proceeds from Clarke and Marshall's charities for the adult poor, along with some lesser charities, to set up ragged schools was a further occasion of debate, in which there were some bitter attacks on his position.[29] When defeated in the council, Abel took the issue into the wards, and was reported giving talks to raise support against the mayor's policy. The debate was widely reported, but in the *Manchester Courier* we are reminded that Abel was sometimes abrasive and irascible, and excited hostility and resentment among the other councillors against him:

Alderman Heywood urged, with great warmth, the impropriety and injustice of the motion and taunted the mover with having taken very little part in the work of the council. Councillor Robinson took leave to say that his services were quite as useful as those of Mr. Alderman Heywood; and if he had not made as much noise and troubled the council with speeches as often as Mr. Heywood, it was because he was heartily ashamed of the time occupied in that council by speeches which gentlemen of decency never would deliver, and which indecency had not been lessened by Mr. Alderman Heywood. (Laughter)[30]

The argument continued into 1860, and in the council meeting of 18 January in response to a report from the Charitable Trusts Committee Abel put his most detailed case yet against the diversion of money to ragged schools. It is Abel at his most effective; he tried to bring home his point by appealing to his hearers' attitudes to property. He began by saying that he 'did not think it necessary to talk of his sympathy with the education of the people', but that in the case of Clarke's charity, founded in the seventeenth century, the adult poor were the beneficiaries and always had been:

If any one member of the council held an estate which had been in his family since 1626, he would laugh with contempt at anyone who sought to dispossess him; and he (Mr. Heywood) contended that this was just such another right, belonging to the poorer classes of the population of the town of Manchester.- (Hear, hear.)

The discussion continued and occupied the council for four and a half hours, so significant was it considered, but the final vote went in favour of the mayor by four votes.[31]

Abel's efforts, unusually, won praise from the *Manchester Courier* which was 'happy to find that others besides Conservatives, who profess to be friends of the aged and indigent poor, are now taking up the matter in a very proper spirit.' The article finished with a real sting in the tail for the mayor and his supporters:

Now, we do hope that Mr. Alderman Heywood and his friends in the council will go through with this affair; for the zeal, the knowledge of the subject, and the ability which they have already displayed, promise well for those real friends of the poor who would rather support Ragged Schools out of their own pockets than wrest the bounty of our ancestors from its original purpose, in order to be philanthropic at a cheap rate to themselves.[32]

In February the Manchester clergy declared themselves against the mayor's plan. This was a valuable addition to the opposition armoury, though it gave Abel some very strange bedfellows. By mid-February, the mayor had bowed to the force of the opposition and the scheme was abandoned. The Conservatives may have been weak in the council, but they certainly had clout when they united to prevent changes perceived to be inimical to their interests and beliefs. For them the rights of property and paternalism had been upheld, and it could be argued that Abel Heywood and other opponents on the council had been their stooges. But Abel believed that he had scored a victory for the poor. His achievement was recognised by radicals like Edward Hooson; at a meeting in the schoolroom of the Lever Street chapel, with 'great unanimity' and 'cordial approval' a committee was formed 'to raise funds for the purchase of a suitable testimonial to Mr. Alderman Heywood for his successful labours in securing the public charities for the benefit of the poor, in accordance with the intentions of the donors'.[33] Abel had taken on the dominant group in the council and won; the question now was whether he could turn that victory into a more permanent political success.

A test came over the perennial issue of Corporation salaries, when town clerk Joseph Heron's remuneration came under review. Abel was one of those who voted in favour of an increase from £1,500 to £2,000, and for this he came in for censure from his ward, with calls for his resignation. On 15 August 1860 Abel was fully endorsed by thirty or forty of his 'friends and admirers' in the Collegiate ward, when they held a dinner in his honour. Abel felt that the resolution of no confidence was 'one of the most harsh in its character that he had ever received from them'.[34]

The affair was clearly part of a wider struggle for power, and at a dinner in the ward given in honour of Councillor Porteus, their newly elected representative, Alderman Goadsby stated that 'The town-clerk's salary was now becoming not so much a question of salary, as who should be master.'[35] In the long run it seems that the town clerk retained his pay-rise, and the opposition were effectively blocked. When reporting back to the council about negotiations for an Act of Parliament to develop Manchester's railway communications, Abel pointedly remarked that 'The services of the Town-clerk had been beyond all estimable value.'[36]

In view of his commitment to highways, it is perhaps unsurprising that Abel also took a growing interest in issues concerning transport. In its most traditional form, the hackney coach, he participated in lengthy discussions about how to regulate and rationalise the organisation of the burgeoning numbers of cabs in the town. A proposal in 1852 to remove rules that dictated which cabs used which stands, but to regulate fares – making them cheaper – was greeted by opposition from the cab owners. Abel argued that their suggestion for a six-month trial was reasonable, but he also put the moral argument that the cab drivers would no longer be under the control of their masters, and that this would lead to bad moral conduct and dress. The council voted narrowly to abandon the proposal.

In October Abel unsuccessfully proposed a new approach, which was to adopt the principles of free trade and to deregulate the hackney coaches altogether, in terms both of their stands and their fares. The only rule would be that the fares must be clearly displayed on the sides of the coaches. The council voted for the Hackney Coach Committee's resolution for a free-for-all in stands, but regulated fares. But by the spring of 1854 it was felt that the system was failing and the committee itself proposed a free trade in fares; Abel was highly annoyed that they did so without acknowledging that he had already suggested it earlier, and he referred to their action as 'a sort of literary piracy'.[37] By 1858 there was chaos in certain parts of the city due to the lack of regulation and the rise in the number of cabs from 170 to 310. St Ann's Square was a case in point; the police were required to keep order there on Saturday mornings, so 'disgraceful' were 'the scenes' around the coach stands. The situation was somewhat unfairly dubbed 'Alderman Heywood's pet scheme'. Alderman Neild went so far as to refer to it as 'an abomination'. It was agreed to go back to the old system of appointing each cab to a designated stand, even though that system had been found wanting in the first place.[38]

So, it was a case of back to the drawing board, and Abel's response was to begin to investigate the aptly named Mr Train's 'street railway': a horse-drawn tram. In October 1860 the Paving Committee sent a deputation to Birkenhead to see the street railway in action, and they were very impressed, especially as it had already worked well in Paris. Mr Train was to be allowed to trial it from Cross Street to Stretford Road.

It was, however, on railways that Abel spent his most productive energies at this time. As a man who travelled quite often to London in pursuit of his civic duties, Abel took an interest in the development of a second railway route to the capital and he went to London as part of a high-powered deputation visiting the President of the Board of Trade to lobby for an Act of Parliament to allow this development. A major obstacle was rivalry between the railway companies involved, the London and North-Western and the Manchester, Sheffield and Lincolnshire, and Abel and his colleagues worked tirelessly to resolve the issues for the benefit of Manchester.

By 1861 the companies were approaching an agreement to rebuild London Road (Piccadilly) Station in such a way that 'we should eventually have... not only one of the first passenger stations in the kingdom – (hear, hear) – but also a very great improvement in the matter of the goods station'. Abel was again prominent in these discussions.[39] In May, he and Alderman Clark were appointed to act for the General Purposes Committee in reference to the railway bill before Parliament. The Manchester, Sheffield and Lincolnshire Company had agreed to several large projects in relation to a new line, including a new viaduct.

There was severe criticism of the two appointees from Councillor Stracey, who objected to their behaving as 'the dictators to the corporation of Manchester'. He accused Abel of not giving figures because they would 'tell against him', and said that the 'convenience of the inhabitants' of Sheffield Street, which was to be handed over to the railway companies for development, was 'put on one side'. There were further insults: 'The influence of the House of Commons seemed to have sent Alderman Heywood asleep... Perhaps the deputation had been to Bellamy's [Club] and had their feet under the mahogany.' He went on to accuse Abel of being naive in believing in the honour and promises of the railway directors, and ended by claiming that Aldermen Heywood and Clark had been bamboozled and that the companies would make a 'cat's paw' of the Corporation. Nevertheless, the feeling of the council was with the deputation and their report was approved by a large majority.[40] Ultimately the bill before Parliament became law, but the wrangling had to continue, in the first instance to persuade the railway companies to improve passenger accommodation at Victoria Station, where Abel himself had seen passengers discharged onto the tracks less than three feet from a moving train.

As Abel's influence thus grew, so also did his political aspiration. Perhaps aware that the time was not yet ripe for his own elevation to the mayoralty, he focused his attention on the candidacy of his close colleague and ally, and fellow shopkeeper, 'druggist' Alderman Thomas Goadsby. In November 1860 the council met to elect the new mayor in what was to be a 'sharply' contested election between Thomas Goadsby and Matthew Curtis. Abel accepted that he had unsuccessfully proposed Goadsby in the previous year, in his attempt to prevent Mackie's mayoralty from continuing for a third term.[41] This time he enlarged in great detail on Goadsby's 'services and his character', and his efforts particularly as chairman of the Markets Committee. He had also acknowledged to the voters of the Collegiate ward that he and others were making efforts 'to place a shopkeeper in the highest civic position in the city'. The vote was a draw, but the mayor cast his vote for Curtis. Abel was clearly unhappy that his candidate had again failed, and objected to the vote of Councillor Lamb (in favour of Curtis) because he 'had compounded with his creditors in April or May', but to no avail.[42] It must have been a disappointing setback, but Abel was by now a sufficiently experienced politician to realise that such a failure could soon be transformed into victory, given an astute handling of the situation. And so it proved when the following year, on the third attempt, Abel proposed Thomas Goadsby for mayor and he was at last elected, without opposition. It was a hard-won triumph, but it set the stage for Abel Heywood's own elevation to the mayoralty only a year later.

6

Political Aspirations:
The Would-Be MP (1859)

In the heady early years of Chartism, the hope had been that Parliament would respond to popular petition and extend the franchise to virtually all adult men; in the 1840s such hopes were dashed, and Abel Heywood began to seek other ways to achieve suffrage reform. These included participation in the formation of new organisations, such as the Political and Financial Reform Association and the Manhood Suffrage Association, but most strikingly by his involvement in parliamentary elections, initially in support of middle-class liberal candidates, and then in attempts in 1859 and 1865 to enter Parliament himself as MP for Manchester.

Liberal campaigner

In 1846 Abel emerged as a supporter of what was to become the Liberal party and thereafter participated in the electoral campaigns of Manchester's liberal candidates. In order to be accepted in these circles, he was forced to modify his stance on universal manhood suffrage and accept that a first stage towards this would be some form of household, or ratepayer, suffrage and he argued for accepting the granting of the suffrage to the working classes in 'instalments'.

His first appearances in the machinery of national elections came when he seconded a proposal that John Bright, the Quaker Rochdale cotton mill owner and campaigner against the Corn Laws, should be supported as a candidate by the electors of Collegiate ward in the coming election. Bright avowed his support for gradual extension of the suffrage, initially to the heads of households. Abel seconded the resolution because 'he considered he was a reformer of some little standing' and implied that the electorate deserved better than the alternative candidate, Lord Lincoln, 'consisting as it [the electorate] did of the most intellectual, or at all events of a larger number of intellectual men than were to be found in any other town in the United Kingdom'. He hoped they would 'show to the country they could distinguish honesty from sophistry, and real, sterling democracy from that humbug, as he called it, whiggery.- (Applause.)'[1]

Not all those who wanted universal male suffrage were prepared to take the 'incrementalist' route, and another aspect of Abel's political activity was his continuing participation in campaigns to extend the franchise beyond what the liberal middle class were prepared to accept. By the late 1840s there was a bill before Parliament proposing a limited extension based on property-holding. On 10 February 1847 Abel attended a meeting of ratepayers opposed to these limits. As yet, Abel was little used to dealing with parliamentary matters, but he knew where to seek advice and consulted the MP Thomas Dunscombe. As a result, he unsuccessfully proposed a petition to Parliament.

An incident which took place in the election of August 1848 demonstrated how tense were the inter-class feelings in Manchester. This was 'The Fracas in St Ann's Square, on the Nomination Day.'[2] The 'fracas' was caused by the collapse of a barrier in front of the police who were, as usual, present to keep order. The situation escalated and the police reacted by 'driving, with their staves in their hands, the crowd hastily back' until Chief Constable Willis instructed them to cease. There were no apparent injuries and, it was claimed, no lasting ill-feeling.

Abel's assertions in the council showed that this event had created 'considerable alarm' in the minds of some, 'for it had been stated that the mayor, or Mr Bright, or some other person, had ordered the police, and that, acting under those orders, the police had attacked the people'. Abel conceded that this was an accident. The whole affair was inconsequential on one level, but it clearly illustrates the tension and suspicions with which many working people regarded the forces of authority, and also how the middle classes feared the 'mob', particularly at a sensitive time like an election.

Abel continued to walk the tightrope between working- and middle-class aspirations. On 21 April 1848 the burgesses of Collegiate ward had met to form a new society with 'four points', echoing the 'six points' of the People's Charter but in a limited form: household suffrage, vote by ballot, triennial parliaments and equal electoral districts. The new association was formed on Abel's proposal; its president was to be James Kershaw MP, who had said quite plainly that he was in favour of household suffrage. This may well have rung alarm bells for those who hoped that radical leaders would stick to the goal of universal suffrage.

It produced a radical reaction at another reform meeting a week later, largely attended by the working classes. From the platform, Abel seconded a resolution proposing an extension of the suffrage and other measures, but explained that 'He was in favour of household suffrage only as a means to get universal suffrage... He advocated the necessity of going for household suffrage, in order to gain the co-operation of the middle classes in an agitation for an extension of the suffrage.' These remarks were heckled by Chartists and the meeting became rowdy, but the resolution was passed by a large majority; most of those who favoured the extension of the vote to all men accepted that this was not going to be achieved in one step.[3]

Abel was keen to gain favour with the electors and the elected alike at this period, and in 1849 he earned positive comment in the *Manchester Times* for his organisation of a public dinner for 500 gentlemen as 'secretary to the dinner committee'; the guests of honour were the two Manchester MPs, John Bright and Thomas Milner Gibson. It was an elaborate affair: 'The tables were decorated with confectionary ornaments, fashioned into Chinese temples, rustic cottages, castles etc.' Abel also got himself noticed stewarding, and then reading out letters of apology from those who were unable to attend.[4]

His hard work feeding the liberal elite bore fruit. He appeared among the middle-class liberal community as one of the platform party at a meeting of the Parliamentary and Financial Reform Association in Manchester on 16 April 1851, supporting the re-election of Milner Gibson and Bright as MPs for Manchester. Then at a 'Great Reform Meeting' of over 10,000 people, held in the Free Trade Hall on Wednesday 24 September 1851 to receive a deputation from London of the Association's leaders, Abel, for the first time in such exalted company, proposed a resolution. He spoke in favour of the working and middle classes showing mutual trust and proposed rather vaguely 'a cordial and energetic action amongst all Reformers; and organising a branch of the National Parliamentary Reform Association to co-operate with the council in London'. His seconder was his old Chartist comrade, James Scholefield. It is likely that Abel's proposal had been discussed and approved even before the meeting took place. By collaborating with the middle classes, he was thereby forced to take the line of incremental reform and play the game by their rules.[5] Perhaps they also saw the benefits of allowing such a known and respected radical, albeit one with a great deal of ambition, a place in their deliberations as a means of curbing his zeal and bringing his working-class following into their camp.

By 6 April 1852, Abel had gained a place on the election committee, which was very large, for the liberal candidate for South Lancashire, John Cheetham. He was also on the general committee supporting the return of liberals John Bright and Thomas Milner Gibson for Manchester, and duly reported on his progress as deputy chairman of the Collegiate ward committee on 22 June. It was a modest beginning, but he was now in a position to make local contacts in the circle of national politics. So it was that, having also attained the exalted position of alderman in the Manchester Corporation, he was among a select 400 who gained admission to a reform meeting on 24 January 1854. The Free Trade Hall was being rebuilt, and the alternative venue, the Albion Hotel in Piccadilly, was far too small for the large numbers who wished to attend, so admission was by ticket only. The 'Manchester School' gathered to hear the MPs Milner Gibson and Bright (Manchester) and Richard Cobden (West Yorkshire) speak on the issues of the day and in particular on their joint manifesto as to the proposed government reform bill. They were also invited to speak about the situation in 'the East' and government policy on Russia and Turkey; Britain was of course on the verge of a war against Russia in the Crimea.

This meeting reflected the preferences of middle-class liberalism for modest reform and more representation for the industrial cities of the north, and the speakers were all, to a greater or lesser degree, in favour of peace as in the best interests of those same cities and their trade. Bright in particular denigrated the idea of war, and then went on strongly but vaguely to advocate an extension of the franchise to as many working men as possible. That was all the support for 'universal manhood suffrage' Abel was likely to get in such a gathering. Yet his forbearance brought him acceptance, and when there was a similar such gathering on 28 January 1856 at the Corn Exchange, Abel was for the first time allowed to sit on the platform, among the 'top brass' of the liberals.

Yet he still kept the faith with the working classes; the meeting in Ancoats on 24 January of the working men 'for a reform of parliament and of our military system' has been discussed earlier. As well as focusing on the war, the purpose of the gathering was 'to pass resolutions and a petition in favour of a reform of the representation of the people, as laid down in the people's charter'. Abel also called for the ballot, which he said was essential to protect the working classes against intimidation, 'which was extensively exercised at Manchester elections, by both parties'.[6]

Candidate

There was a dramatic change in the political weather in Manchester in the mid-1850s. Both Bright and Milner Gibson were increasingly unpopular in Manchester because of their hostility to the war with Russia. The electorate was seemingly all for Palmerston's aggressive tone in foreign policy. So, at the end of a New Cross ward meeting, while proposing a vote of thanks to the chairman, Abel made a remarkable statement:

> Mr. Alderman Heywood.... stated that if Messrs. Gibson and Bright were thrown out, he would, at the next election, offer himself to represent the working classes of Manchester. Speaking of traitors, he said that there were some even amongst the working classes; there were working men who would have deserted Feargus O'Connor himself.... The meeting broke up in great confusion.[7]

It is not clear whether this announcement had been planned, but certainly the matter must have been under consideration by Abel himself; despite repeated attempts in the 1850s to reform the electoral system, even household suffrage was making little headway in Parliament, and by invoking O'Connor's name he made it clear that he would represent Manchester in a new and more radical way.

It appears that Abel had not entirely given up on Milner Gibson and Bright, however, and he was one of the vice-presidents listed in the press on 21 March supporting their re-election. The following week on one of the election days at an open-air meeting in Stevenson Square, called to testify to public confidence in the MPs, Abel took the chair. Milner Gibson addressed particularly the non-electors present, who he argued should be given the vote as well as a cheap and free press.

He cited how he and Bright had opposed the government because it had let the people down, using as his example the treatment of soldiers in the war in the Crimea. Although Bright was too ill to attend, the meeting ended with a vote of confidence in the two MPs, which was 'carried most enthusiastically'.[8]

Despite the apparent support for Milner Gibson and Bright among the non-electors, James Aspinall Turner and Sir John Potter were returned for Manchester. Therefore, having made his candidature in the next election in such circumstances a matter of public knowledge, Abel now needed to prepare for that eventuality. He did not give many formal lectures, so it may be significant that he chose to deliver one on 'Manchester and Some of its Improvements' in April 1857 at Cheetham Town Hall, immediately after the election. Admission was free, to make it accessible to all. The topic allowed him to expound on the achievements of his own Highways, Paving and Sewering Committee.

In advance of a new Reform Bill which was in the offing, Abel appeared amongst names from all over the UK as a member of the Parliamentary Reform Committee, based in London. Supporters of electoral reform were encouraged to agitate, in an unspecified manner, for a ratepayer franchise and a redistribution of seats, combined with the ballot and triennial parliaments and the abolition of the property qualifications for MPs. When a new Manchester Reform Association on these lines was established at the start of February, supported by middle-class liberals such as Edmund Potter and George Wilson, but also by a leader of working-class Chartist opinion, Edward Hooson, Abel was chosen to be one of a committee of nineteen who would draw up resolutions for the constitution of the association.

Abel was not, however, the only potential liberal candidate for the next election. By the summer of 1858 Thomas Bazley and Thomas Fairbairn had stated their intention to stand, and this was discussed at a meeting of the liberal electors of Collegiate ward on 10 August at which Abel presided. Although no reference to his own position was made, Abel took the opportunity to disparage the abilities of the present members:

> The great disparity between the intellectual powers of the present members [Turner and Potter], and those of the previous members [Bright and Milner Gibson], was as great as the disparity between the telegraphic communication just established between this country and America, and the simple telegraph of Tim Bobbin in his history of 'Tummus and Meary.'[9]

Neither was he slow to express dissatisfaction with Fairbairn, who opposed the ballot. There was discussion as to the health of one of the present MPs, Sir John Potter. According to the *Manchester Times*, it was Abel's opinion that Potter would not stand again, if his health did not recover. However, he spoke highly of Bazley, particularly his belief in education for all classes. The *Manchester Guardian* reported that there was also talk of the desirability of persuading Richard Cobden to stand, but Abel dismissed that, as Cobden had pledged himself in writing to stand for Rochdale. The meeting ended satisfactorily for Abel; a resolution was upheld that Fairbairn was unfit to represent the liberal electors of Manchester, and his name did not appear on the list of candidates.

Despite the fact that many working-class men were non-electors, they continued to wish their voice to be heard. In November 1858 nearly 4,000 of them were reported to have gathered in the Free Trade Hall at a meeting initiated and funded by working men (in the guise of the Working Men's Provisional Committee), chaired by Abel and supported by the United Kingdom Alliance. The aim again was to discuss parliamentary reform with the intention of having some input into Lord Derby's expected bill in Parliament. Abel explained that, although middle-class men could speak, the resolutions would be made and seconded by working men so that they fully represented their views. The ex-Chartist leader Edward Hooson proposed that a new political reform association be set up in Manchester, and interestingly the meeting ended with cheers for Messrs Milner Gibson and Bright, who were still clearly held in esteem by such activists.

The new body became the Manhood Suffrage Association. It met at the People's Institute in Heyrod Street on 7 December, when Abel again presided. He proceeded to recap the current position on parliamentary reform, opining that it was on the issue of how wide the franchise should be that there was the greatest disagreement, but that this organisation would be pursuing the aim that every man who was 'supposed to be sane (for some writer had said that no man was sane) should have the privilege of voting'. A letter from John Bright was read out, warning that the key issue was not the extent of the suffrage, but the distribution of seats, and that they must not let the former engage their interest to the detriment of the latter. But there was clearly a strong tide in favour of the more radical line, even in defiance of a very popular reformer.

Many anticipated that 1859 would see the fall of the minority Conservative government of Lord Derby. The campaigning for electoral reform which continued into the new year was therefore coloured by the anticipation of an imminent general election. There were two bills before Parliament; that of John Bright, which proposed to increase the number of voters from one million to two and a half million, and that of Lord Derby's government (led in the Commons by Benjamin Disraeli), which was largely concerned with creating a more uniform county and borough franchise.

At a meeting with George Wilson in the chair in the Free Trade Hall on Tuesday 15 March, under the auspices of the Lancashire Reformers' Union, Abel contrasted Bright's bill with the government's: 'Mr Bright's measure was something like real flesh and blood in proper habiliments; but the proposition of the government was a shadow dressed in a crinoline. (Laughter.) He, as an inhabitant of Manchester, protested against the crinoline system – (Laughter)...' He also claimed that Bright's bill was only fulfilling what had been the original institutions of the country, in that Lord Brougham and others had expressed the view that 'the householder... was the constitutional franchise in boroughs prior to 1832'. In this way, Abel attempted to convince even those of a very conservative disposition that Bright's bill was 'no innovation on the constitution'.[10]

Two days later, on Thursday 17 March, there was a public meeting in the Town Hall in response to a requisition originated by the Lancashire Reformers' Union to consider how to promote electoral reform in the light of the Conservative government bill. Abel Heywood spoke first, and, despite noise from the audience, was still careful not to scare off potential allies by overtly advocating universal manhood suffrage. He referred back to the Great Reform Act of 1832, saying it had been understood that those who had been instrumental in obtaining reform would unite with the working classes to win a further extension of the franchise. The current bill, he argued, was 'a monotonous thing' as it changed nothing really, even though it was intended to make the county franchise uniform with the borough one. He suggested it could have been less monotonous if the suffrage had been extended to 'every man able and fit to give a vote', which was just sufficiently vague that it avoided explicitly advocating universal suffrage.[11]

By the third week in March 1859, the election was approaching, and it seemed as if Abel would take his usual role when he was announced as a member of the committee for ensuring the re-election of Thomas Milner Gibson and John Bright as Members of Parliament for the borough of Manchester. However, in early April a requisition was drawn up to Mr Alderman Heywood, and according to the *Manchester Guardian* by 11 April he had 'consented to become a candidate' himself.[12] In a speech to supporters four days later, Abel elucidated for public consumption his version of what happened. He referred back to the promise he had made two years earlier when he had seen Milner Gibson and Bright cast off as candidates. 'In the sorrow of his heart' he had then declared that in a future election 'he would test the working men themselves as to whether, when the opportunity served, they would vote for one who had through the whole of his life been devoted to their cause and to their service.' When asked to offer himself as a candidate, he agreed to do so provided there were sufficient support.[13]

A meeting chaired by Edward Hooson was held in the Union Chambers on Dickinson Street with the object of securing 'the election of Mr. Alderman Heywood for Manchester'. The origin of this proposal was said to be with the Manhood Suffrage Association, but they would need the help of other groups to achieve their aim. In justification of this move it was stated that 'Mr. Alderman Heywood had taken a very active part in municipal affairs, and understood the feelings of the working classes and a great portion of the citizens of Manchester.' In support of this, those who had canvassed for the requisition reported that they had had a very positive response, with only four people refusing to sign, and a few sitting on the fence until they had seen Abel's election address. That very evening in only an hour and a half they had received fifteen pledges and thirty-four promises of support.

It was also agreed to ask for the support of the Lancashire Reformers' Union (LRU), as it was very influential and as Abel himself was 'a prominent member of that Union'. It was considered unlikely that they would actively oppose him, but there was doubt as to whether they would give their positive support. The warning voices were listened to attentively:

> Mr Merriman spoke highly of the qualifications of Mr. Alderman Heywood, but he did not think it possible to carry him. The Lancashire Reformers' Union had determined to solicit a gentleman whom he would not name, to stand; and Mr. Alderman Heywood was one of the persons who concurred in the invitation, and said he would support that gentleman against any other person. He did not think the Union would adopt the plan of the meeting; yet there might be a chance, because there was the possibility that one of the two Liberal candidates that the Union was likely to bring forward would not come.

It emerged that the gentleman in question was Robertson Gladstone, older brother of William Ewart Gladstone, and that indeed Abel seems to have committed himself to support his candidacy. A committee was set up for Abel's campaign, but in an amendment it was agreed that this would only be carried out if the LRU came on board.[14]

Despite this, when the LRU refused official backing, Abel's supporters set up a committee which 'pledged itself to use every effort to promote Mr Heywood's election', which it proceeded to do by appointing officers and preparing for canvassing.[15] On the same day 'A True Reformer' penned a letter to the *Manchester Guardian* on the topic of 'Abel Heywood, Robertson Gladstone and the Reformers' Union.' This correspondent was clearly of the opinion that the LRU council (which he equated with the middle-class Anti-Corn Law League) was playing a double game, and was inimical to the candidacy of Abel Heywood, the people's 'champion'. The letter ended:

> It is to be hoped that the simple-minded working men who are labouring against such fearful odds to return their great champion [Abel Heywood] in this city to Parliament, will not place too much faith in the promises of gentlemen, whose 'rules' are so elastic and variable. ... Messrs. Hooson and Co. may rest assured that in no place is their candidate viewed with more jealousy and dislike than in the chambers of the League.[16]

Abel's supporters met again on 15 April, this time in the large room of the Free Trade Hall, although they did not manage to fill it; there were reportedly about 2,000 working men present, who had gained admission by free tickets. With Abel's frequent ally on Manchester Council, Alderman Goadsby, in the chair, the platform party included radicals Dr John Watts, W.P. Roberts, J.R. Cooper, Elijah Dixon and Edward Hooson. When he appeared, Abel was 'cheered loudly'. Thomas Goadsby elaborated on Abel's qualities as the best person to represent their 'advanced political opinions'. He refuted potential objections to Abel's 'humble origin' by pointing to his reputation, property and sympathies with progress and good government. If returned, he would go as 'the unflinching advocate of the bill of John Bright, for the reform of the representation of the people'.

When Abel spoke, he stressed that he only wanted to stand for this 'onerous and important' position if he had the support of both the working and middle classes. He stated that he was not a party man, but depended on principles. In particular, he supported the Bright reform bill so that the issue of popular rights should be settled for perhaps even half a century. The meeting resolved to adopt Abel as their candidate, and the campaign began. The committee met daily at 87 Market Street under the secretaryship of ex-Chartist R.J. Richardson and the chairmanship of Robert Falkner, with radical lawyer W.P. Roberts as election agent.

Abel accordingly published his address on the same day. He stressed that he was standing by popular demand, and that he was well qualified as a resident of Manchester for forty years who had worked his way up 'by untiring industry' to 'a moderate competency'. He reminded readers of his part in the campaign against the stamp duty on newspapers, and linked his name to Milner Gibson, who had joined the fight. His twenty years of work on the council was cited as evidence of further public service. Beyond the core focus on political reform, Abel stated his opposition to secret diplomacy in foreign affairs, and that he would 'visit with the severest censure' any minister who waged war without first consulting the House of Commons. He also declared in favour of free trade. But he showed his radicalism by ending with the 'sincere hope that, whatever may be the result of the polling, the numbers will allow that the independent electors of Manchester are not afraid to trust the great working class of this country with political power'. That his view was inimical to those sympathetic to Conservative government is demonstrated in a letter to the *Manchester Courier* which described both Abel Heywood and Thomas Bazley as 'rampant chartists' and 'republican and revolutionary characters'.[17]

Thomas Bazley, one of the two sitting candidates, was considered by the radicals to be a suitable 'running mate' for Abel Heywood because he was in favour of the Bright reform bill. Accordingly, when the Bazley camp met to plan their campaign there was considerable discussion on the topic. The liberals were afraid that there was a danger of splitting the liberal vote to the detriment of Bazley, as Turner too was standing for re-election. Thomas Goadsby spoke up in favour of Bazley's joining forces with another 'exponent of the same principles'. The meeting failed to reach a suitable conclusion on the matter, a state of affairs which several of those present considered very dangerous to Bazley's interests.[18]

Abel's solo campaign was well underway by 19 April when he appeared at two ward meetings, in St Luke's and St George's. His responses to questioning in ward meetings are instructive with regard to his views on a variety of burning issues. Besides reform, he was quizzed on other matters; he supported the Maynooth grant to the Irish Catholic seminary, and was in favour of the Marriage with a Deceased Wife's Sister bill; he was against church rates and would vote to disestablish the Church of England; he did not believe MPs should be paid or that a borough should pay election expenses. At the St George's ward meeting, he spoke confidently about his hopes of winning a seat in Parliament.

He must have been highly encouraged the following day when, at a meeting in Cheetham Town Hall consisting mainly of middle-class men, having selectively explained his policies stressing those in favour of a redistribution of seats, free trade and a fair property and income tax, they voted to support his candidacy by two to one. He asserted that he wanted to be answerable to his electors and also to speak clearly and unambiguously, and he emphasised that he would not 'coalesce with the party either of Mr. Turner or that of Mr. Bazley'.[19]

Nevertheless, that same day, at a meeting of Turner's committee, fears were expressed that Bazley and Heywood were sometimes canvassing jointly, although there was no formal coalition. They did however plan for the eventuality, subscribing the massive sum of £3,000 at the meeting to pay either Turner's expenses, or the election expenses of a second candidate, should one be needed to counter a joint threat from Bazley and Heywood. Abel's candidacy clearly had the other liberal candidates rattled.

Abel's campaign continued optimistically; another meeting, this time in working-class Ancoats on 21 April, saw unanimous support for him. However, perhaps significantly, the numbers attending were only moderate. Abel told the meeting that 'he desired to be no dumb waiter in Parliament; he would there speak plainly and honestly the feelings and the wants of the working classes'. However, he wanted to represent more than one class, and said that he had been promised 'hearty support' from many of Manchester's 'highest men' and that 'shopkeepers without number had expressed the joy they felt in, for once at least, having the opportunity to go to the poll for one of their own class'. D. Donovan opined that 'if the 7,000 or 8,000 working men stuck together, there could be no doubt about Mr. Heywood's triumphant return', and the chairman of the meeting, Edward Hooson, said he believed it very likely that Abel would top the poll. Abel was keen to show that this would all be achieved fairly, and 'wished it to be understood that he would not consent to payment for a single cab. If there were twenty voters ready to vote for him – and if their votes would secure his return, while without them he was sure to lose – he would not pay an ordinary cab fare for them.' The meeting ended with 'loud applause'.[20]

Further supportive meetings were organised in Bradford and Beswick, and St Michael's and St Clement's wards. In St Michael's he reminded his hearers that their ward had been his earliest home in Manchester as a 'very humble boy'. He reported that there had just been a decision (this was by the Turner camp) to bring a fourth candidate, Captain Denman, to stand in the election and that the latter had been described as a Conservative. Mr Turner was termed a Palmerstonian, Mr Bazley a representative of Mr Bright, and Abel himself was characterised as the representative of the Chartists, but he 'denied that he came forward on Chartist principles' and claimed instead a desire to represent all classes. He also touched on the question of an alliance with another candidate; he claimed that unbeknownst to him the 'parties' who invited him to stand had made an application 'to one of the two representatives' – he would not state which, but it must have been Bazley – to see if there were any chance of 'an amalgamation'. The result of this was not passed on to him until after he had announced in the Free Trade Hall on 15 April that he had no coalition with any other candidate. In this way, Abel appeared sympathetic to a popular middle-class candidate, but still maintained his independence for the benefit of the working-class electors and non-electors in his audience.[21]

The election

The day before the poll, Friday 29 April, saw the nominations take place on a cold and windy morning at 10 a.m. in St Ann's Square. The crowd attending, estimated at up to 20,000, was unusually large 'and the excitement was intense'. Each candidate was proposed with a speech by a key supporter, citing their virtues and suitability to represent Manchester.

In his 'corner' Abel's supporters included Dr John Watts, George Wilson, J.R. Cooper, W.P. Roberts and Elijah Dixon. It was Thomas Goadsby who proposed Abel Heywood, as 'a man who was essentially and most truthfully a man of the people'. His character was described as one of 'indomitable energy and perseverance, and self-denial'. To cover every base with regard to his record as a bookseller and publisher, it was admitted that he had been accused of selling 'free-thinking publications' but argued that in the past twenty years he had 'sold more Bibles and Prayer Books than all the other booksellers of Manchester put together'. His efforts to gain a free press were touched on, as was his role in helping to quell trouble in 1842. Goadsby also seemed to link the names of Heywood and Bazley, despite the previous denials of an alliance. The seconder of Abel's candidacy, Dr John Watts, argued that until then Manchester had been represented by the employers, and that now was the chance for the 95,000 heads of households who were working men in Manchester to have representation by 'a true and thorough working man'. The response was encouraging; even the Tory *Manchester Courier* recorded that Watts's words were met with 'great cheering'.

After the nominations, the candidates themselves spoke. Abel did not hide that his ultimate aim was 'for every honest man of Manchester [to gain] admittance within the pale of the constitution', or that he supported the secret ballot, a redistribution of seats and shorter parliaments. He denied that he was a 'revolutionist' on the grounds that no one had done more to 'preserve order' than he had, but made much of his work to ensure the freedom of the press. Abel also suggested reasons why voters should be less than happy with his rivals; he implied that their commitment to reform was recent, and later he particularly attempted to undermine the 'conservative' candidates. With regard to Captain Denman, he jokingly made much of the fact that he was not a Mancunian: 'Had the gallant captain ever navigated the Irk. – (laughter) or sounded the depths of the Medlock? – (Renewed laughter.)' Despite the repeated denials of a formal alliance with Bazley, the middle-class Liberal candidate, he appealed to the electors to 'return him, together with Mr. Bazley, by a triumphant majority'. He then ended with an appeal to liberal principles, progress and free trade. Abel must have been only too aware that to stand a chance of election he must gain the support of the middle classes, and his references to middle-class Liberal Bazley indicated a hope that by connecting their names together he would enhance his own chances. The nominations ended with a show of hands; Bazley seemed to have the most support, with Abel Heywood a close second.[22]

The *Manchester Courier* provided information about how the polling was organised, explaining that there were fifteen polling places in the city. Hourly reports were sent to the headquarters of each candidate giving the state of the voting so far, which was of course only possible because the voter announced his choices for each of his two votes openly. From these returns it was clear that voting peaked in the mid to late afternoon, as excitement mounted.

The turnout at 18,334 was much greater than in 1852, when the figure stood at 13,291; it was even greater than 1857 when it reached 18,014; this reflects the comments in the press that 'there was a good deal of excitement'. But Abel with 5,420 came third, and therefore missed being elected, and that by a substantial margin of 1,791. Bazley was hugely successful, polling 7,434, and Turner would accompany him to Westminster with 7,211 votes. Denman polled the lowest at 5,158.

Voting figures were published for each candidate in each ward, and in no ward did Abel come top of the poll. Nevertheless, he came second in poorer areas – St Michael's, Collegiate Church, St Clement's, St George's and Bradford and Beswick. What is clear is that Abel stuck to his pledge not to spend money on cabs to get his voters out; the other candidates had expended large amounts but he had spent nothing on this and had conducted his election with, in his own phrase, 'unusual purity'. In the more affluent St Ann's ward, there was a perhaps significant objection to a vote, when one elector was said to have first voted for Turner and Heywood, then to have changed his choice to Turner and Denman. It was also recorded that this occurred in several cases. It seems at least possible that some undue influence was being exerted against votes for Abel Heywood. There was also some evidence that Abel's supporter Dr John Watts acted improperly in the Town Hall polling station for St James's ward, when he tried to push through the vote of an elector whose identity was dubious. Alderman Shuttleworth, the presiding officer, had to call a policeman to remove the doctor, who beat a hasty retreat before he could be apprehended. In the event, the number of votes for Abel probably indicated that many of the working-class voters had supported him; what had let him down in the end was the flight of the much larger middle-class vote.

In view of his stated belief in the run up to the poll that he would be elected, it might have been expected that Abel would have been devastated at his defeat. That he apparently was not might imply that he had indeed suspected that when the day came the middle classes might find it a step too far to put their name to his candidacy. His speech in the wake of the poll at 5 p.m. was upbeat. He gave it on the steps of the Peel monument in front of the Royal Infirmary. Accompanying him were some of the middle class who had given their support: George Wilson, Jacob Bright (brother of John) and S.P. Robinson. He said he was pleased not to come last in the poll and 'considered this a great success, looking at the short time he had been before the public as a candidate'. He praised the patriotism of those who voted for him and the spirit in which the whole election had been conducted. The number of votes polled for him, he thought, was all the more telling in view of the way he had conducted his election without cabs, and he was pleased to note that he did top the poll for a large part of the day in Collegiate and Bradford wards. Wilson thought that in the circumstances the number of votes Abel had gained was 'quite unexampled'. He ended with a ringing call to unite in preparation for the next contest so that 'they would, at the next election, have the satisfaction of sending Mr. Heywood as their representative to parliament'.[23]

The Tory *Manchester Courier* was only too keen to exploit what some may have regarded as Abel's faux-pas in using the monument for his speech. His choice of position brought censure from conservatives, ostensibly because it was considered disrespectful and hypocritical to climb on the monument. As early as 7 May the *Manchester Courier* published a letter from an anonymous author about the matter, claiming that double standards were used when ignoring the behaviour of the Heywood camp, compared to the arrest of an old Bowdon philanthropist, Mr Wood, who had tried to take a rest on the steps on a hot day and been taken before the Nuisance Committee and fined.[24] Not content with this, two weeks later the paper published a poem about the Peel monument affair which included the following verses:

And where, think you, those heroes got
To spout their wretched "stuff?"
Upon a statue steps? Not they!
That was not high enough;
They climbed upon the upper plinth
Of Robert's monument,
And though so high 'twas evident
They were not there content.

For while they stood beside of "Peel"
'Twas very plain to see
They would have mounted on his head,
If such a thing could be;
And others – men of lesser note –
They madly scrambled o'er
The figures round the monument,
An act ne'er done before....[25]

In contrast to the sarcasm and carping of the *Manchester Courier*, the *Manchester Times* was glowing in its praise of Abel Heywood's showing. He was described as 'the nominee of the unenfranchised thousands'. The article continued: 'Mr. Heywood's position on the poll is a real triumph, which shines all the more gloriously for the circumstances under which it was achieved.'[26]

Aftermath of defeat

Whatever he may privately have felt about the election, Abel now had to pick up the threads of his political activities, and this consisted of a series of large meetings of middle-class Liberals, at each of which Abel took his place on the platform. A soiree was held for the triumphant Richard Cobden as MP for Rochdale in August. Abel did not speak at the meeting, but he attended in the illustrious company from Manchester of Sir Elkanah Armitage (Mayor of Manchester, 1846–48) and George Wilson. He continued his association with the Lancashire Reformers' Union at a meeting in the Free Trade Hall on 27 October. The meeting pledged to continue the fight for an extension of the suffrage. However, the focus now began to fall on financial, rather than political, reform; they also added a resolution for a review of taxation so that the burden would fall most on property and not on labour. However, it may well be a symptom of the disillusion felt by reformers after the election in May that the meeting was not well-attended, and according to the *Manchester Courier*, which was of course not sympathetic, numbers of people left before its late conclusion.

This was followed in December by Abel's attendance at a soiree held by the Financial Reform Association in honour of Bright and Cobden (who was unable to attend due to illness) in the Philharmonic Hall in Liverpool. The aims of the Association were set out by the chairman, Charles Robertson, and he expressed the key Liberal ideals of free trade and the abolition of indirect taxation. This body also supported the more radical ideal of progressive taxation; direct taxes on citizens in proportion to their means and property.

Abel did not neglect the grass-roots entirely; he chaired a meeting of the Ardwick branch of the Lancashire Reformers' Union. In his opening speech, he accepted that the government would not concede manhood suffrage.[27] Indeed the Liberal government of the anti-reform Whig Lord Palmerston was unlikely to pass any kind of franchise extension, and Abel pragmatically accepted that there was more to be achieved in other arenas. For now, therefore, he turned his attention to local politics, as expressed in his activities in the council and other civic bodies. Manchester was facing a disastrous economic situation by 1861 with the advent of the American Civil War and the resultant cotton 'famine' in the region, and Abel was prominent in the work carried out to alleviate the situation. He also now set his sights on moving up the civic ladder and by the end of 1862 had become Mayor of Manchester.

7

Mayor of Manchester (1862–63)

While still keeping a weather eye on the wider political situation and intending to present himself as a candidate in the next general election, Abel focused in the meantime on his career in local politics. Having helped his colleague and fellow-shopkeeper Thomas Goadsby into the mayoralty in 1861, it was his turn to be elevated in the following year. We may surmise that it was not to everyone's taste that this forceful and sometimes divisive and awkward character should be chosen. On 18 October 1862 it was reported that 'a considerable number of members of the city council' had asked Goadsby to stand again for mayor, but he had declined because 'the idea of a one year's mayoralty is popular in the council' and he did not want to disturb 'the harmony which at present prevails by his name being brought forward in opposition to that of any other gentleman'. This would suggest that there was another serious contender, and indeed the report continued that 'Alderman Heywood is likely to be elected Mayor for 1863.'[1] Goadsby marked the end of his tenure, as was usual, by giving a dinner at his home, Throstle Nest in Stretford. The guest of honour was Richard Cobden, now MP for Rochdale, and Abel and others were also invited. The plight of the cotton workers, which was acute in the face of a lack of cotton imports from the warring United States, and the consequent need to extend fundraising was discussed at length. This was to be the great theme of Abel's mayoralty.

Election as mayor

The election for the new mayor took place at noon on Monday 10 November in the council meeting, where there was full attendance and also an overcrowded public gallery. Alderman Neild, who was by now considered to be the 'Father of the Corporation', spoke in complimentary terms of Abel's record of service to the council, particularly citing his work on the Paving Committee where he had, characteristically, 'boldly grappled with every difficulty that assailed him'. Neild acknowledged that he and Abel did not always agree, but stated that the latter had always treated him with 'courtesy and patience', and had always listened to opposing arguments carefully and was prepared to change his opinion. He went on to praise the support Abel had given him at the time of riots when he, Neild, was mayor (1840–42); 'without seeking popularity or applause, Mr. Heywood did what was right, because he saw it was right'. The seconder, Councillor Grundy, added that 'the language of adulation would be as unbecoming to him as it would be distasteful to Mr. Alderman Heywood' but that the mayoralty would be 'a fitting crown to a long public life devoted to the welfare of the people'. He mentioned how Abel's name was known to many in the north of England, and was familiar to every inhabitant of Manchester. When the resolution was put, it was passed unanimously, 'the "ayes" were given with unusual vigour and unison, the "noes" being conspicuous by their entire absence', and Abel was received by the council members 'rising and applauding'.

At the start of his speech of acceptance Abel demonstrated his commitment to the poor before all else. His very first point was about the challenges which would face him as mayor in view of the widespread distress currently in Manchester and all the cotton areas. But he also showed his respectability as a 'lover of constitutional government' by reference to the imminent majority of the Prince of Wales, being also keen not to 'diminish the halo and the glory of the reign of Queen Victoria'. Abel accepted the mayoral chain as the symbol of the council's power, and promised that 'it never shall be sullied, or its brilliancy suffered to fade'.[2]

The cotton famine

His immediate preoccupation was the fight to alleviate the distress among the people of Manchester, continuing work already started earlier in 1862. Indeed, there is the possibility that Abel's election at such a time, surprisingly unanimous as it was, was the response of those in power to the threat intrinsic in such a crisis as the cotton famine. If social dislocation were to be avoided, the council needed to choose a mayor who would be decisive and organised, who was wholly committed and whom the poor perceived as a friend. Mass meetings of the populace were already taking place in Stevenson Square; the next step might well be riots and violence if the situation were not handled with care by a figure of authority who could convince the people that he would act in their best interests. Abel Heywood was just such a man, and he immediately rose to the occasion.

Abel was clearly exercised about the issue as early as May 1862, attending a meeting of cotton workers in Great Ancoats Street at which he persuaded them not to set up a committee to raise cash from workers in employment, who he pointed out could ill-afford to pay. Instead, he explained to them how they should exploit the resources of the Poor Law, and of the District Provident Society, as well as use the soup kitchens which had been established as 'he had visited them himself, and could testify to the excellence of the soup that was sold there'.[3] He promised them that the Poor Law Guardians would not use the hated 'Labour test' in the case of unemployed cotton workers, who were deserving cases. However, some reports seemed to belie this: 'The men and women who appear before those committees as applicants are treated as if they were standing in the dock of a criminal court...'[4]

He advocated getting money from the rich through organisations which the rich themselves established, as 'it was very well known that the poor could not get subscriptions so well from the rich as they rich could get from each other... The rich knew almost the length and breadth of every man's pocket...' He honoured those who made every effort to be self-sufficient and not to appeal to the Poor Law, stating that 'A little suffering now and then did us good; there was no doubt about it. It made us think, and made us better than we were before.' He suggested the formation of another kind of committee, one which would inform the Poor Law Guardians of the names of people in need who, through pride, had not asked for help and were therefore bound to be considered deserving. Abel's proposals were well received and five men were elected to form such a committee. Despite his views, Abel did accept a request from the Shaftesbury Relief Fund, an operative committee collecting subscriptions from the employed in aid of the unemployed, to become their treasurer.

Large amounts of money were raised all over the country, particularly in London by the Lord Mayor's Mansion House Fund, but it was in Manchester that the relief operation really got underway. A general central Relief Committee, usually chaired by the Mayor of Manchester, had been established on 20 June 1862 in Manchester to raise funds. It appointed a central executive Relief Committee, chaired by the Earl of Derby, the leading nobleman in the north-west. This had the task of distributing the money to local committees in the distressed areas of Lancashire.

In November it was 'in at the deep end' for the new Mayor of Manchester; on the very afternoon of his election Abel attended the general Relief Committee and took over the chair. He inherited this position from Thomas Goadsby at a time when the committee was facing a crisis due to the inadequacy of funds. Abel lost no time in trying to remedy the situation and on 12 November he helped to establish a new Manchester and Salford canvassing committee set up for the purpose of soliciting subscriptions from the more recalcitrant members of the community. Abel was appointed its chairman and it would meet every day at 11 a.m., such was the importance and urgency of its remit. There was no time to relax, as on the evening of election day Abel was present at the prize evening for the Manchester Rifle Volunteers, from which any money raised was to be donated to the relief fund.

By 28 November, Abel was writing to all the clergy and ministers of religion asking them to make regular collections amongst their congregations. On 1 December he attended the weekly meeting of the executive committee, which reported on its receipts (£46,000 in the last week) and disbursements. The following day he appeared at the Lancashire meeting called by the Lord Lieutenant and held in Manchester Town Hall; he thanked the Earl of Derby for the complimentary way he had described the behaviour and fortitude of the working men, as well as the manufacturers and the merchants, and went on to explain that 'pauperism was increasing at the rate of upwards of 10,000 persons per week'. Manchester, he said, had already given nearly £100,000 for relief, and he successfully proposed that since the calamity was proving longer-lived than had at first been expected the subscriptions should accordingly be increased.

On the same day, Abel chaired a special meeting of the canvassing committee. It emerged that they had £210,000 in the fund, which only equalled nine days' wages, but some were concerned that such a large amount in the bank might put off potential donors. Abel said he would urge the executive committee to increase the funds given out, though agreed that 'they must be cautious in the distribution of funds, and only give that which was barely necessary'.[5]

By Christmas the relief fund had reached over £400,000, the equivalent of £46 million today, but still insufficient to meet fully the needs of the unemployed. To encourage further giving, lists of donors and how much they had subscribed were regularly published in the Manchester press. They were varied and very long, and included Abel's wallpaper company, Heywood, Higginbottom and Smith, who for instance were listed on 2 May as donating the substantial sum of £70, along with Abel himself who gave £20.[6] In all, between 1862 and 1864 the Relief Committee distributed over £800,000.

In an attempt to expand Lancashire's cotton supplies, on 9 July 1862 the Viceroy of Egypt, source of a superior cotton, had been welcomed on a visit to Manchester and received by the mayor, Thomas Goadsby, and the Corporation in their robes. Even the ladies were invited, and Mrs Goadsby and some others were seated at the end of the council chamber. On 21 January 1863 the Manchester Chamber of Commerce met in the mayor's parlour in the Town Hall under Abel's chairmanship. The purpose of the gathering was to present an address to the Governor of Queensland, where cotton growing had lately commenced with notable success. Emigrants to Queensland from Britain, moving in large numbers to escape the current hardship, were expected to provide more labour and also a market for British exports.

Efforts did not stop there; by August the council were discussing a proposal to provide employment for able-bodied unemployed operatives. Abel warned against holding out false hope to the poor. He also spoke strongly against the labour test, which as the workers had feared was being used in a heavy-handed way to humiliate applicants for assistance. A deputation to the Poor Law board led by Abel in November successfully sued for a government loan of £220,000 under the Public Works Act. It was to be spent on additional waterworks, the purchase of land for the creation of a new public cemetery, paving streets and improving public highways in Ardwick and Cheetham, and for 'sanitary purposes' in Chorlton. The intentions were laudable, but in practice it seems that the numbers employed were disappointing; by April 1864 only 4,838 men had been directly engaged, as opposed to a forecast of 27,000. On the other hand, the public works did benefit Manchester's infrastructure, adding 400 miles of good road, more public parks and recreation grounds, and an extension of the sewage and drainage system.

Even after his mayoralty ended in November 1863, Abel continued to attend the Relief Committee and to take particular interest in the public works. At the meeting on 16 November he stated his support of the Poor Law board policy of providing employment particularly for the unskilled, and on 2 December in the council meeting he called on the Corporation to work to reduce 'these monstrous mortgage charges which the government exacted on loans to help the unemployed through job creation'.[7]

The Relief Committee also involved itself in job creation by way of 'sewing schools' for women and girls, and advertised an appeal for old and new clothing and other textiles to be sent, which the railway companies had agreed to transport free of charge. In the winter of 1862/63 it was estimated that over 41,000 women and girls were attending sewing classes.[8] They were encouraged to feel valued by the provision of a Christmas tea, such as that for 'the Ardwick sewing girls', funded by subscriptions. This was accompanied by a meeting at which the mayor presided and spoke.

Meanwhile, in a further attempt to avoid social dislocation and potential threats to authority, on 3 December 1862 evening 'entertainments' for unemployed male workers commenced in a large room at Lamb's Mill in Ancoats. Between 800 and 1,000 working men of all ages and grades gathered in an orderly and enthusiastic manner to hear a lecture by Professor Roscoe of Owens College on 'The Air We Breath'. Abel attended the meeting, and was met with 'one of the most hearty outbursts of cheering that has greeted his worship since his election'. He could not resist the opportunity to play the crowd a little, by quoting to them some of the criticisms by doubters about the wisdom of raising subscriptions for the benefit of the workers. He cited arguments that this would result in greater pauperism, and would demoralise working men, making them reluctant to go back to work. His audience were voluble in their denials; he told them that he himself did not agree with such views because he felt 'that the working men of this country desired nothing better than fair play and hard work'. He went on to praise the Poor Law Guardians for their efforts and in particular for providing educational opportunities for those in receipt of relief, and even carried his audience with him so far as to get applause for the guardians and the ratepayers. The audience apparently enjoyed the lecture, which was 'so simple that it was brought within the range of the meanest capacity'. The gathering ended with the singing of glees.[9]

On New Year's Eve a significant meeting of workers was held in the Free Trade Hall on the subject of the American Civil War. Its aim was not, as might be expected, to express dissatisfaction at the hardship caused, but to show support for the anti-slavery northern states. It had been called by working men, and the platform party included Thomas Bazley, MP for Manchester, prominent Manchester radicals Dr John Watts and Edward Hooson, and an escaped black US slave 'Jackson', who had been President Davis's coachman. Abel chose to attend in an unofficial capacity, but was spotted in the body of the hall and invited to chair the meeting because of his 'connections with the working classes in the past, and their esteem for him', though the fact that he was the mayor was probably also a factor. The meeting proceeded to condemn slavery and the southern United States for rebelling to create 'a nation having slavery as its basis'. It went on to send an address to President Lincoln supporting his attempt to preserve the union and abolish slavery. Abel, as chairman, was asked to sign the address and as mayor to transmit it 'with an expression of its [the meeting's] earnest hope that England and America may ever remain knit together in the most intimate fraternal bonds'. Jackson, the ex-slave, was called upon to speak and he duly thanked the gathering for 'their sympathy with the negro'. Although reference was made to the hardships suffered by the Lancashire cotton workers, the overwhelming sense of the meeting was of support for the actions of the northern United States.[10] In this way, the working men of Manchester showed to the country and the world that principles of liberty were even more important to them than economic well-being. It was such sentiments that helped to win over politicians like William Gladstone to the cause of electoral reform in Britain, by showing that the working man was responsible and sober, being motivated not by base animal instinct, but by integrity and principle.

In token of friendship, in February a United States vessel, the *George Griswold*, was sent to Manchester by the New York international relief fund, laden with flour to relieve the sufferings of the poor. Abel as mayor was to join Mr Maclure of the Relief Committee and Mr Fleming of the Chamber of Commerce in inviting the ship's officers, led by Captain Lunt, to an address at the Town Hall accompanied by a lunch. On 4 March the Mayor and his 150 guests sat down to a 'costly banquet'. The cargo had been distributed in kind by the Relief Committee to the localities where it was needed.[11]

In accordance with the developing respect amongst the wealthy for the fortitude and probity of the suffering working classes, when the Manchester and Salford Co-operative Society met under Abel's chairmanship for its annual meeting on the New Year's Eve, he promised that he would support the claims of distressed co-operators to receive help from the relief fund without being forced to sell their shares 'at a sacrifice'.[12] However, forbearance was not considered practical when the Relief Committee, chaired by Abel, met on 19 January 1863. The Earl of Derby had drawn up a list to define who were the rightful recipients of relief, and anyone who had even the smallest saving or investment was to be obliged to realise them wherever possible to sustain themselves, and was only eligible for relief when actually destitute. The committee passed this as the only possible approach in the current circumstances.

Although Abel had from time to time expressed a reluctance to see workers emigrate, by April it was necessary to accept that emigration was sought by a great many unemployed workers, and he therefore presided at a meeting in the Town Hall to discuss how best to facilitate this. Help, Abel noted, was being given 'without any concert, and without any of those specific arrangements which it appeared to himself and others ought to be adopted, so as to prevent the possibility of the population of this part of the country being transported to other shores without having the means of existence on their arrival'. The meeting agreed to set up, under

Abel's chairmanship, the Manchester Emigrants Aid Committee, effectively to co-ordinate and organise emigration. By 23 April the committee had made grants to outfit 130 individuals who had gained free passage to New Zealand and was planning a fundraising drive to promote emigration to the British colonies. They had an offer from Victoria in Australia for assisted passages for 306 adults, and to equip them would cost a further £1,100.

Abel continued to support the establishment of public kitchens for the use of workers and was prominent both at the opening lunch of the Gaythorn cooking depot, and also at the end of January at a ceremony to honour its founder, John Pender MP. It provided 'good and cheap' food at cost price.[13] It was with the purpose of relieving distress among the clerks and warehousemen, secondary victims of the slump, that a new dining rooms company was set up under Abel's auspices (having once been a warehouseman himself, he may well have had particular interest in that group) at a meeting in his parlour in the Town Hall.[14] By July larger premises were opened at 9 Oldham Street with a dinner at 3s a ticket, presided over by Abel as mayor.

Such provision for those in work was all very well, but the numbers of unemployed who could not afford even modest charges were burgeoning. By June the Poor Law Guardians were in considerable disarray and the middle classes and small manufacturers were also in peril. The work of relief continued unabated for the next two years.

The royal marriage

Although the cotton crisis was the defining aspect of Abel's mayoralty in 1862–63, it was not of course the only matter with which he had to grapple. At the other end of the social scale from the impoverished cotton workers, there were developments in the royal family which required attention; in particular, the majority of the Prince of Wales on 9 November 1862, and his marriage to Alexandra of Denmark on 10 March 1863. As ever, Abel demonstrated enthusiastic loyalty and was keen to celebrate both; at the end of 1862 he commissioned a marble bust of the prince, who had agreed to sit for it, by the sculptor Marshall Wood. It was 'colossal' as it was calculated for a figure about twelve feet high, but was considered a good likeness and a skilled work of art, despite the 'bland' nature of the subject. Abel presented it to the council on 7 October, expressing the desire that it commemorate the prince's coming of age, and that it might be seen with the busts of the Queen and Prince Consort which were already in the Town Hall.[15]

The prince's forthcoming marriage was the topic of discussion by early February in a sub-committee of the General Purposes Committee; suggestions as to how to celebrate the marriage in Manchester were elicited from leading merchants and employers. Abel put himself in overall control of events and chaired meetings for several weeks before the marriage. Ever the committee man, he suggested another committee should be appointed, this time consisting of 'gentlemen', which might combine with the sub-committee because the council did not feel able to take full responsibility for any expenses which might be incurred. It was perhaps with a view to sharing costs that it was also suggested that the celebrations should be combined with those of Salford.

As this was a wedding, and therefore could be deemed the province of women, the ladies too were busy, preparing a gift for the bride. About twenty of them met on 20 February, presided over by the mayor, in his Town Hall parlour. They were led by the mayoress, Ann Heywood, and included Mrs Elizabeth Goadsby, wife of ex-mayor Thomas Goadsby, who five years later was to become Abel's second wife. The chosen piece was a 'magnificent opal bracelet, set with emeralds and diamonds', valued at over £500.

In his official notice of the proposed celebrations, Abel ended with a somewhat ominous prohibition that 'the use of fire-arms, of every description, within the city, is strictly forbidden'. The authorities did not want any trouble from malcontents or criminals. Indeed, their fears about firearms were not unwarranted; a John Foy, for instance, who took his wife and friends out in a cart to see the city's illuminations was killed in Peter Street when the horse shied and threw them all out of the cart. 'It was found that he had carried a revolver pistol in his pocket, with one of the barrels charged, and that the force of the fall had caused it to go off. The shot had penetrated his lungs…'[16]

In the end, the celebrations were quite remarkable, and surely helped to lift the spirits of the depressed city as much as to show off its greatness and honour royalty. Most of the entertainments were provided free of charge to the public; for those in search of outdoor fun there was access to the Belle Vue Gardens and Pomona Gardens and in the evening there were firework displays in both for an hour. For those in pursuit of more intellectual pastimes, the Royal Institution, the Botanical Gardens and the Natural History Museum were opened free to all. Troops of the line and volunteers assembled in Peel Park for a twenty-one-gun salute and a *feu de joie* at noon followed by a parade through Salford and Manchester. Bells were rung in several city churches.

But perhaps the most impressive feature of the celebrations was the evening illumination of all the Manchester Town Halls and other municipal buildings, businesses and homes, including Ardwick House, the home of Abel Heywood, which sported a Brunswick star and 'AA' for Albert and Alexandra. The gas company had agreed to supply gas for the illuminations at a cheap price and it was boasted that Manchester had much larger gas pipes than Salford to accommodate the demands of display. The press reported in great detail each building's illuminations. The Town Hall was splendidly lit with four pillars 'festooned with lights, crystal feathers, and star 10ft. high, elaborate scroll-work from one end of the front to the other, a bead light on the string course, and two 9ft. royal stars, with AA in centre of each'. Surprisingly perhaps, there were very few accidents with the gas and the fire brigade, though ready to act, was not called for. This may have been due to careful planning and the thought given to the accommodation of the crowds expected, estimated at half a million.[17]

To defray costs the sub-committee had aimed to raise £1,000 of which any surplus was to be given to the district provident society for relief work. Disappointingly, in the event only £425 could be collected, as many pleaded inability to pay.[18] Despite the financial difficulties, the tone of the reporting suggests that the whole day was a great success, with only minor hitches, and large numbers of citizens participated, wearing 'wedding favours' to show their loyalty.

For Abel personally, there resulted a social triumph when he, along with Alderman Curtis, was presented by Prime Minister Lord Palmerston to the Prince and Princess of Wales on Wednesday 13 May 1863, at the levee held on behalf of the Queen. It may be surmised that this was one of those occasions where Abel took stock of just how far he had come in life.

Inevitably, there must have been those who were bitter and angry at the expense of the occasion, and who saw the rejoicings as a mark of callous indifference to the current destitution and starvation. In honour of the marriage a meeting of unemployed operatives was planned in Stevenson Square to allow them to show their thanks to the people of New York for the gift of food brought on the *George Griswold*. Mr Denison, the chaplain of the ship, would attend and 15,000 loaves would be distributed after a march from the square to Kersal Moor. A turbulent meeting took place and the bread was seized in the square and thrown about, one loaf hitting Mr Denison on the head. 'Mr. Edwards said that the promoters of the meeting thought that on such a day of rejoicing something better might be done than give an empty pageant to the starving poor.'[19] It is hardly surprising that there were undercurrents, but the press gave them relatively little attention.

Thus, there were two defining aspects of Abel's mayoralty: the cotton crisis and the royal wedding celebrations. Both were apparently managed effectively in Manchester; the press, even the frequently hostile *Manchester Courier*, was throughout supportive and uncritical of the authorities, which may be construed to have reflected conservative middle-class opinion. The views of the poor are harder to ascertain, but the incident in Stevenson Square certainly indicated that there was bitterness and disorder bubbling below the surface.

Mayoral duties

There were many 'bread and butter' aspects of office which Abel managed to fit into his busy schedule. First among these was his chairmanship of the council at which he appeared regularly, but rarely (and uncharacteristically) said much in discussion, keeping his promise at his election to maintain a studied impartiality. As mayor, Abel was also Chief Magistrate for the city, and accordingly attended regularly at the Quarter Sessions. The magistrates dealt with crimes which were too serious for the Manchester Police Courts, such as burglaries, theft, fraud and assaults. It was reported that the current hardship had not raised the overall level of crime, though some of the fraud related to money obtained from the Poor Law Guardians or from charitable monies intended to relieve distress. There were other court duties too; on 23 March Abel was sworn onto the grand jury at the

South Lancashire assizes at St George's Hall in Liverpool. One of the cases they were to try was a serious robbery from the Bank of Manchester, but there were also murders and the dreaded 'garrottings'. There was also the job of attending the Manchester gaol sessions, which regularly reviewed the state of the prisoners and the prison, and the accounts; in addition, visiting justices were appointed to inspect the prisons and in April Abel was among them.[20] Likewise Abel attended the inspection of the Manchester police force. The force gained a glowing report, as they were able to march about in columns very impressively and were 'a healthy and vigorous body of men'. Abel was full of praise, adding that 'he knew well their character as constables, and with many of them he was personally acquainted. He thought he could say with perfect truth that there was no other borough possessed of a finer body of men than the Manchester Corporation…'[21]

Mayoral duties also meant that Abel took an interest in matters which were not on his usual agenda, in particular the Arts. In January he attended the soiree of the Manchester School of Art in the Royal Institution, at which it was noted that the current slump was taking a toll on its finances, and, with modern echoes, there were concerns that London art establishments were being funded at the expense of those in the large towns like Manchester. Again in April, Abel was listed at the head of the local educational board of the Society of Arts, and as such he attended the annual meeting of the school and proposed the adoption of the treasurer's accounts. Abel's role in encouraging the Arts also embraced literature and on 17 October 1863 he convened a meeting at which a committee was formed under his chairmanship to plan celebrations for the tercentenary of William Shakespeare the following year. It was suggested that they might establish some Shakespeare scholarships at Owens College and the Grammar School. Rather less highbrow in the world of theatre was his patronage and presence at Newsome's Alhambra Circus on Portland Street for their presentation of *Cinderella or the Little Glass Slipper* on the occasion of a 'Fashionable Box Night'.

Having attended other mayors at their homes for dinners, Abel provided hospitality at Ardwick House on several occasions throughout this mayoralty. The guest lists reflected his interests at the time, as well as those whose views he might find helpful, not to mention personal friendships. On 19 February it was an eclectic gathering: it included the engineering magnates, William Fairbairn and James Crossley; James Prescott Joule, Henry Roscoe and other academics and scientists; the mayors of Liverpool and Salford; the Manchester town clerk Joseph Heron, the city surveyor, the stipendiary magistrate and the County Court judge; various members of the clergy, notably Unitarian minister William Gaskell, and Abel's own son-in-law, husband of his eldest daughter Jane, Robert Trimble, a Unitarian linen merchant with a close involvement in the volunteer movement.[22] In March he invited a very different group, including his older brothers, William and John, and the radical Dr John Watts. A gathering in May was very diverse, since the guests included pillars of the establishment such as the Vice-Chancellor of the Duchy of Lancaster, Sir James Kay-Shuttleworth, Bart., and with him Ernest Jones, the radical ex-Chartist. On 15 October there was a special dinner at which the guest of honour was the Lord Mayor of London, who of course was carrying out sterling work for the Lancashire unemployed through his Mansion House fund; it was specifically stated that the other guests were invited there to meet him. Accordingly, the list included Manchester's recorder and town clerk, with a large group from the council of six aldermen and seven councillors, and others who included Thomas Sowler, editor of the *Manchester Courier*, and Alfred Waterhouse, who was later to become the architect of the new Manchester Town Hall. In political life it is always wise to maintain cordial relations with the powerful, and Abel continued to attend banquets where such persons might be met with. On 25 July, he took his place amidst a throng of over 500 gentlemen in the Corn Exchange who were dining to celebrate the foundation of a grand new masonic hall in Cooper Street.

Social campaigns

Abel demonstrated the tenacity and energy for which he was known in continuing to promote many of his ongoing campaigns. Sewage had long been a topic close to his heart; even as mayor he had continued on occasion to attend, though not to chair, the Highways, Paving and Sewering Committee. In April 1863 he joined a group of visitors with the Scavenging Committee of Manchester in Hyde to study the Patent Eureka Sanitary System, a process to concentrate human manure, then spent an hour enjoying hospitality.

In education, his support of the Mechanics' Institution was unabated and at their annual prize-giving he was among those who addressed the students. On this occasion it was reported that he regretted that those in the school of design had not produced 'the requisite beauty of pattern' which meant that manufacturers had to go to Paris for designs: 'We ought not to be compelled to go to foreign markets to obtain that which our own population should be able to provide.'[23] Abel also participated in the oversight of the Manchester district schools for the orphans of warehousemen and clerks as chair of its annual meeting in the Athenaeum. The school provided for twenty-eight pupils and Abel stated his belief that it should accommodate at least four times that number and receive more support. In evaluating the school, he believed that not only financial considerations should be taken into account, but also 'the mind which had been cultivated… and sent out to make its own way in the world'.[24]

At the other end of the educational scale, Abel also supported the development of Owens College (later to evolve into the Victoria University of Manchester). On 17 April 1863 he attended the lecture of Professor Williamson, FRS, on life in the depths of the ocean and gave the vote of thanks at the end. After the talk there was the opportunity to examine specimens of such creatures through microscopes, which Abel would surely have enjoyed.[25]

Meanwhile, he continued to take an interest in 'rational recreation' for the working classes. In June he opened a bazaar in the Royal Exchange which was raising money for St Matthias's working men's club on Silk Street in Salford. In his address, he explained the need for such clubs due to legislation which allowed men to finish work at 6 p.m., thereby increasing their leisure needs. He believed that 'Working men were more social than any other class, because there was not that distinction created by position amongst them as there was amongst other classes.'[26]

This was all of a piece with an increasing support for teetotalism. On 30 May 1863 the *Manchester Courier* carried an announcement that Abel as mayor had been requisitioned by ratepayers to hold a public meeting to consider the bill then before Parliament which proposed to ban the sale of alcohol on Sundays. Abel accordingly called a meeting on 1 June and took the chair. The meeting agreed to support Sunday prohibition and to present their resolution to the House of Commons. Abel was chosen to meet up with deputations from other towns and see the Home Secretary, Sir George Grey, to urge the government to support the bill.

When the United Kingdom Alliance for the Total Suppression of the Liquor Traffic held its tenth annual meeting in the Free Trade Hall in October, Abel again was prominent as chairman, and as such he spoke about the success of the movement so far. He referred to the principles which the Alliance sought to inculcate in the public as 'correct truth', and he explained that the weapons used were 'those of reason'. The meeting went beyond Sunday prohibition, and resolved to campaign for a 'permissive prohibitory law' so that the sale of alcohol could be altogether banned if the owners and occupiers of property in the district wished it.[27] In accordance with such views, when Abel joined a group of magistrates at the New Bailey on 28 August to hear applications for licences to sell spirits, they refused all the applications; he seems to have been 'swimming with the tide' on this matter.[28]

He was also active in the campaign to abolish public hangings, 'which in the ordinary course of things might be expected to take place here after the new assize courts have been opened', holding a meeting in his mayoral parlour on 29 January 1863 at which he stated that 'he should regret to see the time when executions took place in Manchester…' The meeting resolved to memorialise the Home Secretary to ask for executions to be carried out in private, within the New Bailey prison.[29] Abel led a very high-powered deputation which met Sir George Grey on 30 April to discuss the resolution, and the goal was achieved in 1868.

When the 1863 municipal elections were held, it had already been established as early as September that Abel was not planning to stand for re-election as mayor. Perhaps he had found the experience gruelling, in the light of the ongoing cotton famine; indeed, in his speech at the end of his tenure he referred to 'the extra labour entailed by the Relief Committee'. Moreover, there is the likelihood that he found chairing council meetings frustrating because he was unable to speak out plainly as he had been wont to do. When the new mayor was elected on 9 November, Abel immediately resumed 'his old seat at the bottom of the centre table'. Alderman Neild spoke in praise of Abel's mayoral record, though some phrases were somewhat noncommittal: 'he had occupied the civic chair so worthily that the honour and dignity of the office and the interests of the city had suffered nothing in his hands'. Nevertheless, he also spoke of how Abel had made a 'strong impression upon all who had had anything to do with him' and 'had earned the very high respect of individuals who sat in high places'. He said that Abel's actions were not for his own aggrandizement, but that he had discharged his duties 'faithfully, honourably and most laboriously'.

In his reply, Abel, reflecting this assessment, focused on matters which affected the poor of the city, and began by praising the working classes for their calmness in the face of distress. He was gratified that this had been recognised by the Earl of Derby, whom he said he accordingly regarded 'with the greatest veneration and affection'. Unafraid to refer to more earthy matters, Abel went on to assess the 'sanitary condition of the city', in that there was an abundant supply of water and light, but 'they were deficient in the means of removing the *excreta* of the city'. He encouraged the council to face up to this and to work so that 'the death rate might be materially diminished' and referred to schemes under examination to utilise the city's refuse.

The celebrations for the royal marriage merited a mention, but were not dwelt upon. A particular point was to thank Joseph Heron, the town clerk, for his help and 'unvarying kindness and great generosity'. Having referred to his position as Chief Magistrate, Abel said he was pleased that his judicial role would continue as a Justice of the Peace. He also made a significant reference to 'the necessity... for a new Town Hall'.[30]

When the Liberal *Manchester Guardian* reported that Abel Heywood was to be mayor again in October 1876, it was recalled that this first period in office had been marked by the inception of Albert Square, the purchase of land for a cemetery, the opening of the Philips Park Road to Bradford, the reorganisation of the fire brigade, and public rejoicings and illuminations for the marriage of the Prince of Wales which 'made it pleasantly memorable'. It is telling that no mention was made of the terrible cotton famine which was probably its most obvious feature for the ordinary workers of the city, and for Abel himself. That the newspaper ignored it demonstrates how different his approach was to that of his more middle-class peers.[31]

Abel's mayoral year had been marked by dramatic highs and lows. When it concluded, Lancashire was still in the grip of a terrible depression, and his relief work continued after his time as mayor. He had demonstrated that he could be trusted to take an impartial stance in council meetings, and that he was a steady hand on the tiller in times of potential upheaval and peril. Due deference and recognition had been shown to royalty, and any such ill-feeling this might have engendered had been kept successfully in check. All in all, Abel had established himself as a man who could be trusted to carry out difficult tasks under difficult circumstances both efficiently and effectively. His calls for a new Town Hall and his record as mayor helped to lay the foundations for his great task of the later 1860s and '70s: the design and construction of a municipal palace fitting for the government of a great metropolis.

8

The Emergence of the Liberal Elder Statesman (1860–76)

While the 1840s and '50s were the decades when Abel entered the lower middle class and espoused the liberal beliefs common among that group, the 1860s and '70s saw the maturing of that commitment, albeit on the radical wing of the Liberal party. The period of mayoralty over, Abel resumed his work on the council, and in 1869 he played a prominent role in a royal visit by the Prince and Princess of Wales. He also continued his support of the many philanthropic and moral campaigns focused on the poor. He had not forgotten the struggles in Europe, and was not allowed to forget those closer to home in Ireland. Matters did not proceed without interruption, however, as he again stood for Parliament in 1865, and took an active interest in the election of 1868. By that time he had set the ball rolling on the construction of Manchester's tramways, and was immersed in the development of the new Town Hall site.

The council

On 9 November 1871 Abel nominated William Booth as the new mayor, and his supporting speech affords some insight into what he perceived should be the current priorities for the council. As 'essentially a Manchester man', a phrase which held great meaning for contemporaries, the manufacturer Booth had been active in Sunday school education and the Sanitary Association. Abel expressed the hope that he would improve the sewage system, and in particular would look into 'how that immense sewer, the Irwell, could be remedied or improved'.[1] Although Abel was clearly aware of the shortcomings of local government in Manchester, some of which were caused by duplications and overlapping of departments in need of rationalisation and reorganisation, he was also keen to maintain the power of the council as the representative body of local opinion. In 1872, Parliament was discussing a controversial Public Health Bill. Abel spelled out the problem as he saw it: the Health Committee would be given extraordinary powers to spend money on hospitals and other medical assistance, over which the council would have no control.

But Abel was particularly interested in the 1860s and '70s in the council's role in developing transport. As in so many areas, Victorian Britain was struggling to get to grips with the new demands created by technology. On 16 February 1860 discussion in a public meeting focused especially on the poor accommodation in Manchester's railway stations. The manufacturer Robert Hyde Greg recited a catalogue of failings at London Road Station; the access was dangerous, the station itself was dark, there were no proper waiting or refreshment rooms, and the turntable was liable to sweep the passengers off, and indeed there had been one fatality. There was great confusion and delay of trains, and people could easily get on the wrong train or be left behind. There were calls for the directors to take more responsibility for the accidents and injuries which occurred to passengers and for an inspectorate to be set up to ensure safe accommodation; the beginning of 'Health and Safety' culture can be detected in such sentiments. Abel, in the body of the hall, then spoke up in a more conciliatory tone by proposing 'this meeting has no desire to urge any unnecessary expenditure on the part of the railway companies; but hereby declares its opinion, that a large extension of the railway stations in this city is an imperative and public necessity…'[2]

A council meeting in 1866 demonstrated the huge issues surrounding railway development in an established city such as Manchester. The matter of a bill set before Parliament by the Manchester, Sheffield, and Lincolnshire Railway Company to establish a central railway station on Portland Street was raised by Heywood on behalf of the General Purposes Committee. The council was clearly overwhelmed by the complexity of the question of how to develop provision and what the priorities should be. There were many vested interests: the railway companies, still in fierce competition with each other; the property-owners, whose warehouses were threatened; the railway-users who wanted efficient services; the residents living close to proposed developments, where noise and dirt would increase and house values would fall. Abel expressed support for the principle of a great central station, but felt that the Portland Street site would leave the Stevenson Square area of working-class Ancoats without railway provision, and he feared the city would be divided into two by the new lines required, like 'a kind of China wall'.[3]

Abel was keen enough to be included on a deputation to Westminster to present the council's opposition to the scheme proposed in the bill in the House of Lords. They reported to the council on 1 August that the Lords had rejected the bill. Abel took the opportunity to attack the railway company for its attitude to the council, since in the past the latter had given 'accommodation to railway companies without exacting greater remuneration. They had been charged with erring on the side of liberality.' He particularly took exception to company director Edward Watkin referring to the council satirically as an 'august' body, and claimed Watkin had implied that they were acting out of private hostility to the company.[4]

Abel's commitment to effective railway development was not limited to the glamour of meetings with bigwigs in London; he also undertook inspections on the ground. In 1872 he went with Councillor Greenwood and the town clerk to inspect the proposed line of the Lancashire and Yorkshire Railway Company from Victoria Station through Cheetham Hill, Prestwich and beyond. They made very specific technical recommendations to the railway company for the height of bridges, the width of viaducts, the siting of railway crossings and the construction of fences. In this case, they appear to have had a satisfyingly successful impact, in that the town clerk reported to the council that clauses effecting the recommendations had been put into the company's bill before Parliament.

Although Abel spoke in the council increasingly as deputy chairman of the General Purposes Committee, he was still active as chair of the Highways and Paving Committee, such as approving the trial of a new steamroller on Peter Street. This was an age of experiment and innovation; Abel was required to be ever open to new machinery and constant change. Quite frequently he had to deal with situations where roads and railways met. In the early 1870s the council was exercised about the Midland Railway Company's request for a level crossing on Great Ancoats Street. There were lengthy negotiations. Ominously, it was pointed out that a railway crossing had been allowed in Salford by a parliamentary committee, against the wishes of the Corporation, and therefore to oppose the Midland Railway was probably pointless.[5] By February 1872, clearly exasperated, the General Purposes Committee proposed that the council empower them to negotiate a deal for a level crossing 'and so avoid the necessity of an expensive contest' because the company had given notice that they intended to apply to Parliament. But the council rejected this suggestion. This is just one example of the kind of difficulties presented by the technological development of transport clashing with the wishes of the council, with which Abel and the committee had to grapple.

Meanwhile, by the end of the 1860s the city began to take an interest in the establishment of a tram system on the lines of those already in use in Copenhagen and Brussels. Abel supported the idea of some general government guidelines, but was characteristically *laissez-faire* in backing the principle that the local council should actually be in control in their own city through the appointment of a committee. Apparently, he had visited Liverpool to look at their tramways and declared that 'such a system of locomotion would be of great usefulness in this city', especially in view of the fact that the Manchester Carriage Company was to bear all the costs of laying the rails. Again Abel showed his awareness of the necessity for adaptation and change when he opined that whether the council agreed with it or not, 'he was quite certain that tramways would yet be laid down throughout the country. It was not likely that we should continue to go on in the same jog trot way with regard to our road, as we had observed for hundreds of years.' Despite his convictions, the council was not convinced at this stage, and opted to put off making any decision by referring the matter to yet another sub-committee of which Abel became chairman.[6]

After lengthy arguments, and jaunts as far away as London, Edinburgh, Glasgow, Leeds and Liverpool, and also extensive talks with Salford Council, on 11 September 1874 Abel's committee recommended that the city should build tramways up to the city limits, and five routes were specified. The recommendations were finally accepted at 1.30 a.m. on 6 January 1875 and construction work began the following December.

Whereas full council meetings were open to the press, the council was still arguing about whether other meetings should be similarly opened up, and in December 1866 there was a move to allow the press to report on the General Purposes Committee. This was supported by Abel, who argued that 'publicity of proceedings was the purifying process in the life of public bodies… It was not a question of speeches being reported, but of information being given to the public.' However, the resolution was defeated by thirty-four to seventeen.[7]

This desire for the Corporation to show transparency and integrity in all its dealings brought Abel into unusual conflict with Joseph Heron, the town clerk. In 1846 the council had decided to increase Heron's salary so that he could be compensated for giving up his own legal practice in favour of his Corporation duties. In 1871, having served the council in what was generally agreed to be an exceptionally distinguished career, Heron accepted a directorship in a public company, the Nantyglo and Blaina Ironworks Company Limited. Abel, who seems hitherto to have enjoyed cordial relations with him, argued that to take on such a role in a public company went against the express understanding which the council had with him, and also against the town clerk's own previous words (which Abel offered to quote if necessary). The limitation on outside employment extended to all officials employed by the Corporation, and Abel feared that the example now set would influence other employees and undermine morale.

Both men were keen to stress that they were not taking the discussion personally, but Heron argued strongly in favour of his acceptance of the position, as commensurate with his understanding of his role in the Corporation. Mr Fox Turner, a new councillor, defended the record of Heron and took Abel to task. He sarcastically contended that, if they were drawing up the specification for a new town clerk, 'Mr Alderman Heywood… might perhaps claim to prescribe for him what he should and should not eat and drink, for what points he should play in chess – (a laugh), – or whether he should pursue a Malthusian policy in his domestic arrangements.– (Laughter.) But the present case was quite different, and called for the allowance of some latitude.'

The council agreed that Heron's case was special, and he was 'thoroughly exonerated… from any blame in the matter'. But they did not want any formal resolution passed, apparently because this was an exceptional situation and the rule of not allowing Corporation employees to take up other employment still stood.[8] Thus was an important principle, as enunciated by Abel, upheld, while at the same time due recognition was given to the exceptional work done by Joseph Heron on the council's behalf. Whether the relationship between the two men survived intact is another matter. When a proposal was made to increase the town clerk's salary in January 1875, Abel tried to rebuild relations with Heron and could not praise his work too highly, but continued to insist on the correctness of his own position:

Finally, let him say he had a profound esteem for the Town Clerk... He (Mr. Alderman Heywood) had done on various occasions things from which other gentlemen shrank. He had complained – and he thought justly – of the Town Clerk; but he had complained because he loved the Town Clerk, and loved the position which he occupied; and when he had complained it was only that the Town Clerk might see that the course he (Mr. Alderman Heywood) recommended was the best and most honourable. – (Hear, hear.)[9]

The royal visit of 1869

The royal visit of July 1869 was perhaps Abel's most prominent moment in the later 1860s as a member of the Corporation; the Prince and Princess of Wales were received at his new home, Throstle Nest in Stretford, where he was now residing with his second wife, Elizabeth Goadsby. Preparations began in May 1869, when Abel joined the sub-committee to plan the reception of the royal couple jointly with the Royal Agricultural Society, which was to hold its show in Manchester under the patronage of the Prince of Wales. On 20 July the royal couple visited the agricultural show at Old Trafford, arriving from the Earl of Ellesmere's house at Worsley by royal barge on the Bridgewater Canal. They landed in Abel and Elizabeth's garden:

> To the request of the Earl of Ellesmere Mr. Alderman Heywood and Mrs. Heywood gladly acceded, that a landing stage might be erected at the foot of their garden close to Throstle Nest Bridge... A number of ladies and gentlemen had been invited to assemble in the garden, and waited with most loyal patience in the hot sunshine during the hours that elapsed... before the arrival of the procession. The bridge was covered with gay bunting, the Prince's feathers, and His Royal Highness's and the Princess's arms. Flags and streamers also floated from poles and lines in and about the garden.... After their Royal Highnesses were seated, Mr. and Miss Heywood [Jessie, Abel's youngest child, then aged 17] approached the carriage door, and the Princess was pleased to accept a bouquet from Miss Heywood...

The *Manchester Courier* added the detail that Abel and Elizabeth:

> conducted [the Prince and Princess of Wales] from the landing place to their carriage. His royal Highness the Prince of Wales, before driving off, entered into conversation with Mr. Heywood, to whom he expressed his thanks for and admiration of the excellence of the arrangements which had been made for his reception.

Later in the day the royal party embarked at Throstle Nest for the return to Worsley. It can only be imagined how gratifying it was for the Heywoods to have been invited to the entertainment held that evening at Worsley Hall where they hobnobbed with the local aristocracy and indeed with the Prince and Princess themselves.[10]

Social campaigns

Even in the midst of all the excitement of his council career Abel did not neglect the plight of the working class and in the spirit of 'self-improvement' he played an active part in the establishment of the Manchester Working Men's Club in 1864, taking on the post of treasurer. As an introductory offer, the club provided 'rational recreation' in the first week free of charge every evening from 6 p.m. This included concerts, games and gymnastics. That this was not an isolated instance is demonstrated by Abel's support for a conference in 1871 held in the mayor's parlour and chaired by the Bishop of Manchester with the purpose of promoting the spread of working men's clubs in the 'great cotton districts of the North'. The workers were to be allowed to show that they were capable of running their own institutions, a principle established by Abel and his fellows way back in the 1820s in the Manchester Mechanics' Institution, and which he had ever since expressly supported.

The following year saw the inauguration of 'the Art-Workmen's Exhibition', of which Abel Heywood was also the treasurer, in the Royal Institution on Mosley Street. In his address, he emphasised that such an exhibition, which had been the brainchild of the artisans themselves, could prove wrong those people who thought that the finest workmanship and artistry could only be had in London. For this reason, he believed that this should be a permanent institution for the edification of workmen.

With the advent of the Paris exhibition of 1867, Abel supported the plan of the Metropolitan District Association of Working Men's Clubs and Institutes to send workmen from Manchester, alongside others from across the country, to the event. He chaired the meeting at the Mechanics' Institution at which it was explained that costs would be kept as low as £4 by gaining the use of a building in Paris for accommodation, and providing a package to include a week's keep, admission fees and travel. There would also be the opportunity to visit French factories. A committee was set up to further this project, and Abel chaired it when it met every Monday.

He sympathised with the 'friendly society' aspects of worker organisations, supporting the Oddfellows at a meeting in Heyrod Street to establish a widows and orphans fund in 1861. Perhaps surprisingly, in view of the local focus of most of his activities, Abel firmly expressed his support for the 4,000 agricultural workers led by Joseph Arch in eastern England who, in 1874, were locked out by the farmers in their agitation for the restitution of 1s a week to their wages. When a committee was formed for Lancashire, Yorkshire and Cheshire to support them, Abel Heywood was its chairman.

However, he was to be found far more frequently supporting efforts towards co-operation rather than towards combination, celebrating the success of the Manchester and Salford Equitable Co-operative Society at the end of January 1865 in the Free Trade Hall. He also demonstrated eagerness to support local co-operative societies in 'outreach'. When the Prestwich group funded and presented a free 400-volume library to the town, Abel's birthplace, he presided on 25 February 1865 at the opening, expressing the hope that the number might increase to 2,000 by the end of the next year, and if not 'he should be "obliged to fill up the gap himself"'.[11]

Abel's concern for the living standards of the working classes was also undiminished as he continued to strive for healthier streets and houses and better provision of parks, hospitals and most especially education, all the while continuing to campaign for temperance. By 1865, there was again the threat of cholera, which focused the minds of the council on public health provision, especially the unhealthy overcrowding of housing and the prevalence of cellar dwellings. Manchester's mortality rate was reported as twenty-nine per 1,000, which compared favourably with Liverpool at thirty-five, but unfavourably with most other large cities; Birmingham was quoted at eighteen. The argument was put that people had been allowed to stay in cellars rather than to turn them out into the street during the cotton famine, and that the failure to eliminate the 3,700 cellars still in existence was therefore not due to concern for the owners of the properties, but for their poor tenants.

That cellar dwellings were 'objectionable' was an opinion which Abel maintained throughout, and he contended that the council should continue to decrease their number, and also that of crowded garrets, until they ceased to exist.[12] He supported his view by quoting at length from a lecture he had attended given to the Social Science Association on conditions in Ancoats. Over 65 per cent of the houses there were still 'single' (back-to-back), and were filthy, damp and in some cases 'ruinous', and therefore 'wholly unfit for human dwellings'. In Manchester there were estimated to be 25,000 such houses. This was attributed to the failings of the sanitary department, which needed a complete re-modelling, and the lack of a 'responsible medical officer of health'.[13] Perhaps in response, by March 1868 the council was appointing just such an officer and Abel spoke strongly in favour of the candidacy of John Leigh. He made light of the apparently 'advanced years' of Mr Leigh (he was 52), being a councillor of 56 himself, and 'he ventured to say that he would have greater confidence in a member of 50 years old and beyond, than he would in some of the young ones. (Laughter.)' Mr Leigh was duly selected and became the first Medical Officer of Health (MOH) for Manchester.[14] When the Manchester Improvement Bill came before the House of Commons' committee in 1871, it was not a surprise that Abel accompanied the town clerk, Joseph Heron, and others to represent Manchester and press for the passage of the legislation; it succeeded as 'a mere matter of form'.[15] Abel carried his arguments beyond the council; at a meeting of the ministry to the poor, chaired by William Gaskell, minister to the

Cross Street chapel of which Abel was now a member, he supported the 'arduous' work of the mission, but pointed out:

> It was not only important to consider the moral condition of the poor, but also the condition of their homes. He... thought that the missionaries in connection with that Society would be of essential service in enabling the [Health] Committee successfully to carry on their work, if from time to time they forwarded them information of the existence and locality of the unhealthy dwellings which they might visit.[16]

It was not only improved homes that were important to ensure a healthier population. Having supported the foundation of the first baths in 1849, by the 1860s Abel was leading the way to spread the availability of such institutions. He presided over the 1864 meeting of the Manchester and Salford Baths and Laundries Company, and in 1866 made a spirited contribution to the meeting; the company had only been able to pay a dividend of 3 per cent to the shareholders, and Abel had his piece to say on this, recommending that the Turkish baths section be closed and the management be reviewed. 'He did not know whether the thing was dying out, but it was evident they should be "washed out" if they went on at the present rate. (Laughter.) He hoped to see new life infused into the management.'[17]

The response of the meeting was to add Abel's name to the list of directors, presumably in the hope that he might be the agent of the 'new life'. By the following year Abel was pleased to note at the annual meeting that there was an increase of over a thousand 'washers' (users of the laundry). By now the company had six establishments and Abel became company chairman.

By the summer of 1877, during Abel's second term as mayor, in accordance with his oft-expressed views as to the role of the council in services to help the poor, he had succeeded in agreeing with the company that the baths and washhouses in Leaf Street, Stretford Road and Mayfield, in Ardwick, be sold to the Corporation. The Corporation was also proposing to construct new ones at New Islington under the auspices of the now established Baths and Washhouses Committee.

All too often when illness did strike, it led to unemployment and destitution. In an attempt to address this, in the early 1850s Abel had begun to take an active interest in the Manchester hospitals. The most prominent was the Royal Infirmary, then sited on Piccadilly; by the summer of 1850 he had become a 'House Visitor and Inspector of the Infirmary'. As mayor, Abel had supported the Manchester General Hospital and Dispensary for Sick Children and in 1865 he was also in attendance at the annual meeting of the Manchester Eye Hospital and became a 'visiting trustee'. In 1866 it was found that the Lock Hospital was in financial difficulties. The hospital treated women infected with sexually transmitted diseases, as well as children. The Bishop of Manchester was anxious to ascertain that the women were 'deserving' and not 'vicious' poor, but was assured that they had been infected by their adulterous husbands. Abel's opinion on the matter was that the subscribers should be asked to double their offerings to avoid people who needed help being turned away.

In view of his strong commitment, it is unsurprising that Abel continued his crusade for education into the 1860s and '70s. He supported a variety of approaches towards the education of the masses. He was still frequently to be found patronising schools for poor children, and in 1869 he appeared on a sub-committee of the council which made proposals for the establishment of industrial schools in Manchester for children who had fallen foul of the law by begging, or who were destitute or in bad company. The aim, which in many ways sums up Abel's belief that education was the way to redeem the working classes not only from poverty but also from immorality, was to 'remove… from the streets and byeways of our city those unfortunate and partially-destitute children who are at present receiving their first lessons in vice and crime, but who, by such means, might be trained up for honest work and respectable citizenship'.[18]

By February 1870, Gladstone's Liberal government was preparing a national Education Act. The National Education League (NEL) met in the Free Trade Hall at a packed meeting by ticket only; Alderman Rumney chaired it and Abel Heywood appeared on the platform. He seconded a resolution to support by all constitutional means the NEL plan to establish free schools supported by local rates and government grants, managed by the local authorities on an unsectarian basis, with the compulsory attendance of children not otherwise receiving education. Although Forster's 1870 Education Act is now widely acknowledged to be the foundation stone of the modern state education system, to contemporaries it was fraught with problems, particularly surrounding religious issues. It seems highly likely that Abel and his colleagues would have been disappointed in the form the Act finally took; Anglicanism appeared to be favoured and education was still not free or compulsory.

A new departure in the educational opportunities of the workers, strongly backed by Abel Heywood, who 'had taken great pains to make himself thoroughly acquainted with the subject', was the establishment of a variety of museums in Manchester. True to his scientific bent, Abel introduced a proposal in the council in 1865 for the adoption of the Museum of Natural History in Peter Street, with the purpose of opening it free to the people. This would finally bring to fruition negotiations with the Natural History Society, which had continued for the past fourteen years. In 1866 the council discussed whether the Queen's Park Museum should be open on Christmas Day and Good Friday. Abel, predictably, was for opening because 'when work was suspended the people must go somewhere, and it was better they should feast their eyes and improve their tastes in a museum than in a pothouse'. On this occasion, Abel's view, entirely consistent with his unsuccessful championing in the 1850s of music in the parks, prevailed by a large majority; music was considered to be a frivolous entertainment, whereas museums were thought to encourage sobriety and morality.

By the 1860s Abel was a keen temperance campaigner, seeing abstinence as an intrinsic part of the amelioration of the material and moral standing of the working classes. The statistics cited by Donald Read cast light on why this movement was so popular amongst Victorians of the working as well as the middle classes. The average national annual consumption per man, woman and child was rising towards a peak in the mid-1870s of 1.3 gallons (almost 6 litres) of spirits and 34.4 gallons (over 156 litres) of beer. In the saying of the time, for the poor drink was 'the shortest way out of Manchester'. Abel recommended the adoption of the 1864 Public Houses Closing Act which prevented the opening of pubs between one and four in the morning, citing a case which had come before him as a magistrate, where at a 'night-house' about forty 'ladies and gentlemen' had assembled at 2.30 or 3 o'clock 'for the purpose of drinking'. Because they did not create a disturbance, there was no real case against them, and it was dismissed. However, 'he had his doubts as to the respectability of the parties – and his own ideas as to the object they had in being there'. The council agreed and voted unanimously in favour of adopting the Act.[19]

In 1865 Abel took the chair at the formal opening of Trevelyan's Temperance Hotel on Corporation Street, an elegant and imposing Italianate six-storey edifice with over sixty bedrooms, not to mention conference and other rooms and a restaurant. Alcohol was strictly forbidden, and 'the not unknown custom at temperance hotels, of being permitted to send out for spirituous liquors, should they be required for "medicinal" or other purposes' was not to be allowed. It was hoped that by providing such an excellent hotel, young men might be removed from the temptations of drink present in ordinary restaurants, and that merchants would be enabled to do business 'without the bottle', avoiding 'the custom of having a decanter on the warehouse table, for the use of customers'. After the speeches 'the room was speedily cleared for dancing, greatly to the satisfaction of the young ladies and gentlemen who had been clustering outside the door waiting for the announcement that all the speeches were at an end'.[20]

By now, Abel clearly believed that government action was also a part of the solution to the problems of alcohol, and in 1871 he chaired a meeting of the National Reform Union which was addressed by Sir Wilfrid Lawson MP on the subject of legislation to prohibit the liquor traffic where the ratepayers supported such measures. Gladstone's 1872 Licensing Act was a response to such demands, though as with the Education Act it did not go far enough to satisfy campaigners.

Much of Abel's effort was focused on causes that do not evoke surprise, were part of his general trajectory into Liberalism, and were increasingly mainstream as the political and economic climate around him evolved. However, he continued to describe himself as a 'Liberal radical' and one of the ways in which this was substantiated was his espousal in the 1870s of women's suffrage.

There had been signs that his sympathies were not hostile to a recognition of women's role outside, as well as within, the home. As early as the 1830s, commensurate perhaps with his Owenite views, he provided an outlet in his shop for tickets to 'Lectures by a Lady', Mrs Hamilton from Scotland, on that most unwomanly and controversial of topics, the Political and Religious Rights of Men and Women. Her talks included disquisitions on the Bible in relation to women, women's education, and very prominently, the application to her theme of phrenology (divining personality and aptitudes from head-shape). By 1861 there were strong indications that Abel supported the idea that women should be educated and able to train in medicine. At the Bolton Mechanics' Institution fundraising soirée, Abel offered an exceedingly generous £300, with an offer of another £200 'on condition that classes were opened for the instruction of females as well as males'.[21] He also subscribed towards the founding of a female medical college in London and was the agent for the publication of letters supporting the replacement of male midwives with trained women doctors.

In 1867, very few people thought it was feasible or desirable to give women a vote in national elections; in the Second Reform Act of that year, John Stuart Mill's proposal to include women in the franchise was soundly rejected in Parliament by 196 votes to 73. However, by the early 1870s the climate was changing; women could now participate in local municipal, Poor Law and school board elections. Moreover, in Manchester, Lydia Becker had established the Manchester Women's Suffrage Committee. And on a personal level, Abel had married (in 1868) Elizabeth Goadsby, who was a keen proponent of women's rights.

Manchester Council in 1870 petitioned the government in favour of a bill to remove the electoral disabilities of women. Some councillors expressed fears because in the school board election it was reported that some unscrupulous agents had taken women voters in Ardwick to pubs and got them drunk before escorting them to vote. The solution offered was the secret ballot, which was needed before 'these poor creatures' should be given the suffrage. The council voted to take no further action on the matter. Abel, in view of his frequent volubility on questions on which he held strong views, was silent and he did vote for the successful resolution; it does not seem that at this point he was campaigner for votes for women at all costs.[22] By 1873 the council discussion had become an annual event and Alderman Murray argued that it should be characterised not as an 'annual resolution' but an 'annual farce'. On this occasion, Abel supported the petition to Parliament.[23] Perhaps his wife's influence was gaining ground.

Abel was clearly not opposed to women's suffrage in principle, and in 1871 and 1874, for example, his shop was one of the outlets for tickets for meetings of Becker's Manchester National Society for Women's Suffrage. When it held its AGM in 1874 Mrs Abel Heywood agreed to 'preside' at a tea table at the evening 'conversazione'. It seems fair to suppose that she also attended the daytime meeting, and it is possible that she was accompanied by her husband.

But in the mid-1870s Abel had not yet clearly nailed his colours to the mast on women's suffrage. It may be that he, like many of his Liberal colleagues, refrained from open support because their leader, William Gladstone, had declared himself against the suffrage bill of 1870, which proposed women should be given the vote on the same terms as men. Moreover, as yet most men (about 60 per cent) could not vote and perhaps he shared a fear among the proponents of male universal suffrage that giving the better-off women the vote (i.e. on the same terms as men) might jeopardise the movement to give all men the vote, and therefore disadvantage the poor. Liberals, among whom Abel by now counted himself, were also worried that these women might vote Conservative, and that to enfranchise them might be detrimental to their party.

The Fenians

Manchester became notorious for Irish terrorism on 18 September 1867, with the 'rescue' of Fenian prisoners on their way to court, just outside the works of Heywood, Higginbottom and Smith.[24] The Fenian prisoners were smuggled to safety in the United States. On breaking into the prison van the terrorists had shot dead the policeman inside, Charles Brett. His funeral was symbolic of the public mood: on 22 September, with full honours from the fire brigade and the police, the streets were lined with crowds numbering an estimated 40,000 or 50,000 people, and many of the Corporation attended, including Abel.

The council held a special meeting to discuss the situation on 25 September, at which Abel was keen that they should avoid saying anything that might inflame the situation. He also took pains to stress that the outrage perpetrated by the Fenians had nothing to do with the working classes or 'a very large proportion of the Irish' in Manchester.[25] Nevertheless, large numbers of Irish were rounded up and their initial examination for committal took place before the magistrates in the city court, among whom Abel Heywood was to be found.

The heightened sense of threat also had a personal impact on Abel; in October the newspapers reported that there had been a Fenian attack, in the form of an attempted shooting by a man dressed as a brickmaker, on his nephew the Deansgate publisher, John Heywood. It was believed in some quarters that this was not a matter of Fenian revenge, but was more likely to be a reprisal for an article he had published, which had upset the brickmakers. The other possibility was that this was a case of mistaken identity; both Heywoods lived at this time in Stretford, and Fenians would certainly have reason to want to take revenge on one of the magistrates at the committal. The truth of the matter seems never to have been ascertained and the perpetrator remained undiscovered.

In the end three men were publicly hanged for the murder of Charles Brett on 23 November, a cold, foggy morning, outside the New Bailey prison. The scene was set for the election of the following year when Gladstone focused his Liberal campaign on the Irish issue, and in particular on the disestablishment of the Irish Anglican church, and Abel accordingly fell into line with that policy, which he may also have regarded as a first step towards English disestablishment.

Perhaps as a result of the ill-feeling engendered, by 1872 it was feared in the council that the reputation of the city was at stake due to 'scenes in certain parts of the city'. Abel had attended a discussion by the justices on the day previously, and said he thought 'faction fights' were not a new phenomenon entirely, but that they had taken a new turn in that they now reflected religious divisions, by implication between Protestant and Catholic:

> What used to be called 'scuttling' fights had been more or less carried on between the youths of different districts for at least 45 or 50 years, within his knowledge, without the interposition of any religious animosity. It was said that such disorderly scenes were extending in the neighbourhood of St Michael's, Ancoats, and elsewhere, even among adults prompted by religious hostility.

The authorities were particularly worried by the seriousness of the fights and the damage to property, and the involvement of girls and young women; all of these features were felt to be novel and a threat to social stability, and therefore there was serious talk of recruiting special constables and asking for reinforcements from the Home Office.[26] It seems, though, that the existing agencies managed to hold the situation together and the alarm eventually subsided.

Foreign affairs

The war between Denmark and the emerging state of Bismarck's Germany exercised radical Liberals like Abel, Ernest Jones, Dr Watts and others of a more moderate persuasion such as Thomas Bazley and Thomas Potter. Their preoccupation was for Britain to remain unentangled from events in Europe, and not to interfere in the expansion of German power, so that trade might continue unencumbered.

Abel had done his homework, and condemned treaties made secretly by the government and not put before Parliament, the elected representatives of the people. He cited the example of the London Protocol of 1852, which stated that Denmark must not try to bind the province of Schleswig-Holstein more closely to itself, and which might therefore become the pretext for war, but had not been put before any of the people involved in the dispute, and therefore could not tie the British to any commitment to armed intervention. He concluded by supporting the resolution that Britain should maintain neutrality. This was indeed the line taken by the government, and Bismarck continued to manipulate events in Europe, proclaiming the German Empire in 1871.

But the event which made the biggest impact was the assassination of President Lincoln on 15 April 1865. He had become a hero in Manchester because of the perception that the American Civil War was fought to abolish slavery, and was now seen as having died for the cause. The Union and Emancipation Society held a meeting in the Free Trade Hall to express condolences to his wife. So many wanted to attend that two meetings had to be held in different parts of the building, at which Abel assured his listeners that slavery was doomed. On 3 May the matter was discussed in the council. Abel saw the assassination as part of a wider issue and linked it into his ideas of legitimate power:

> This was not an ordinary crime. It was a blow aimed at the official life, he might say of the whole world; for if those who were appointed to office by the voice of the people were to be subjected to the blow of the assassin, then none who occupied prominent official positions would be safe.[27]

Even after the great outpouring of sympathy in 1865, interest in the American Civil War continued in Manchester, and on 22 January 1866 Abel was on the platform at a gathering of the Union and Emancipation Society, which was held to mark its own dissolution. Professor Goldwin Smith lectured 'Upon the Civil War in America'. He shared the sublime optimism of his audience about slavery: 'The immediate result of the victory had been the downfall of slavery, not only in the United States but everywhere and for ever. (Cheers.)' That this had been achieved by a country where every man now had a vote was not lost on the audience.[28]

Free trade

As a businessman, Abel displayed a classic Liberal support for free trade and was a proponent of its benefits for all. It was a burning issue in this period with the negotiation by Richard Cobden in 1860 of a key trade agreement with the French and Gladstone's free trade budget of that year. In 1861 Abel Heywood had proposed a resolution in the council to recognise Cobden's achievements for Manchester, especially most recently for 'his eminently successful services, by which commercial intercourse has been extended between the people of France and England, and the cause of peace greatly promoted'.[29]

In the same period there was a related agitation to abolish the tax on paper, which was seen by Liberals and radicals as one aspect of achieving a free press and furthering the freedom of the people. Indeed, in view of his history and his trade, it is unsurprising that Abel attended meetings on this subject outside Manchester itself; when the people of Stalybridge met in July, Abel was there to condemn the stance taken by the Lords in rejecting the abolition of the tax, which was symptomatic of the aristocracy's disregard for the perceived rights of the people. In the end, by making the 1861 budget a 'single money bill' Gladstone rendered it much harder for the Lords to reject it, and therefore the repeal of the excise on paper was at last successful. Abel's hero had delivered.

Mortalities

On 2 April 1865 Richard Cobden died. The council agreed that they would be formally represented at the funeral in Sussex by the mayor and two prominent elder statesmen, Sir Elkanah Armitage and Abel Heywood. Abel was keen to extol the virtues of the deceased and characteristically noted that 'as a statesman his name would be a landmark for future generations'. The city raised a subscription for a statue to commemorate Cobden's achievements; Abel was appointed treasurer.[30] When the statue was inaugurated in St Ann's Square on 22 April 1867, Abel spoke of Cobden as someone 'who had moved the world' and had universal significance for 'the great principles of liberty'.[31] For Liberals, the doctrine of free trade was not just about taxes, but about fundamental freedoms and world peace, and Cobden had amply proved his credentials as a star in the Liberal firmament.

A few months later the same men set off south again for an even more distinguished funeral, when the prime minister, Lord Palmerston, died on 18 October. The Manchester Council was much more muted in its lamentations than it had been for Cobden, though they still requested citizens to close their businesses at the hour of the event. By this time, Palmerston had become the bulwark of the Whig Liberals against the attempts of Lord John Russell and others to extend the franchise to the working classes. His death opened a window of opportunity for reformers; in the election of 1865, Heywood stood again as the radical Liberal candidate on a platform of universal male suffrage, and the very next year Russell and William Gladstone introduced a Liberal bill for a modest extension of the suffrage; the times were changing.

In 1870 Abel lost another near contemporary with whom he had a significant history, George Wilson, one of his chief supporters in 1859 as a parliamentary candidate. Abel attended his funeral as a representative of the Reform Union executive, in which the deceased had lately been prominent, and of course they had earlier shared support for the Anti-Corn Law League, of which Wilson had been chairman. Abel's devotion to his memory may be judged by his presentation to the council of a bust commissioned by Mary Wilson, George's widow, early in 1876.

Such losses must have brought home to Abel the proximity of his own mortality; these men were his near contemporaries, his colleagues and some of them his friends, and their demise surely made its mark. Abel was not to know that he still had seventeen years ahead of him in 1876. It may be noted that when he was offered the mayoralty for a second term in the autumn of that year, he referred to what appears to have been a period of depression which had deterred him from seeking office again; though in the end he did, of course, accept the nomination.

9

'Old Blazes': The 1865 Election

At end of the general election in 1859, Abel, the manhood suffrage candidate, had stated his intention to try for election again, and in the following years he had become a much weightier figure in local politics, holding the office of mayor in 1862–63, becoming a magistrate and collecting several directorships of companies. It was understandable therefore that he had high hopes in 1865, particularly as the cause of electoral reform seemed to be gaining ground, with the establishment in 1864 of the middle-class Reform Union and its working-class counterpart, the Reform League. Gladstone's declaration in favour of a franchise extension in the same year can only have encouraged Abel and his fellow reformers to believe that their time was coming.

Reform agitation

They had worked very hard in the preceding years to reach this point. When Lord John Russell presented proposals for reform in Parliament, the Manchester campaigners had hastened to support him. At the annual dinner of the St Michael's Ward Reform Association in January 1860 and at the meeting of the council of the Lancashire Reformers' Union the following month Abel voiced his backing for those struggling in Parliament, especially John Bright, at that time MP for Birmingham:

> Alderman Heywood said that no one cared more for the ballot than he did. But he regarded the voting power as a question of principle; while he considered the ballot as a means of simplifying elections and preventing abuses. Mr. Bright had stated his willingness to take what could be got got [*sic*] this session; and his (Mr. Heywood's) advice to all the friends of Mr. Bright was, 'Take Mr. Bright as your guide, and support him to the utmost of your power.' (Applause.)[1]

When the Reform Bill of 1860 was presented to Parliament, the Lancashire Reform Union sent a deputation under George Wilson to London to put the case for more MPs for the county than were on offer in the bill. Abel spoke against a clause which rendered the payment of poor rates compulsory before an elector could vote, as this would effectively disenfranchise 'large bodies of the working classes'. Russell replied that there was no chance of carrying a bill that went any further than the one before Parliament, though he agreed to consider the points raised.[2] In the event, lacking the support of Prime Minister Lord Palmerston, the bill was defeated.

By 1864 Abel was back in harness in the reform struggle, and taking his part in organising a National Reform Association conference in Manchester. Further, on 25 October 1864, when the National Reform Union was set up by the middle classes in Manchester, Abel duly took his place as one of its vice-presidents. When the NRU met in November Abel criticised reformers for their failure to support John Bright 'when they had seen him day after day attacked in the most virulent and most vilifying manner', or indeed Richard Cobden, 'who had lived and fought with them'. His hope for the NRU was that it would adopt a definite and united policy and only follow really committed leaders like Cobden and Bright 'who fairly and honestly represented them'. Otherwise, he warned, the Liberal party might lose their influence in the country.[3]

At the end of November he attended a meeting of working men in Pendleton organised by the NRU and successfully encouraged them to unite with the NRU in support of its aims for a ratepayer franchise, the ballot, redistribution of seats and a three-year parliamentary term. Working-class support was going to be hard won, and Abel was a valuable asset as a man who could bridge the middle–working class gap, and working-class attendance improved thereafter.

However, there were continuing divisions. When Abel, representing the NRU, attended a meeting in Failsworth for the working-class supporters of reform in February 1865, Ernest Jones excused himself with a letter which explained that he 'felt unable to attend… from a difference of opinion with the conveners, arising out of his dissatisfaction with the National Reform Union'. Abel made a 'long and animated' speech, reviewing the reform campaign from the early nineteenth century. To reconcile his audience to middle-class priorities he advocated a redistribution of seats because he claimed it was the inequality of power which was preventing a full extension of the franchise. 'So long as this inequality existed, no more than a very moderate measure of reform could be wrung from a parliament so composed – (loud cheers).' He concluded that while 'the vote of Buckingham… neutralised the vote of Manchester', manhood suffrage was unattainable.[4]

Yet on 9 May 1865 he appeared on a manhood suffrage platform in the Free Trade Hall chaired by Edward Hooson, and attended by such stalwarts as Elijah Dixon and Ernest Jones. The previous evening a reform bill had failed in the Commons and Abel explained that Robert Lowe, a key Liberal opponent of franchise extension, was elected by a mere 103 voters in Calne; he had a reputation as a difficult man 'and probably on the evening he made his much talked of speech he was in one of those excessive bad tempers for which his friends gave him credit.

(Laughter.)' It was proposed that a deputation attend a reform conference planned for the following week to urge the adoption of manhood suffrage as the basis of the national movement. Abel was to be included on this deputation, which might have been expected to put him in an awkward position in view of his pragmatic approach in the NRU.[5]

Quite what the working-class activists made of Abel's varied stance on franchise extension is not clear. They must surely have been aware that he was far more disposed to a 'softly, softly' approach when he addressed the NRU. It is possible that they understood that he needed to adopt this position in order to win sufficient votes to be a viable candidate in the next election, but that he was fundamentally in favour of manhood suffrage and would do his utmost to achieve it once he took his seat at Westminster.

The candidate

His chance came in July 1865. With James Aspinall Turner, MP for Manchester, on the verge of retirement, the Liberals had invited Thomas Bazley to stand again, and proceeded to deliberate upon a second candidate. Abel was proposed by a working man called Crossley, and supported by radicals J.E. Nelson, Ernest Jones and Edward Hooson. Other prospective candidates included R.N. Philips, Jacob Bright (brother of John), George Wilson and Edward Miall. Indeed, a letter by radical Robert Cooper to George Wilson of 21 May showed that Abel's camp had discussed the possibility that he might stand down in favour of Wilson:

> You [Wilson] will win if you will only say yes. Decide then at once and I am sure Abel Heywood will not stand. He has told me so and declares he will move 'heaven and earth' to carry you. Heywood has a prior claim to Miall, and should you decline, he shall have my help, and that of the large majority of the advanced radicals...[6]

A Liberal committee was appointed to make a choice from amongst these candidates. They reported that approaches to Wilson and Philips had been refused, and so they recommended the adoption of Thomas Milner Gibson. Abel's name was mentioned, but this excited both support and strong opposition. By 5 June Abel was running his own independent campaign from Swan Court, Market Street, much as he had done in 1859. He put his all into it, with ward meetings all over Manchester at a rate of two a day. His election committee met daily, and 'gentlemen' were invited to make donations towards the expenses of the campaign to his committee, led by H.M. Steinthal (chairman), Councillor Ingham (treasurer) and Robert Whitworth (hon. secretary).

Abel published his address on 6 June. He referred to his showing in 1859 as 'satisfactory', and recorded his public activities since, 'directed towards the advancement of the labouring classes in the acquisition of knowledge, the necessary preparation for the exercise of a greater share of political power'. This may well have been by way of riposte to Liberal opponents of suffrage extension, such as Robert Lowe, who pointed to the educational unfitness of the workers. He recapitulated his principles, unchanged since 1859. The manifesto was carefully constructed to appeal to as wide an audience as possible. For the radicals, it appeared to promise that Abel would work for manhood suffrage in referring to 'the fullest extension of the franchise to the people', but it was worded to reassure moderate Liberals, by alluding to Gladstone's take on suffrage extension which, as his bill the following year demonstrated, was not intended to rush the issue at all. Continuing the theme, Abel's manifesto advocated triennial parliaments and the ballot, and covered all angles by supporting the abolition of 'absurd inequalities' in the present system, which could be taken by radicals as referring to the right to vote, but could also mean the unfair distribution of seats, which was closer to the hearts of the moderates.

Abel also brought out aspects of his economic policies which could appeal to both working- and middle-class voters. He stated his belief that national expenditure must be reduced 'to relieve the overtaxed commercial and industrial classes'; he supported full development of free trade to end the taxation of 'the necessaries of life' and the obstruction of trade. Although he avowed his nonconformist beliefs, he stated he was 'not an enemy of the Established Church', but he did favour the abolition of church rates. In education he was less equivocal, and advocated a national and unsectarian system. He ended with promises that if elected he 'would not flinch in the manly discharge of the duties imposed upon me', but would exert himself to establish 'Peace, Retrenchment, and Reform' – the great rallying cry of Gladstonian Liberalism.[7]

A free public meeting was organised in the Free Trade Hall to gather the 'friends' of Abel's candidature together. Robert Cooper wrote again to George Wilson expressing his resistance to Abel's intention of running against Milner Gibson, and the strong influence in his camp of the temperance lobby:

> My Dear Mr Wilson
>
> The aspect of affairs have changed. Milner Gibson, I am told, will be brought out. I therefore told Heywood's Committee to delay their proceedings as it would be utter madness to run Heywood against Gibson, – that he had a prior claim to Heywood, and I would not lend myself to splitting the genuine reformers in order to exclude so eminent and so useful a man as the old colleague of John Bright. The majority were obstinate at the Committee meeting last night, and Heywood himself amongst the rest. They would run Heywood against Gibson even to lose. I retorted that it would not only be defeat – it would be humiliation, and I would not share in it. I retired, especially as Heywood joined in the cry against Gibson, after giving me to understand he would not stand against Gibson. – The majority last night were nearly all Alliance [UK Alliance] men. He is completely in their hands – I have requested not to be announced as a

speaker at the Free Trade Hall on Monday next, and I would urge upon you not to preside at the meeting as you will be asked to do. It would be amusing[?] to the common enemy to see George Wilson chairman of a meeting to oppose Milner Gibson. At present you will doubtless hold off from Heywood's Committee as I feel I ought to do.[8]

The gathering on 19 June was advertised for electors and non-electors with the ostensible purpose of adopting a second Liberal candidate for Manchester, but of course in reality proposing that the second candidate should be Abel Heywood. Wilson was indeed approached to chair it. But he did not appear again in Abel's camp, and the chair was taken by Max Kyllman. The loss of Wilson's support was to cost Abel dear.

The Liberals hit back with an advertisement on the day of the meeting encouraging attendance to vote against Abel's candidature. He was accused of seceding from the Liberal party, 'after being outvoted by large majorities in the Liberal selection committees'.[9]

Apparently, the meeting was well attended, but it did not fill the gallery of the hall. Ernest Jones proposed that they should adopt a candidate who would promote a full enfranchisement of the people and civil, political and religious equality, in a speech which described Abel as 'the recognised popular advocate of the principle of manhood suffrage in Manchester'. He hoped that 'the first knell of Tory trickery and Whig exclusiveness would be sounded by the citizens of Manchester, through the hands of Mr. Heywood, as their representative in parliament. (Loud cheers.)' Next, W.P. Roberts proposed the formal adoption as candidate of Abel Heywood alongside Thomas Bazley. He reminded the audience that Abel lived amongst them and 'they know him and his wife and children as friends and fellow-citizens', that Abel had polled more votes in 1859 than any candidate had ever polled in Manchester, and that this had been done without recourse to bribery or treating. He also dismissed the rights of any other candidates to represent 'the democratic forces of Manchester' unless they had been accepted by such a public meeting as this one.

When the resolution was adopted, Abel rose to speak. Reminding his listeners of the circumstances in which he had previously stood for Parliament, he said he had lost the election because of those wards where 'broadcloth' was dominant.[10] He believed that it was important to send men to Parliament who held firm views about reform: 'if they sent men who would not go downward with the suffrage, they might whistle jigs to a milestone, and expect them to dance, before they would get reform in parliament. (Cheers.)'

It was not all plain sailing for Abel, however. There were suggestions that Abel's candidature was premature, reminding the audience about the Liberal split in 1857, but they were booed and hissed. The chairman struggled to control the meeting, and when in response to questions Abel stated he favoured the disestablishment of the Church of England there was great applause, and the audience became rowdy.

Eventually Abel was allowed to inform the meeting that he would vote for the Permissive Bill (allowing local prohibition on alcohol) and that he was against the payment of MPs. When a final vote was taken, it was carried 'by an overwhelming majority' and Abel proclaimed 'I *will* go to the poll.'[11]

Meanwhile the Liberal committee of selection was still in disarray. Their slowness in announcing a candidate to run with Bazley was regarded by the Conservatives as a golden opportunity to win a seat, and the letters column of the *Manchester Courier* at this time included missives urging action to 'preserve the country from republicanism' and prevent Manchester from 'abdicating its proud position in the country'.[12]

On 26 June at a meeting of Liberals an appeal was made by Henry Rawson to Abel Heywood to give up his candidacy in favour of supporting the candidature of Thomas Bazley and another potential candidate, Jacob Bright. 'He did not think that Mr. Heywood would be the man to divide the Liberal party.' Rawson said he would have supported Abel if he had thought he had any chance of winning, but he did not want to back a 'hopeless battle'. J.E. Nelson wrote to George Wilson at length about the situation in the Liberal committee:

> Dear Sir
>
> The Self Elected [the Liberal committee] have turned up another Card in order to show that they can dispose of the representation of Manchester, but in Mr Jacob Bright they are as far from a candidate as if they had taken under their patronage the Prince of Wales – this is the first time the Reformers have attempted to choose one of the Candidates from the Ranks of the Retail traders...
>
> It is quite manifest that the old leaders are afraid of pitch in Mr Heywoods candidature... Fear in Mr Bazley's friends [might] lead them to plump and Heywood's doing the same the Whig and Tory party might take both seats... When the [Anti-Corn Law] League Triumphed many went over to Whiggery and Toryism, and indeed in this wealth producing age this must be expected after every wave of true Progress. He that endureth unto the End shall be saved. The Knavery that could impose on Mr Mial that he had been invited by the Ward Committees when said Committees have never been convened since 1859 will stick at nothing. Meanwhile we work away and laugh at their floundering in the mire.
> JE Nelson[13]

His scorn for the Liberals who sought to put up Jacob Bright to run with Thomas Bazley was manifest, and he was concerned that those who would otherwise vote for Bazley and Heywood might 'plump' or vote for someone else, leaving the way open for Whigs (aristocratic Liberals) and Conservatives to triumph.

Meanwhile, Abel, undaunted, continued to hold ward meetings. In St Clement's ward, which had put him second in the poll in 1859, he addressed the electors in the Temperance Hall in Fairfield Street. His address, tailored as ever to his audience, focused firstly on the Permissive Bill and 'the morality of the people'. In contrast to his reported answer on 19 June that, if elected, he would vote for the bill's second reading he now, a week later, said he would not support it for Manchester, because the people of Manchester were not yet persuaded, and he certainly did not want to interfere with the rights and liberties of the people. He was clearly hedging his bets.

He proceeded to elucidate his opinions on disestablishment, stating that he thought all religions should be supported equally, and that disestablishment for the Anglican Church would actually strengthen it because church rates drove people away from it (later, in St Michael's ward, he said he supported the disestablishment of the Irish Church, too). He suggested he would not give any grants to religious bodies. He would not support the fortification of Canada, and was broadly in favour of the Ten Hours Bill for factories and a Sunday closing bill. Asked about the franchise, he stated he would support a £5 property qualification, but that he favoured the fullest extension possible. He claimed that he did not want to represent any interest group, but all the people of Manchester, and that he was so committed to work hard for them that, if he were elected, he would cease to work in his publishing and distribution business. He would not go so far as promising to oppose the business of any government which did not adopt reform, saying that he would judge each measure in the light of its benefit or otherwise to the people.

He claimed to be prepared to give up his candidacy for George Wilson or R.N. Philips, a safe offer as they had both already refused to stand, but would not countenance giving way to Milner Gibson or Miall. According to the *Manchester Guardian*, he seemed to offer to run alongside Jacob Bright.[14] A notice was placed in the press reminding the public how Bright had supported Abel in 1859:

> Mr. Jacob Bright said he rejoiced that Mr. Bazley had been placed in such a proud position, but he should have rejoiced ten times more if Mr. Heywood had been by his side...A great deal had been said about Mr. Heywood's position. Was he not an intelligent, honest man, and a man of business? Then what more could they want?[15]

Abel gave the audience his version of the inner workings of the election when he claimed that, having been asked many times since the last election to prepare himself to stand again, when Mr Turner announced his retirement he was suddenly informed that he was unelectable as he had 'entirely lost the confidence of shopkeepers and the labouring classes'. He also asserted that the Liberal split had been caused by the circumstance that circulars to attend the selection process had been sent out selectively, omitting his (Abel's) friends, thereby excluding them and him from the selection process. Their response, he implied, was to set up their own selection process.[16]

In the last week of June, in the St Michael's ward meeting, the chairman, Councillor Worthington, who had known Abel 'since he was a lad', stated his opinion that 'the aristocratic portion of the Liberal party objected to him because

I

he was a shopkeeper; and if he had been a merchant, he would have received the Liberal aristocratic support'.[17] Abel's campaign publicly taunted his opponents with having convened neither ward committees nor a large meeting in the Free Trade Hall. On 30 June this was accompanied by a paragraph reminding Manchester of all the promises that had apparently been made in 1859 after Abel had made such a good showing in the election and, it was claimed, enabled Thomas Bazley to top the poll. It ended with Liberal leader George Wilson's 1859 affirmation of Abel's significance: 'They have placed before the constituency a man whom in future no candidate, or combination of candidates, could afford to disregard.'[18] Still defending the rightness of his candidacy, on 3 July at Newton Heath, Abel added that 'there was scarcely one gentleman in the House who could be said to be a representative of the working classes'. By implication, this was a role which he would fulfil.[19]

The *Manchester Times* of 1 July did not accept these versions of events, and blamed Abel for the Liberal split, claiming that he had already planned to stand 'whether his candidature was favourably regarded or otherwise by the majority of the Liberal party'. It warned that the split could allow a Conservative candidate to win a seat, but feared that Abel was determined to stand. 'Our city might be saved this ignominy by the retirement of Mr. Heywood, who has come to the front unsolicited by any save a small section of his party; but we confess that we have no hope of the display of so much wisdom and discretion.'[20]

Robert Cooper wrote again to George Wilson on the subject of Bright's candidacy, and indeed in his version of events Abel was by now determined to stand come what may. Cooper also feared he could win Whig, and even Tory, backing as well as that of the Catholics and the temperance lobby. It seems that even Abel's closest allies were unsure as to whether his candidacy was wise. Indeed, Cooper had become markedly hostile:

Do you not think the nomination of Jacob Bright a very happy one? it ought to have united all the parties, – the Gibson, Miall and Heywood sections. The withdrawl of Miall was wise and generous, and the retirement of Heywood ought to have followed.

I told him so, and appealed to him with all the earnestness and candeur[?] of old friendship to resign. As yet, he has refused.

Indeed, I am beginning to suspect that in order to revenge himself upon those whom he conceives have injured him, he will coalesce with the [*illegible*] clique. If he does, I shall despise and denounce him. To get into Parliament by the help of false Whigs and malignant Tories will eternally disgrace him and deservedly so. He is clearly wanting in that magnanimity and good sense for which I gave him credit.

I would beg of you to impress upon the Bazley and Bright Committee not to commit the blunder of 1857, by holding their opponents too cheap, and especially if the Catholic party go against Jacob Bright – this should be ascertained......

The Tories, Whigs and Catholics added to the Alliance party will be a <u>strong</u> coalition <u>and must</u> <u>not be despised</u>. Will you put this view before the Committee?[21]

Cooper's disillusion raises the question of how other erstwhile supporters were feeling, and likely to vote when the time came.

The Conservatives were still disorganised. Letters to the *Manchester Courier* from 'a Liberal Conservative' and 'JF' threatened they might vote for Abel Heywood, in one case as a protest vote, and in the other because 'he at least is an honest Radical, and will not try to lower the influence of England abroad' (having attacked the other Liberals over their opposition to the Volunteer movement and their lack of patriotism). The situation continued unresolved, however, and *The Times* of 4 July reported that Abel was 'likely to have a fair support from the Tories in the event of the Tories not bringing out a candidate of their own, not that they can approve such an advanced radical, but because the Whig-Radicals having had the representation in their hands ever since Manchester was created a borough they would prefer a change in any direction to none at all'.[22] One 'Conservative voter' expressed abhorrence of the 'clique at Newall's buildings [the moderate Liberals]' and explained 'Mr. Abel Heywood's politics are none of mine, but I believe in his honesty of principle; and I would rather swallow his manhood suffrage and all his Radicalism, and plump for him, than stand quietly by and submit without a struggle to that overbearing, domineering clique.'[23]

Abel could not fail to be aware of this potential support from Tories, which was increasingly mentioned when attempts to create a Tory candidate in Admiral Denman (Captain Denman in 1859) ran into the sand. When he addressed electors and non-electors in Oxford and St James's wards at the Athenaeum, Abel was quick to deny misrepresentations of his policies which the Bazley and Bright camp had circulated. He had come third and last respectively in the poll in these wards in 1859, and must have been keenly aware of the need to allay fears about his radicalism in this climate. Bills claiming that he wanted manhood suffrage, the Permissive Bill and separation of Church and State, and would accept 'nothing less', were misleading, he stated. He even argued that 'he believed the only proper way to obtain the extension of the suffrage was by gradual degrees'. He would support a Conservative government reform bill and, unless a better bill was proposed, he would not join any party to throw Lord Derby out of power. For the Permissive Bill (on pubs), he would vote for it, but as a magistrate he would continue to show no injustice to the interests of licensed victuallers. With regard to the Church, he did think religious equality was in the best interests of the people, but had never taken part in any movement against the Church in the last twenty years, and had refused to subscribe to the Liberation Society which campaigned for disestablishment. The Conservative Romaine Callender junior was extremely supportive of Abel's candidacy and quipped:

It was said that Mr. Heywood was not quite good enough for them. He did not know whether the objection applied to his personal appearance - (laughter) -

because although they were a Radical set of people, they had been more than ordinarily favoured by men of good personal appearance. (Renewed laughter.)... Seriously however, he expected that the root of the matter was that Mr. Heywood was not a cotton spinner; that he had not an enormous mill; but if he had not the same number of guineas or spindles, he had what was far more important, and that was the amount of brains which were in his head. (Cheers.)

The meeting voted its confidence in Abel Heywood, but with some vocal opponents.[24] However, although many Conservatives continued to favour him as a conscientious and honest local man, it must have been a blow when the Licensed Victuallers and the Wine and Beer Trade Association opted to support Bright.

At a meeting on the next evening in the Collegiate ward Abel, speaking from a window of the Fleece Inn, was enthusiastically received. By now it was beginning to be said that he was an independent candidate 'who was not under the wing of any party'. He was sufficiently confident to tell his audience that 'in the settlement of great questions there must of necessity be great compromises'. When he stated that he was never an enemy of the Established Church, but was in favour of religious equality 'as far as public opinion was prepared for it', and that 'he would not vote for the separation of Church and State and thus sacrifice the property of others' his hearers were sufficiently politically aware that they commented:

'Only fishing for Tory votes!'
'And he'll have them!'
'Very good fish too!'[25]

The election was not without its lighter side, and in July the election notices included some of the puns the Victorians so enjoyed:

Is Manchester to be disgraced by sending to Rochdale for a Representative [referring to Jacob Bright], so long as we have a Citizen 'Abel' and willing to represent our views fearlessly and faithfully?
    Representation of Manchester – 'Jacob' will not be 'Abel' to mount the 'Ladder,' even with the assistance of his 'Big Brother,' 'John.' [Bright][26]

Three days before the poll, having for the preceding week or so advertised the venues for the Heywood campaign ward committees, Abel's camp was appealing for more canvassers who were interested 'in the independence of the constituency' to come forward to visit electors in their homes. A new Whig-Liberal candidate had thrown his hat into the ring, in the person of Edward James, the Attorney General of the County Palatine of Lancaster, who Abel's supporters said was a fake Liberal and was really a Tory. It must have been of some concern that there was now a candidate who might take some of the Tory votes which had hitherto been promised to Abel. In his address to electors and non-electors at the Wellington

Hotel, Abel referred to Bright's accusation that he was of 'a chameleon-like character' and 'a trimmer', because he seemed keen to catch the Conservative vote.
Abel dismissed this as 'sour grapes'. But there was good news from another quarter;
at two meetings of temperance reformers it was decided to support both Thomas
Bazley and Abel Heywood.[27]

A meeting was called of the working men that evening in the traditional place,
Stevenson Square, to listen to Ernest Jones and discuss the fitness of Abel Heywood
as candidate for Manchester. Abel arrived after a few minutes and focused his
speech on the desire for reform, whipping up the crowd by reminding them that
those opposed to reform argued that the poor were not interested in the election;
he found the support for which he hoped; he had not lost the 'common touch'.
But many of this audience were unenfranchised.

The election

Two days later the nominations took place. Abel was proposed by Alderman Bowker,
who stressed his record in Manchester by saying that his name was a 'household
word'. He reminded the listeners of Abel's origin in the working classes, and how by
industry, energy and talent he had raised himself. He denied that Abel had 'coquet-
ted' with the Conservatives and that they had therefore promised to vote for him,
claiming that Abel was 'an independent man... not connected with a clique or party
of men, and totally untrammelled'. The crowd was reminded of Abel's earlier role
in suffering for a free press. Initially supportive, the audience began to feel that the
speech had gone on long enough, and got impatient; he finished amid cries of 'Time.'
The seconder was Councillor Ingham, who stressed that Abel was an independent
candidate who actively wanted 'to put down the spirit of dictation and a clique' – a
dig at the Liberals. They brought their candidate out to assert the 'manhood of the
city and the independence of the city'.[28]

Much later, in the *Manchester Times* of 28 April 1877, 'Verax', the *nom de plume*
of the paper's editor, recalled the day of the nominations and how in Market Street
handbills were distributed casting aspersions on Abel's integrity and moral standing, probably by referring to his 1840 prosecution for selling obscene works. A
member of the committee of Bazley and Bright was heard to refer to Abel as 'Old
Blazes', which Verax interpreted to be used in a familiarly affectionate sense, as it
was 'coupled with the admission that the Alderman was "a plucky old Cock after
all"'. Nevertheless, Verax, in retrospect, felt that Abel was not treated fairly, and that
in the interests of winning the election things were said by his rivals that ought
not to have been said.[29]

The proposers of Bazley, Heywood and James were all received with cheering
and support; but according to the *Manchester Courier* Jacob Bright 'was received
with marked disfavour'. It must have been a blow to Abel that James was seconded
by Romaine Callender, who had spoken out so strongly in Conservative circles in

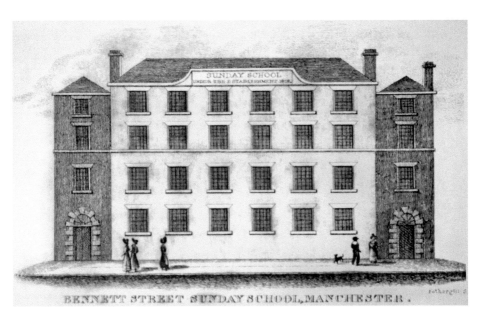

1 Bennett Street Sunday School. (Image from an old print)

2 Manchester Mechanics' Institution, 1827. (Image from an old print)

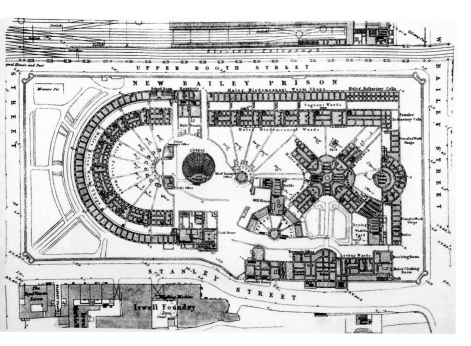

3 New Bailey Prison. (OS, 1848)

4 Reading the Riot Act at Manchester Town Hall, 1842. (Image from the *Illustrated London News*, 1842)

5 Portrait of Abel Heywood in 1863 by A. Bottomley in Manchester Town Hall. (Image courtesy of Andy Haymes and Manchester City Council)

6 Elizabeth Salisbury Heywood. (Image from an old drawing based on a photograph)

7 The Albert Statue, 1867.
(Photograph by Jacqueline
Banerjee, www.victorianweb.org)

8 Statue of Oliver Cromwell,
1875. (Author's photograph)

9 Cross Street chapel.
(Image courtesy of
Manchester Cross Street
chapel)

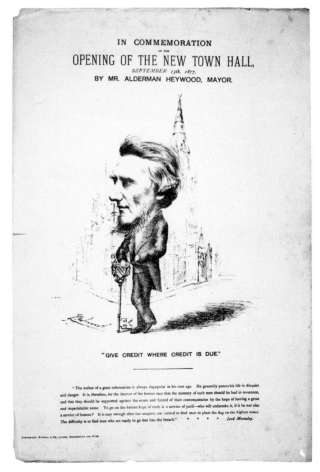

10 J. Ashworth, cartoon
poster for the opening of the
Town Hall. (Image courtesy
of John Rylands University
of Manchester Special
Collections)

1 J. Macgahey, *The Trades Procession*, 15 September 1877. (Image courtesy of Manchester Art Gallery)

2 The Liberal Reform Club. (Author's photograph, courtesy of Tatton Estates)

13 The Liberal Reform Club in the 1880s. (Image courtesy of the University of Toronto and *Internet Archive*; www.victorianweb.org)

14 Bust of Abel Heywood in the Town Hall, 1880. (Image courtesy of Andy Haymes, Manchester City Council)

15 Gravestone of Abel
Heywood, grave D128,
Philip's Park Cemetery.
(Author's photograph)

16 Portrait of Abel
Heywood in 1889 by H.T.
Munns in Manchester
Town Hall (Image courtesy
of Andy Haymes and
Manchester City Council)

favour of Abel himself. The prospect of winning Tory votes suddenly looked much less likely. As it was expected that Thomas Bazley would be elected, the possibility of a second representative from the 'moderate Liberals' was a distinct danger. Callender did not entirely abandon Abel, however, as he finished his speech with a call for the electors to vote early 'as one side for Mr. James, the moderate Liberal candidate, and for Mr. Heywood, the man of the people'.

Abel's address, 'very warmly received', reminded the audience first of all that he was 'the unflinching advocate of popular rights' and a 'townsman'. He tackled the issue of the Liberal split head on and in his favour put it that he had been the second candidate to come forward (so why did they bring forward a third?), and had been the object of 'foul slanders'. He clearly perceived Bright as his main rival, and made much of the fact that he was a relative outsider who had no record of service to the people of Manchester, which was of course one of his own strong points. 'They might as well have sent for the man in the moon as sent for Mr. Bright (Cheers and laughter.).'

In the customary show of hands, Abel was said in some reports to have dominated the vote, but the crowd would have included many non-electors.[30] The *Manchester Guardian*, hostile to the Liberal election committee, which it called 'the old tyranny', pointed out that the show of hands had conclusively refuted any assumption that Bazley and Bright were the choice of the 'people'. It launched into a major attack on the way that Abel was repudiated and Bright brought in, and said that although it did not share Abel's opinions on public affairs, 'he will not fare worse to-day for being unmistakably an ill-used man'.[31]

The nature of the 'ill-use' was to be found in a final appeal to Liberal voters issued by the Bazley and Bright committee reminding voters that Abel had won Conservative support by underhand means and that 'Mr. Heywood holds opinions in direct antagonism to those which Mr. Heywood himself has openly advocated.' He was thus accused of lacking personal integrity. In the eyes of their opponents this only made the Liberals seem even more 'dictatorial'.[32]

On the morning of 13 July, Abel must have entertained hopes that he would be a member for Manchester by nightfall. The candidates posted up their calculations of the voting on each hour. That the figures may have influenced tactical voters there is no doubt; the public took an avid interest in them and would have used them in their decisions.

Indeed, this was explicitly the case. According to the *Manchester Courier* around midday it had become obvious to the Heywood camp that they were not going to win and at 2 p.m. they apparently declared using placards around the city that voters should 'plump' instead for Edward James. However, there was more to this, as on the following day Abel claimed that it was his opponents who had gone so far as to 'propagate the falsehood that I had retired, by which hundreds of votes were lost to me'. If this were the case, then the poll was subject to the worst 'dirty tricks'. Abel also hinted that, as in 1859, he had not used untoward means of gaining support, as he claimed, 'Had I been reckless as to the means used or the expenses incurred, the poll would have been very different.'[33] This would appear to be supported by the accounts for the campaign published on 22 September. Abel's expenditure amounted to £781, as compared to that incurred by Thomas Bazley and Jacob Bright of £3,500 and by Edward James (in only three days) of £2,346.

However, Thomas Bazley had been the front-runner from the start, and polled 7,909 votes. Edward James, after a slow start, had overtaken Jacob Bright around 2 p.m. and was elected as the second member with 6,698. Bright had gained 5,562; and Abel had come a dismal fourth with 4,242. It was observed that, although the voters' register standing at over 22,000 included 4,000 more names than in 1859, the total number of votes cast was 2,500 fewer, and that therefore many electors had 'taken no active interest in the election'. No analysis of this phenomenon is given, but the ill-feeling in and against the Liberal factions must have played its part in alienating potential voters.

For Abel, the result was even more dispiriting in that he had received well over 1,000 fewer votes this time than in 1859. He addressed his supporters, led by Max Kyllman, Councillor Ingham, Mr Smith, Ernest Jones, J.E. Nelson and Edward Hooson, at 5 p.m., not from the Peel statue this time but from a low wall in front of the Infirmary. The first thing he said was that he intended to fight again, and this was clearly not just a casual statement as he repeated it twice later in his speech and was encouraged with a cry of 'Go it, Abel lad'. He attributed the lack of support from gentlemen who had promised it in the aftermath of 1859 to 'snobbishness', 'that feeling which would not allow a man to represent this city unless he wore broadcloth - (Hear, hear); - unless he occupied some great warehouse here. - (Applause).'[34] That he was putting a brave face on it seems to be indicated by the fact that he did not attend the official declaration of the poll the following morning; even Jacob Bright was present, despite being 'most unmistakeably groaned', but it seems that Abel was unwilling to face the public again so soon after his crushing defeat.[35]

The Second Reform Act 1867

Abel was ever optimistic, and in the following year he was to be found again working in the cause of reform. The death of Lord Palmerston in October 1865 had opened the door to renewed efforts, and the new prime minister, Lord John Russell, lost no time in the introduction of a new bill, presented in the Commons in 1866 by William Gladstone. It must have been hard for Abel to find himself working with Jacob Bright, but he steeled himself and proposed that the executive encourage all NRU branches to hold meetings and prepare petitions to be presented in support of the bill.

However, by mid-June the bill, limited though it was, had run into trouble. Elements in the Liberal party led by Robert Lowe had joined with the Conservatives to vote it down, much to the fury of reformers in Manchester. The

Liberal government resigned, and an emergency meeting of the NRU was called in the Free Trade Hall assembly room to discuss events. A resolution was passed expressing the hope that the Queen would not select a new prime minister, but would dissolve Parliament and hold an election to allow the people to express their feelings on the matter of reform, and Abel was called upon to move the adoption of a memorial to the monarch accordingly. The *Manchester Courier*, as might be expected, bore somewhat hostile witness to these proceedings, reporting in particular that, as well as placarding the walls of the city with announcements, 'in order effectually to get up the steam, a band of music in a gaily-decorated carriage, played, after the manner of a travelling circus, through the streets, a previously unheard-of proceeding in Manchester'. Nevertheless, the paper gave the meeting very generous coverage, detailing what was said by delegates from all over the north of England and Wales. A Great Reform Banquet in the Free Trade Hall was organised on 20 November 1866. Abel was one of the vice-presidents of the banquet over which George Wilson presided.

Whilst active thus in the Reform Union, Abel was also a participant in the activities of the working-class Reform League which continued to espouse manhood suffrage and the ballot. There was as yet no election, and the Queen prevailed upon Lord Derby to form a Conservative government, led in the Commons by Benjamin Disraeli. Abel chaired his local League meeting in Ardwick, which was very well-attended, mainly by the working class. In his introductory remarks, he discussed how so-called Liberals had let down the cause of reform, and 'had uniformly stemmed the progress of political and other reforms during the whole of their lives'. He stated that he would support anyone who gave reform to the country, whatever their party.[36]

In March the following year, the Conservatives introduced a Reform Bill which was very similar to Gladstone's, which they had voted down. They were a minority government, and it was not expected that they could last long, or that they could pass their bill. At a meeting of the NRU on 26 April 1867 there were resolutions of gratitude and support for Gladstone's attempt in the Commons at reform the previous year and condemnation for the present Conservative bill which was so limited. All Liberals were asked to prepare for widespread agitation throughout the country to secure a suitable Reform Act. Abel was called upon to propose a resolution thanking Liberal MPs who had supported an amendment by Gladstone to the Tory bill. It would have removed a clause preventing those who paid rates as part of their rent (compounders) from voting; such men tended to be poorer, and the bill as proposed would exclude them from the franchise. Gladstone's proposal was defeated in accordance with Disraeli's intention to 'dish the Whigs'. Those who had supported the Tories in this, who included Edward James, the MP for Manchester, were 'denounced' for their 'traitorous conduct', though Abel successfully proposed to tone this down to 'deploring the vacillating conduct' as James and the others might still return to support for Gladstone.

The manner in which Disraeli eventually pushed through his Reform Bill was to allow several amendments from radical backbench Liberals and so win over that group to vote with that part of the Conservative party who were prepared to countenance reform. So when the radical Liberal Grosvenor Hodgkinson re-introduced a compounders amendment, Disraeli allowed it to be passed, with dramatic consequences for the extension of the franchise.

The Reform Bill was expected to increase considerably the Liberal vote. Disraeli's solution to this problem was to redistribute seats and redraw boundaries to mitigate its effects. In June Abel was among 1,000 citizens from a variety of political backgrounds who requested that the mayor call a meeting which would petition for an increase in the number of seats to represent Manchester, and the date was fixed for the 24th. It turned out to be a 'stormy meeting'. Abel joined the platform party. Mayor Neill and Thomas Bazley MP made appeals for the city to present a united face on this issue. A representative from the (Conservative) Constitutional Association spoke in favour of the current redistribution scheme, but the 'frantic uproar' with which his words were received prevented his being heard properly. The Constitutionalists attempted to give like for like when Ernest Jones rose to speak, and the mayor had to threaten to bring in the police to restore order.[37]

After further wrangling in the Lords, with attendant local protests, the Reform Act became law on 15 August. It has been suggested that most MPs were not really aware of the implications of what they were doing in passing the 1867 Reform Act. The prime minister, Lord Derby, himself described it as 'a leap in the dark'. It enfranchised close to one and half million men in the boroughs, bringing the proportion of male voters up to around 30 per cent. It was a significant instalment, but it was by no means manhood suffrage, and the struggle continued.

The united Liberal party

Ever since the Derby government had taken over in 1866 it was in a minority in Parliament. It was expected that there would soon be a general election and in Manchester there was considerable jostling for position. Letters to the press in April 1867 had speculated that both Bazley and James were planning to retire, and therefore the field would be open for others. One correspondent opined that Abel Heywood 'is to be shelved, in order to unite the Liberal and Radical sections, if possible'.[38] When the Conservatives succeeded in passing the Reform Act and Disraeli became prime minister a general election was staved off until December 1868. Nevertheless, in Manchester there was a by-election in November 1867 due to the death of Edward James.

Although Abel had always expressed the intention to stand again for Parliament at the next opportunity, he did not put himself up for election either at the by-election of November, or at the general election of December 1868. While it may be true that he was 'shelved' in the interests of unity, there were other factors.

These were personal; his wife, Ann, died in tragic circumstances on 26 June 1867, and Abel probably did not feel in a position to continue with the demands which would be imposed on him by a such a campaign. The report of the *Manchester Times* suggested that there may have been a (possibly related) health problem. Abel did not publicly state any reasons for this about-turn, and there were some, probably unaware of the circumstances of Ann's death, who felt that he had been let down and put under undue pressure not to stand. His decision was of great benefit to the moderate Liberal party, who could now claim to be the 'united Liberal party', and there was feeling abroad that he had been abandoned by heretofore supporters, in particular the UK Alliance, at the behest of 'a few merchants'.[39]

Meanwhile, working on the assumption that Manchester would get its third MP (which indeed it did), the Reform League council and the Trade Unionists Political Association met in early July. They agreed unanimously to ensure the registration of working-class voters, that such voters should be entitled to nominate at least one of the three candidates for the Liberals, and furthermore that Ernest Jones should be adopted as that candidate.

From the speech which Jones made on accepting this offer, it seems that he may have pointed out Heywood's claims to the position, but that his scruples had been allayed: 'he felt that the interests and claims of another gentleman had been duly considered; that those claims had received every consideration' and so he was enabled 'with a clear conscience' to accept the honour conferred upon him.[40] The Reform League had discussed the situation with Abel and he had accepted it; by November his committee were attending a meeting of the 'united Liberal party' in the Free Trade Hall to support Bazley and Bright. The latter having agreed to stand as candidate to replace Edward James, his committee and that of Abel Heywood joined together to form a joint election committee.

It must have been a bitter pill to swallow for Abel, who had given his all on two occasions, and now that there was a real chance of success for a working-class candidate because of the number of working men with votes he was obliged to give place to another, admittedly long-committed, radical. But the pill was sugared; he had an honoured place as deputy chairman on Bright's election committee, and chaired the one set up in Collegiate ward. Moreover, his sacrifice was recognised by the candidate when he addressed the electors in Cheetham ward. 'He thanked Mr. Abel Heywood for having so generously associated himself with their party, and he believed that if he was returned he would be deeply indebted to Mr. Heywood and his party for their assistance and support.'[41] When Bright addressed the Ardwick electors, Abel chaired the meeting of his neighbours and began by stating his position:

Mr. Alderman Heywood... said that in occupying the chair that night he considered he fulfilled, in relation to the party with which he had been connected all his life, a fair and proper place. (Hear, hear.) He did not consider that in relinquishing for a time the position which he sought some two years ago he was forfeiting his claims if he was ever again asked to come forward as a candidate.

Perhaps to allay public concern by eliciting an explanation, or perhaps to show that he was still his own man even though he was supporting Bright, he then proceeded to question the latter about a statement he was reported to have made referring to Disraeli's premiership in which he 'expressed his sorrow that a British Parliament was led by one of that degraded people, the Jews'. Bright chose his words carefully, and did not outright deny that he was prejudiced, but it is instructive that Abel clearly thought that it was important that he should not appear so; it is a common view of Victorian society that what today would be called anti-Semitism was normal and accepted, but this was not always the case. Moreover, Abel himself did not want to be tarred with that brush.[42]

Bright won the by-election. On the afternoon of the poll, when the result was clear, Abel was cheered in Bright's committee room as 'the gentleman who had kept the Liberal party of Manchester together, and thus led to the election of Mr. Jacob Bright'. His response referred to his unstinting support of Bright's campaign and there was a cry of 'You will go together next time.' He urged the Liberal party to maintain its present unity, to keep up its presence in all the city's wards, and to show they stood for the whole community. When he had staked a claim for the workers in the business of Parliament; his speech ended amid 'loud cries of "Mr. Heywood for the third member for Manchester"'.[43]

By the following autumn, in October 1868, it was becoming clear that the minority Conservative government now led by Benjamin Disraeli would be going to the country in the near future. Whatever Abel's hopes, on 21 October the *Manchester Guardian* bore announcements from the 'united Liberal party' that those wishing to help in the canvass for Bazley, Bright and Jones should present themselves. The notice was signed by chairman Sir Elkanah Armitage, and deputy chairmen Sir James Watts, Thomas Ashton and Abel Heywood. The machinery of Liberal campaigning was cranking into motion, but Abel was not to be a candidate.

A major platform for the national Liberal campaign in this election was Gladstone's policy of disestablishment for the Irish Anglican church, in the aftermath of Fenian outrages in Manchester and London. On 17 November the united Liberals succeeded in getting Bazley and Bright elected, but the poll was in fact topped by the Conservative Hugh Birley with 15,482 votes. Ernest Jones had come fourth and polled 10,746 votes. The *Manchester Courier* was predictably delighted with this result, and attributed it to the pro-Church of England feeling in Manchester. The Liberal *Manchester Times* blamed the lesser showing of Bazley and Bright, and possibly also the failure of Jones, on the candidacy of Mitchell Henry, who put himself up as a Liberal outside the auspices of the united Liberals and therefore split their vote. However, this result was also a harbinger for the future of Manchester elections, and symptomatic of a developing popular Toryism, characterised by Disraeli as 'Tory democracy'. In particular, the workers had responded to the Tory anti-Catholic and anti-Irish stance, at a time when the Fenian outrages were still fresh in the people's minds.

Abel had apparently thrown himself wholeheartedly into the united Liberal party, and ideas he had expressed with regard to party organisation were put into effect in Manchester where the Liberals were quick to grasp the significance of the creation by the Second Reform Act of a mass electorate. In 1870 branch clubs were established in Ardwick and Chorlton-on-Medlock, with facilities for all classes, a model repeated elsewhere.

When the next election was declared for 5 February 1874 the Liberals again selected Bazley and Bright as their candidates. When they both addressed a meeting in the Corn Exchange, Abel presided. He also appeared on the long list of vice-chairmen on the election committee for south-east Lancashire of Messrs Rylands and Taylor. In an era when Conservatism generally was enjoying a revival across the country, the Manchester results did not buck the trend; it is likely that Manchester Conservatism was boosted by the celebrated 'one nation' speech given by Disraeli in the Free Trade Hall, in 1872. In a very close election, with just over 1,000 votes between the top of the poll and the bottom, the city elected two Conservatives, Hugh Birley and William Romaine Callender, and only one Liberal, Thomas Bazley, with Jacob Bright on this occasion being unsuccessful.

However, on the death of Callender in 1876, Bright was supported by Abel Heywood as the Liberal candidate in the resulting by-election in February. Several of the ward meetings exhibited a novel aspect of the new electorate; there were many Irish Catholics in attendance, asking questions about Irish and religious policy. Abel was alive to this newly enfranchised interest group and mentioned that he had been active in Irish interests for thirty years.[44] In a speech at the Corn Exchange he stressed that 'They [the Liberals] must raise the Liberal standard; they must swear by that standard, and not allow one single shred of it to be torn from it.'[45] Bright was returned in the face of opposition from the Conservative, Powell. The Liberals had begun their fightback, and Abel appreciated fully that this could only be done in unity.

On his death in 1893 the *Manchester Guardian* summed up Abel's parliamentary candidacy, explaining that it had failed because he was in some ways ahead of his time, and of relatively advanced years. He had insufficient appeal to 'a ruling section' of the party and 'his politics were never exactly of the current type'. He was not quite in line with the Manchester School, and 'though he was a Radical he had some sympathies which brought him on some points very near to the Tories'. Although he held 'advanced views, he was never a vehement partisan, and his democratic opinions had in them something of a Young England [romantic conservatism] flavour'.[46]

It seems that Abel had by 1870, publicly at least, given up any aspirations to enter Parliament, and he certainly occupied himself in other directions. Most notably, he was by now fully immersed in the great project of the new Town Hall. Perhaps he had decided that there was more than one route to greatness, and as a true Manchester Man he had resolved to find it in the city where he had expended so much personal effort and already achieved so much.

10

The Respectable Family Man

Abel's business success and consequent elevation in the social and political scale was due in part to the support of his family. His mother and a brother, probably John, had continued his business in 1832, when Abel was most certainly not a 'respectable family man', languishing as he was in prison. Later, the backing of his wife, Ann, who reportedly showed a great aptitude for business, was apparently invaluable to his prosperity.

Although Abel does not seem to have had much to do with his elder brother, William, he was very close in early life to the oldest sibling, John. John, who had been his comrade in arms in the disputes of the 1820s at the Mechanics' Institution, after a spell as a handloom weaver joined Abel in business as a paper-ruler until he struck out on his own in 1842. He set up a successful enterprise on Deansgate, carried on by his son and grandson, also named John, similarly dealing in books and other printed matter. Terry Wyke is of the opinion that from 1870 to 1900 John Heywood's was the 'one major book publisher [in Manchester]… whose publishing interests were sufficiently extensive to warrant comparison with some of the larger London publishers'. However, at some point there was disagreement and estrangement between Abel and one of the Johns, a painful family rift.[1]

First marriage and children

Abel's first real step towards respectability was on 27 January 1833, when he married his 'sweetheart', Ann Pilling, in St John's church, off Deansgate. In view of Abel's Owenite beliefs, it is interesting that the ceremony took place in the respectable Church of England. Ann also, to judge from what is probably her baptismal record, was not a worshipper in the established church, but was brought up a nonconformist Bible Christian. The explanation for their choice is that before 1836 marriages outside the Church of England were not legally recognised.

Almost all sources are silent on the subject of Abel's marriage and the person of his wife. Uniquely, Joseph Johnson devotes almost a page to Ann; she is portrayed as the 'true helpmate' of the hero, Abel. Even allowing for exaggeration, it seems likely that Ann was indeed made of stern stuff, as she must have known what she was taking on in marrying Abel; after all, she had read his letters from prison. As so often, Johnson seems to be relaying Abel's own words about Ann, to whom he was still married in 1860 (she died seven years later): 'He mainly attributes, indeed, his prosperity to her advice and assistance.' Johnson goes on to explain, 'Combining great aptness for business, with wonderful shrewdness and penetration of individual character, she was an invaluable associate in the more stormy period of Abel's career, many times being called upon to exercise her strong common sense in cases of emergency.' Indeed, that she supported him in business is demonstrated by the testimony of the government *agents provocateurs* in 1840, who purchased illegal publications from her when she was running the shop.

The couple had their first child, a daughter named Jane, in 1834; she was baptised at Manchester Parish Church (later the Cathedral) on 30 November. Elizabeth followed in 1837, Abel in 1840, George Washington (presumably named as a mark of respect for the first president of the democratic United States) in 1842, and finally Jessie in 1852. There is no available record for the baptisms of these later children, and in view of what we know of Abel's Owenite beliefs, it could be that they had unrecorded Owenite 'baptisms'. From 1831, the family resided at 56 Oldham Street where Abel had his business premises. In the 1841 census record, the presence of two servants and Abel's avocation as a bookseller put the family firmly in the lower middle class. However, Oldham Street itself was an extension of Oldham Road in the poor district of Ancoats, and we are fortunate in having the eyewitness testimony of the reporter Angus Reach from 1849 which gives us a flavour of the environment in which the family lived:

> In returning last Sunday night, by the Oldham-road, from one of my tours, I was somewhat surprised to hear the loud sounds of music and jollity which floated out of the public-house windows. The street was swarming with drunken men and women; and with young mill girls and boys shouting, hallooing and romping with each other. In no city have I ever witnessed a scene of more open, brutal, and general intemperance. The public-houses and gin-shops were roaring full. Rows, and fights, and scuffles were every moment taking place within doors and in the streets. The whole street rung with shouting, screaming, and swearing, mingled with the jarring music of half-a-dozen bands.[2]

Perhaps it is not surprising that the family moved from Oldham Street; from 1844 to 1846 they resided in Broughton Street, Cheetham, and some time before 1 May 1847 moved again to salubrious Ardwick, renting a house belonging to A.H. Burgess, probably 33 Burgess Terrace on Hyde Road.[3] The gross rental in 1848 was £40, which suggests that this was a modestly comfortable residence. In the Select Committee of 1851 Abel no longer described himself as a mere shopkeeper, but as a 'wholesaler'. By the census of 1861 the family was living at the grandly named

Ardwick House in Ardwick Green and Abel was now 'Alderman and papermaker'. By 1861 Jane had left the household because five years before she had married Robert Trimble. Elizabeth, Abel junior, a 21-year-old bookseller, and George Washington, a 'paper hanging manufacturer', were still resident and unmarried. By this time, the family was complete as Jessie had by now appeared on the scene as a 9-year-old 'scholar', who may have been tutored by a 19-year-old 'Lady', Maria Smith from Brixton in Surrey. The family had three servants.

The marriages of Abel's children reflected the family's rising status. Jane's husband, Robert Trimble, was born near Belfast. He became a Unitarian, which denomination the Heywoods had formally joined by 1861, and worked in Manchester for linen merchants. Around the time that he married Jane he joined the Volunteer movement in which he eventually became an honorary colonel. His other claim to distinction was that he was very active in helping freed slaves in the United States in the later 1860s. When he and Jane emigrated to New Zealand in 1875, they settled in Taranaki, near Inglewood, buying 2,000 acres from the provincial government. It seems likely that they were helped to buy this land by Jane's father, Abel; in his will, written in 1883, he talked of his land at Taranaki which was occupied by Robert Trimble. Robert died in 1899 leaving seven children, and Jane lived on until 1925 in New Zealand.

Elizabeth, Jane's younger sister, in 1864 married John Charlesworth, born in 1831 in Middleton, the son of an iron founder. When he married Elizabeth he was an architect with his own business, Speakman and Charlesworth. It seems that he was disowned by his grandfather, Robert Healey, who had brought him up, because of his wife's Unitarian beliefs. The wedding took place in Upper Brook Street Unitarian chapel. John died in 1871 and by 1881 Elizabeth and her three children, Arthur, Anne Stella and Mabel, had moved to live near her father and stepmother in Rosehill, Bowdon in Cheshire.[4] By the time of the 1891 census, she, still with Arthur and Mabel, had moved in with her now-widowed father at Summerfield. She died living in Southport, Lancashire in 1929.

Abel's elder son, also called Abel, began work in the family business on Oldham Street, and in 1871 described himself as a guardian of the poor and a publisher, employing twenty-three men, six boys, five women and nine girls. In 1865 he had married Catherine Johns Woolley, whose father was a 'druggist' and fellow shopkeeper. They lived in Ardwick at 90 The Avenue, and had four children. Catherine died in 1881, and a letter survives in which Abel expressed his shock and devastation at her loss: 'She was cheerful and well one minute and dead the next.'[5] When Abel senior died in 1893, Abel junior took sole control of the business, in which his father had made him a partner in 1880. He was a keen member of the Manchester Literary Club, which championed the Lancashire dialect, participated in the Independent Theatre Society, putting on plays and concerts, and was an enthusiastic amateur photographer. As a walker, he campaigned for a public right of way on Kinder Scout in the Peak District. He died in 1931 and it was noted in his obituary in the *Manchester Guardian* that he had also founded the Manchester Angling Society.

George Washington likewise married into the middle class. Constance Bellhouse's father was an engineer. By the time of the marriage in 1876, George himself was a barrister, having trained at the Middle Temple from 12 January 1866 and being called to the bar on 6 June 1868. He was forging an illustrious career, even producing his own book on *The Common Law and Equity Practice*, published by Abel Heywood in 1871. It is likely that his appointment as a County Court judge for Manchester in 1890 was a source of great pride for his father. He had four daughters, but died at 54, against the family trend of longevity, three years after his father.

Abel's final child was Jessie, born late when her mother was at least 42. She never married, but after a spell living with her sister Elizabeth Charlesworth, emigrated in 1879 to be with her eldest sister, Jane, in New Zealand. Her arrival on the 'Waimate' was not without its difficulties, as she was suffering (with thirteen other passengers) from measles, and the ship was put into quarantine. Jessie lived in New Zealand to the ripe old age of 95 and died in 1947. She was surely her father's daughter, having had a distinguished career there in education, and is still noted today as a herbologist who provided many specimens for the Manchester Museum.

On 26 June 1867 Abel's wife, Ann, died at Ardwick House in dramatic and tragic circumstances. Apart from the bald announcement of her demise, the press were silent on the event. Only by an examination of her death certificate does it become clear that Ann took her own life; the coroner's verdict was that she 'Hanged herself whilst Insane'. Further information does not seem to be available, as the coroner's records for most of the nineteenth century in Manchester have been destroyed. It is therefore unknown whether Ann was really 'insane', for how long and in what form. It may be that the coroner had referred to insanity because, before 1880, to commit suicide whilst of sound mind meant that the deceased could not be buried with Christian rites. In any case, nineteenth-century medical opinion often argued that a sane person would not kill themselves, and therefore someone who did so must be insane. There is no record of Abel's reaction, but it can be surmised that this was at the very least a terrible shock. It certainly must have been a factor in his decision not to stand in the Manchester by-election of that year. Abel and Ann had been married for thirty-four years and she had gone with him through the vicissitudes of his personal and public life, and the loss he experienced can only be guessed at. Her funeral took place apparently in the normal way; she was buried in the nonconformist area of the new Philips Park Cemetery (grave D128), just near the main entrance in a grave which eventually was also to hold the last remains of Abel himself and his second wife, Elizabeth.

Elizabeth Salisbury Heywood

Abel did not spend time in mourning Ann for any longer than was respectable, and he remarried on 26 May 1868, eleven months after her death. It is likely that he had known Elizabeth Salisbury Goadsby, *née* Grime, for quite a few years; she was the widow of his fellow alderman, Thomas Goadsby, who had died in 1866. To judge from her portrait she was not a beauty, but had a characterful look. That she was of strong mind is suggested by her activities and interests; one of her first acts on the death of Thomas Goadsby was to carry out their wish to commission and present a controversial statue of Oliver Cromwell to the city of Manchester, and she was a supporter of women's rights and a fellow campaigner of the suffragist leader Lydia Becker. One obituarist claimed that 'Had she been a man, she would long ago have been knighted for her public services in Manchester.'[6]

Elizabeth was unusual for a respectable lady in having had a dramatic and terrifying experience in her teens which had brought her to public attention in the press and books. It was locally so famous at the time that Abel would surely have been aware of it. This was the fatal launch of the *Emma* on Friday 29 February 1828 in the River Irwell just by the New Bailey prison. Crowds assembled on the banks to see the sight, with two or three hundred people aboard the boat, reportedly mostly young women in holiday clothes. The agent of the New Quay company was William Brereton Grime, and he had commissioned his two daughters, Elizabeth and Mary, to name the ship. When the boat hit the water, it either went in too deep and hit the bottom, or it hit the opposite bank of the river; it ended up on its side, with passengers in the water, and some trapped inside below deck. While Elizabeth and her sister were quickly rescued and brought ashore, several men dived into the water to try to save others. By the end there were thirty-eight bodies laid out on the banks.

The effect of such an experience on an impressionable and sheltered teenager can only be guessed. But it would mean that both she and Abel had experienced traumatic events in their youth which helped shape their view of the world. And Elizabeth also seems to have had to face the death of her child. In 1831 she married Thomas Goadsby, druggist, at St John's church. Their daughter, Marianne, was baptised on 8 November 1835 in the New Jerusalem chapel, Salford, but the little girl died at the age of 3 in 1839. Her death must have had a lasting impact, and in her will Elizabeth left four pieces of jewellery containing Marianne's hair and miniatures of her to relatives, and a marble bust of her by Noble to Owens College.[7] There do not appear to have been any further children.

Thomas Goadsby went on to build up the chemist and druggist business, continuing to keep a warehouse and shop but also with a chemical works at Newton Heath to stock it. By 1847 he was on the Manchester Council, taking on the chair of the Markets Committee. A man of diminutive stature, for which on occasion he was teased in the council, he was a popular public figure. For the rest of his life he was in frequent association with Abel Heywood. In 1861 it was Abel who successfully (on the third attempt) proposed Thomas Goadsby for Mayor of Manchester.

It therefore seems likely that, having heard in his youth what had happened to the *Emma*, Abel may have met Elizabeth during her husband's lifetime at one of the relatively rare social occasions where women were included, such as the ball in 1862 which Thomas Goadsby held for members of the Corporation, and presumably their wives, at Elizabeth's suggestion. She, like Abel, had been active in the effort to alleviate the suffering of the people during the cotton famine, and had formed a ladies' Relief Committee to effect this, for which she had received a testimonial on vellum. The fact that she and Abel married within a year of the death of his first wife may suggest that they had already formed a close acquaintance. It is also conceivable that the shared experience of bereavement may have brought them together. However, that Elizabeth kept many treasured mementoes of her late husband, Thomas, would indicate that she had been very fond of the latter; in her will she left jewellery which contained his hair, portrait miniatures, photographs and an obituary, as well as a testimonial on vellum presented to him by Manchester Corporation.

Elizabeth was a widow of means with a large house at Throstle Nest in Stretford, where she and Abel were living by the time of the royal visit of 1869. The couple seem to have shared similar strong views about the position of women. It is therefore not surprising that she adopted a course common among well-to-do middle-class women, which was to agree an indenture of settlement with her new husband, signed three days before their marriage. Although the details are not stated, this appears to have given her sole control of her estate during her second marriage, which included all the property of her late husband, Thomas Goadsby. In token of his regard for her, Abel gave her an emerald and diamond ring.

Elizabeth sprang from the middle class and she was a very different wife from Ann Heywood. Not only did she pursue her interests in a public fashion, but she also appeared alongside her husband on public occasions. Her notion of holding a ball for councillors and their wives when Thomas Goadsby was mayor set the tone for her participation when Abel became mayor for a second time in 1876–77. She was probably in the public gallery when he was elected and accompanied him on official engagements from the start, such as her attendance at a lecture by Captain Markham on his Arctic expedition. When the illustrious General Grant visited from the US, she attended the luncheon and was toasted by the great man himself. She appeared on numerous other public occasions, usually designated 'the Mayoress', a term which reflected her prominence and also the developing role of women in public life at this time, in which she herself was blazing a trail.

At the inauguration of the new Town Hall on 13 September 1877, she played a prominent part alongside her husband, and at the banquet in the evening was toasted by Lord Tollemache who 'congratulated the ladies of Manchester at having at their head so admirable a person as Mrs. Heywood'. She was lauded in the Reform Club for 'the quiet grace and dignity with which she supported her worthy husband, and received her husband's guests'.[8] The impression is that she threw herself into the role of mayoress at least as enthusiastically as her husband took on the mantle of mayor.

The Albert memorial

In his mayoralty of 1861–62 , Thomas Goadsby had begun a campaign for a memorial for Prince Albert, who died in 1861. Thomas had, out of his own pocket, commissioned a marble statue by the renowned sculptor Matthew Noble, and local architect Thomas Worthington designed an elaborate canopy for it which was financed by public subscription. The monument, originally intended for Piccadilly in front of the Infirmary, was placed in its present site in 1863, in an act of faith that the area would not remain a densely built-up unpaved area adjoining the Town Yard, but would become Albert Square, and boast a grand new Town Hall. In a fraught council meeting in 1863, Abel Heywood used his casting vote as mayor to ensure that this remodelling of the area would go ahead, but lack of funds (at the time of the cotton famine) slowed down the memorial project. Thomas Goadsby died in February 1866, leaving his widow, Elizabeth, to continue with the donation in his name. Further problems accompanied the inauguration of the statue in 1867, which office was declined by the Queen, the prime minister (the Earl of Derby) and the Bishop of Manchester.

On 23 January 1867 two ceremonies were held; in the old Town Hall Elizabeth Goadsby presented the statue, where unusually for a woman she made a speech, which was acceptable because in presenting the statue she was fulfilling one of the last wishes of her deceased husband. The listeners were also touched at her feminine show of emotion when she referred to her own grief – 'too sacred and too deep for utterance'.

A procession made up of male dignitaries with just one woman, Elizabeth Goadsby, then proceeded through streets muddy with thawing snow to Albert Square where the engineering magnate William Fairbairn, regretting the absence of monarchy, unveiled the memorial. A large crowd of 'roughs' had gathered from Deansgate, Angel Meadow 'and other delectable neighbourhoods', and though they were good-natured, they were also so noisy that the speeches could not be heard. The reverence for the prince's memory was perhaps not as universal in Manchester as the speakers at the unveiling intimated.[9]

This statue was expressive of a wholly unremarkable loyalty to the monarchy, and Albert with his interest in industry and modernisation, exemplified in his role in the Great Exhibition of 1851, was a popular figure in Manchester. However, the Goadsbys also had another monument in mind, which was much more controversial; a statue of Oliver Cromwell. The council under the mayoralty of Thomas Goadsby had discussed the idea early in the 1860s, but nothing had come of it before Thomas died; his widow therefore took it upon herself to fulfil her husband's wishes and commissioned Noble to sculpt the Cromwell statue.

Meanwhile she married Abel Heywood on 26 May 1868 in Manchester Cathedral. This is a surprising choice of venue, since by now Abel was a paid-up member of the Cross Street Unitarian chapel, and Elizabeth had been a nonconformist since birth, and there was no longer any prohibition against marriage in the Unitarian church. However, by the admission in the 1870s of no less than the minister, William Gaskell, the Cross Street chapel was said to be 'dingy'. And the cathedral certainly had the advantage of prestige. The relationship between Cross Street Unitarians and the established church was generally relaxed, and in Abel and Elizabeth's case, certainly so.

Elizabeth drew Abel deeper into patronage of the Arts; on 23 December 1868 they attended the annual meeting and prize-giving of the Manchester School of Art, and Elizabeth was singled out for special mention by the chairman, Thomas Bazley MP, who 'congratulated the meeting upon their having amongst them Mrs. Abel Heywood – (applause) – whose liberality and bounty deserved the gratitude of all who were aware of her munificence. (Applause.)' When the prizes were enumerated, there was a set known as 'the Goadsby Prizes', worth £25.11s, donated to the most deserving student for a work of art or for skill, knowledge or proficiency in art. This was the interest from a gift of £500 presented the preceding year by Elizabeth.[10]

By 1877 the School of Art was expanding and Abel was thoroughly on board; in February he presided at a lunch to which the great and the good were invited to discuss the creation of a fund to erect a new school on land already bought on Stretford Road, next to Chorlton Town Hall. It was planned also to set up a permanent Art Gallery and Museum of Art Workmanship. Elizabeth was still a benefactor, and for this purpose was listed as a donor to the tune of £500, the sum given by the ten most elevated patrons, who included the Earl of Derby.

In late November 1876 as mayor, Abel was also president of the Art Union and oversaw the prize draw, held in the Royal Institution. In the following year, the draw itself was carried out by Elizabeth Heywood as the winning numbers were taken from a revolving wheel. How far this was understood to be a double act can be seen from the fact that 'The proceedings closed with a vote of thanks to the President [Abel] and Mrs Heywood.'[11]

Elizabeth continued to support the Arts in Manchester for the rest of her life. The year before her death she purchased and donated a 'fine collection of cloisonné enamels' to the Corporation 'in order that it may be added to the public treasures of the citizens of Manchester'. Elizabeth expressly asked that the enamels be available for public inspection as very rare examples of art manufacture; it was therefore decided that the collection was destined for the Queen's Park Museum.[12]

Elizabeth's munificence also found an outlet in the support of horticulture. When the Royal Horticultural Society held its annual show in Manchester in July 1869, there were prizes worth a total of five guineas donated by Mrs Abel Heywood for Class 34: 'two bouquets for the hand, one for bride, the other ball (amateurs)'.[13] By 1875 the Manchester Botanical and Horticultural Society had set up botanical gardens in Old Trafford which were in deficit; in that year Mrs Heywood became a £20 life member, the only woman in a group of thirteen men. Similarly, in response to a special appeal aimed at paying off the debt the following year, she made a subscription of £20, being one of only three women on a list of over 120 men.

A third good cause in which Elizabeth took an interest was the Governesses Institution and Home on Oxford Road, set up to house those refined ladies who were far from home and might be in need of accommodation due to temporary unemployment; in 1870 there were reported to be sixty 'inmates'. The institution also acted as an employment agency, and had placed ninety-two in 'situations'. At their annual meeting in 1871 Elizabeth joined the general committee, and was still serving in 1883.

This was part of a wider interest in the position of women, and not only did Abel join her in supporting this institution, but also in activities to enhance the education and political rights of women. When Abel, as mayor in 1876–77, presided over meetings of Lydia Becker's Manchester National Society for Women's Suffrage Elizabeth also attended as a member of the committee, proposing the appointment of the new committee for 1877.

Life in Bowdon

Sometime between the census of 1871 and 1874, Abel and Elizabeth moved to their final home at Summerfield in Rosehill, Bowdon, Cheshire. The property, a 'valuable freehold mansion… overlooking the Bowdon Downs', was up for sale by auction on 25 April 1876, but already 'occupied by Alderman Abel Heywood', presumably as a tenant. The advertisement listed over two acres of garden and land, with coach houses, stables, outhouses, greenhouses and vineries. It was a home for a gentleman and Abel's purchase put him among the upper middle classes of the wealthy suburb.[14] There is a rare opportunity to glimpse the domestic arrangements of the Heywoods due to the fact that when Abel died in 1893 the house was again put up for auction and the advertisement carried a lot more detail:

> The house is artistically decorated throughout, and contains spacious entrance hall, vestibule and porch, dining-room, drawing-room, library, morning-room, and butler's pantry, all on the ground floor, six principal bedrooms, and two dressing-rooms on the first floor, and three servants' bedrooms on the second floor. It contains also bathroom, three lavatories, two kitchens, washhouse, and servants' offices on the ground floor, and is well cellared throughout. The outbuildings consist of a two-stalled stable, two loose boxes, harness-room, coachhouse, dwelling-house for coachman, billiard-room, greenhouse, fernery, two vineries, stovehouse, and also a conservatory attached to the house and entered from the drawing-room. The grounds are tastefully laid out and include a large lawn and garden, the latter being well stocked with fruit and other trees.[15]

The census for 1881 confirmed that the couple employed a cook, a footman, a housemaid, a coachman and his wife. The census also showed that the Heywoods were close neighbours of Mary Collier, Elizabeth's widowed younger sister, and her son, Leicester, and also of Abel's widowed daughter, Elizabeth, and her three children. It seems likely that they were well-settled in this comfortable life away from the hectic pace of Manchester.

That Abel threw himself into Bowdon life is demonstrated by his participation in local politics; in March 1880 he appeared on the committee of Liberal candidate William Armitage for the Mid-Cheshire election. They met every day in the Altrincham Reform Club. When electoral boundaries were to be altered in the Redistribution Bill of 1885 there was an open enquiry in Chester Castle into the proposals for Cheshire, which Abel attended in the company of prominent members of the county such as Lord Egerton of Tatton.

He took a leading role in a dispute in the 1880s between the residents of Bowdon and the Manchester South Junction and Altrincham Railway Company over the relocation of the station and ticket prices. A deputation was selected to put their objections to the company, and perhaps not surprisingly in view of his experience Abel was of their number. When they made their report towards the end of June the mayor explained that the deputation had had no real success, and that the most the company would concede was that it would place footwarmers in all carriages. Abel told the meeting that the deputation 'had not been treated by the directors either as gentlemen or as representatives of a large population'. He proposed that he personally would take a second-class 'contract' ticket instead of his usual first class 'and though it might cause him some inconvenience and discomfort, he should consider he was discharging a public duty'. This was a far cry from the days when he travelled to Manchester from Ardwick in an overcrowded omnibus! A proposal that the Midland Railway Company should be requested to build a new line between Chorlton or Urmston and Bowdon was carried; the committee was asked to prepare a memorial to this effect.[16] Abel's position as a leader in local politics was clear.

This was formalised in his chairmanship of the Bowdon local board from at least 1882, in which his expertise from many years on council committees in Manchester was fully exploited. In April 1887 he chaired a meeting of the Bowdon ratepayers discussing whether they should continue to appoint the assistant overseer of the poor, or whether this power should be handed over to the Board of Guardians. The ratepayers of Bowdon did not always accept Abel's recommendations, as was demonstrated in July 1890 when they rejected a resolution to adopt the Free Libraries Acts of 1855 and 1889 for the township. Abel finally resigned from this august body only four months before his death.

The Cromwell statue

Despite the relative distance from the city of Manchester, Abel and his wife continued to participate fully in urban life, aided by the convenience of the rail connection only half a mile from their home. In 1875 Elizabeth established her greatest claim to fame in Manchester when she presented the statue of Oliver Cromwell to the city. The ripples from this were wide and in particular it was claimed that Queen Victoria refused to come to Manchester to open the new Town Hall in 1877 on account of this statue, which glorified the regicide.

The hostile view of Cromwell in Clarendon's history had been challenged by the account of Thomas Carlyle, and his portrayal was taken to heart by the non-conformist middle classes in Manchester. They saw in Cromwell an honest, moral and decisive man of action, a sincere Christian and defender of English liberties. When Thomas Goadsby proposed a subscription for a statue to go in the proposed new Manchester Town Hall in 1860 he was supported by Thomas Potter, Edward Watkin and Robert Needham Philips, all of whom subscribed £100 towards the project. The sculptor Matthew Noble and his wife visited the Goadsbys at Throstle Nest in 1865 and he began research and preliminary drawings. When Thomas Goadsby died, Elizabeth took it upon herself to continue his work and commission Noble.

The Victorian frame of mind was pleased to attribute this to her devotion to the memory of her husband, and while this may have been part of her motivation, Elizabeth was also acutely aware of her own Roundhead connections.[17] In a speech of 25 November 1875 Abel spelled this out:

> There was a propriety in such a statue coming from the hands of Mrs. Heywood. It was this: Sir William Brereton, who was one of Cromwell's generals, and who conducted the siege of Chester, was a representative of the family from which Mrs. Heywood sprang. - (Hear, hear.) ... For himself he had nothing to say; it was all for his wife. The honour and glory belonged entirely to her. He shared it only because he happened to be her husband.- (Applause.)[18]

The delicate question of where the statue should be placed caused much debate.[19] Abel related how on his marriage to Elizabeth she had informed him of her late husband's desire to see the statue in the new Town Hall, but that, as chairman of the New Town Hall Committee, he had immediately perceived that the architect, Alfred Waterhouse, might not accept a huge statue. However, the General Purposes Committee had taken it upon themselves to promise Noble that a place would be found for the colossal statue in the new Town Hall. Abel, much annoyed, claimed that this had delayed the project by six years, but it was finally decided that the statue would have to be outside, and therefore be cast in bronze to withstand the Manchester pollution. Thus began a search for a suitable site.

By now there was an added layer of political sensitivity surrounding the statue due to republican agitation by a few radical Liberals, led by Sir Charles Dilke and Charles Bradlaugh, in the early 1870s. Richard Pankhurst, later husband of Emmeline, chaired the Manchester Republican Club, and the Tory press in response whipped up pro-monarchical feeling with relish. The sub-committee set up to find a site, which included Abel Heywood, after consideration chose the middle of Deansgate where it met Victoria Street and Cateaton Street near the cathedral; this was supposedly where the first blood of the Civil War was spilt.

Despite some calls for a public celebration to mark the inauguration of the monument, Abel stated to the General Purposes Committee on 25 June 1874 that 'some difficulty arose in consequence of the indisposition of the lady who wished to present the statue to the Corporation to have her name paraded before the public of Manchester'. Even some of the General Purposes Committee appear to have been in ignorance as to the identity of the donor, or at least the issue was raised by Alderman Bennett, whereupon the town clerk coyly replied that 'they could not have expected Alderman Heywood to mention the lady's name. (Hear, hear.) He (the Town-clerk) did not think it would be a breach of impropriety to hint who the lady was. The statue was given by a lady who belonged, and he had no doubt was very dear, to Mr. Alderman Heywood. (Applause.)'[20]

The *Manchester Guardian* on 20 November 1875 carried a detailed description of the work. 'The Protector' was in military dress but exhibited an attitude of one engaged in debate with an expression of 'stern dignity'. The *Manchester Times* reporter preferred 'bold and energetic'.[21] The report noted that the Queen and others of the royal family had seen and admired the work, which, including the huge granite pedestal, was in total eighteen feet high and weighed over seventeen tons. The cost of the whole amounted to an estimated £1,600. Elizabeth did not make too much of her own part in all this; the main inscription was 'Oliver Cromwell' with his dates; the words 'The gift of Elizabeth Salisbury Heywood to the citizens of Manchester, August, 1875' were 'in characters so small as to be almost invisible'. On Noble's insistence, the face of Cromwell was to be towards the Royal Exchange, and detractors were quick to point out that he thereby pointedly turned his back on the cathedral, symbol of the power and dignity of the Church of England in Manchester.[22]

The report went on to say how it was not only Elizabeth's wish, but also Abel's that the statue should be presented unostentatiously. By this time, Abel had effectively become a donor too. That he was sympathetic to his wife's intention is not to be doubted, but Victorian sensibilities would not accept that a woman might take this kind of political action without a man at least in support. When Abel provided the explanation to the General Purposes Committee on 25 November, he prefaced it accordingly. 'He thought that some good reason ought to be given why a lady should step out of the path that was generally adopted by her sex and present that to the citizens of Manchester which ought, perhaps, to have been publicly subscribed for.' Thomas Carlyle was invited to the presentation, but old age prevented his attendance. However, in a communication expressly mediated through Abel, he sent his 'cordial compliments', recognising Mrs Heywood's generosity, and expressing interest in her illustrious connections.[23]

At the official presentation of the statue on 1 December, Elizabeth's strong wish for a private ceremony in the old Town Hall was observed, though this was followed by a short public ceremony at the site on Deansgate. The mayor and councillors were invited to attend after their council meeting, as well as a number of ladies and gentlemen, but there was a boycott by some of a Tory disposition.

Abel and Elizabeth Heywood were 'warmly applauded' when they took their seats on the platform of the large hall. Abel then, in Mrs Heywood's name, formally presented the statue to the city and thanked the Corporation. Elizabeth spoke at the Town Hall, where even the acerbic *City Jackdaw* conceded that 'the one tasteful speech of the occasion was made by Mrs. Heywood, who spoke with a touching modesty that was worthy of the personal fidelity and patriotic munificence of which the statue is the expression'. The article gave short shrift to the other speakers, and described Abel's words as 'windy jocosity'.[24] According to the news reports Elizabeth, perhaps significantly, did not once refer to Thomas Goadsby; she spoke eloquently about Cromwell, Manchester and the council, but not a word about the man whose wishes she was popularly said to be fulfilling. But the underlying theme of the rehabilitation of Cromwell that her gift symbolised was expressed most fully in the speech of Councillor Joseph Thompson, who gave a 'Non-Conformist history lesson' to address 'the popular criticisms of Cromwell'.[25]

At the second part of the ceremony, on Deansgate, where Elizabeth unveiled the statue, a large crowd gathered in the rain. They were apparently divided in their response to the monument, as both cheers and hisses were reportedly heard. The mayor, Tory Matthew Curtis, called for three cheers for the Queen and royal family, though whether this was to divert the thoughts of the crowd away from republicanism, or was itself a sort of protest, was not clear.

Even after the unveiling, the press were cynical. The *City Jackdaw* parodied the ceremony; in a mock report it was claimed that there had been plans for a procession of dignitaries, led by 'Abel Spare Bones' bearing the head of Charles I on a platter and leading over 10,000 republicans. This was followed by a skit where Abel and Joseph Heron, the town clerk, went down to Hades to interview Cromwell, only to find that he and King Charles had become the best of friends; the Protector suggesting that Manchester put up a statue to the King as well as himself.

The ripples continued; there was a fear that the statue might need physical protection, and plans were discussed in August 1876 to put up railings with lamps around it. Although it had represented the confidence of nonconformists in Manchester, 'a declaration in bronze of their beliefs and their power to shape the modern city', a hundred years later it was ignominiously demoted by the demands of modern traffic and placed in the park next to Wythenshawe Hall.[26]

Elizabeth's death

Elizabeth died aged 75 at home in Bowdon on 11 January 1887; the cause of death was recorded as 'Debility and Exhaustion (Gastric)' by Dr P.H. Mules. Her stepdaughter, Elizabeth Charlesworth, registered the death, having been present when it occurred. In her will, which she had drawn up in 1883, her personal estate was valued at over £38,764, making her a rich woman, as this was aside from her real estate holdings.

She continued what she had started in life by leaving charitable and artistic bequests. The Schools for the Deaf and Dumb received £200, as did Henshaw's Blind Asylum and St Mary's Hospital and Dispensary on Quay Street; the Governesses Institution benefited to the tune of £100; the Manchester Society for the Prevention of Cruelty to Animals was left £50. In demonstration of her commitment to women's rights, a further provision left £50 to her colleague in the women's movement, Lydia Becker. The Manchester National Society for Women's Suffrage met on 21 January and passed a resolution expressing their regret at her death and praising the public spirit she had shown in her benefactions for the city 'and in her uniform support of the movement for the enfranchisement of women'.[27] More notably, in accordance with her love of art, she left a handsome £500 to the Manchester Academy of Fine Arts, which she suggested should be invested and the interest and dividends be used for prizes. Three paintings, including a Rubens, were bequeathed to the Corporation of Salford, to be displayed in the Peel Park Museum. To Manchester Art Gallery she left paintings, a drawing, statuettes including two of carved ivory which had been shown at the 1857 Art Treasures Exhibition, and, true to the last to her parliamentary ancestry, a bronze of 'Oliver Cromwell viewing the dead body of Charles I'.

All this paled into insignificance when compared to her bequest of £10,000 to Owens College, to be invested and called the 'Elizabeth Salisbury Heywood Endowment'. The key point about this was that it must be used for the provision of instruction for women and girls in the college, or for helping women and girls to enter the college. The money was not to be paid over until women and girls were admitted, or until five years had elapsed, whichever was sooner. At that point it could be used as the governors saw fit, but it must be understood that 'in all cases it is her desire that… the income of the endowment shall at all times be used for the benefit of female students'. Elizabeth also left to Owens College white marble busts by Noble of herself, Thomas Goadsby and 'our late youngest daughter, Marianne Elizabeth Goadsby'. They were to remain in the college 'in perpetuity'.

She chose as her executors and trustees her husband, Abel, her friend John Hough of Chorlton Street, Manchester, a merchant (who in the end did not act), Abel's son George Washington, the barrister, and her nephew Leicester Collier, who was a lithographer. It was to the latter that she bequeathed property consisting of land, houses and buildings as well as rents in Chorlton-on-Medlock. He also received important items such as a silver cup which Thomas Goadsby had given to her, all her photographs, testimonials given to her and to Thomas by Manchester Corporation, silver plate, china, glass, Belique (given to her by Jane Trimble, Abel's daughter), and diaries of her father, her late husband and herself, along with her private papers, which have all sadly been lost to history. She also left Leicester a bequest which he may or may not have relished – 'all such dogs, parrots and other birds as may belong to me at the time of my death feeling assured that they will be carefully attended to by him my said nephew'. She presumably did not have the same confidence in her husband and his family to care for her pets! Touchingly, Leicester also was to have the title deed to the grave of Thomas Goadsby in Salford Cemetery 'and my desire is that such grave shall never hereafter be opened nor will have a body interred therein'.[28]

Her 'dear' husband, Abel, was bequeathed not only the emerald and diamond ring he had given to her before their marriage, but also a diamond and emerald bracelet which had been given to her by Mahomed Said, late Viceroy of Egypt. Although 'not wishing to influence him', she strongly suggested he pass the bracelet on to his son, Abel junior, in his lifetime or in his will.

Elizabeth, who clearly loved jewellery, left gifts of money or valuable jewels to Abel's children and grandchildren, as well as her clothes to Elizabeth Charlesworth and Constance Heywood, with the daunting provision that Abel should arbitrate if they could not agree on how to divide them. The more personal mementoes of her late husband and deceased child all went to her own or the Goadsby family. One aspect of the will worthy of remark is that the grandsons of the family were not mentioned at all; Abel junior's sons Abel and George Basil and Elizabeth Charlesworth's son Arthur were not included in the will, and nor were the three daughters of George Washington, who were very young. Perhaps Elizabeth's main focus was to give the older girls resources which might enhance their independence in the future. She certainly inserted a provision that any property she had left to any female should be 'for her sole and separate use and free from the debts, control or engagements of any husband to whom she is now or may at any time be married'.[29] The residue of her estate was to be divided between Leicester Collier and her husband, Abel Heywood, and after them their heirs.

The funeral was 'unostentatious' at the reported request of Elizabeth herself. As events turned out the cortège started off late over slippery roads and in heavy fog, which put the timetable out. Nevertheless, it was said that many hundreds of persons (although the *Manchester Guardian* said rather 'knots of people') lined the route through the city, who may not have seen very much as 'the vehicles in their passage presented but a shadowy appearance'. The members of the Corporation joined the cortege in Albert Square. There were four mourning coaches; in the first were Abel senior, Abel junior, Abel's elder brother, William, and a Mr Sewell. Also present were George Washington Heywood, John Hough (Elizabeth's friend and executor) and her nephew and heir, Leicester Collier. There was a strong representation from the Corporation, alongside representatives from the School of Art and the Queen's Park Museum.

In the presence of a large number of people, the service at the cemetery was conducted by Revd James Odgers who was the minister at Altrincham Unitarian church. Knowing Abel and Elizabeth personally as members of his congregation, his eulogy in the mortuary chapel was all the more powerful.[30] He summed up her loyalty as 'a Manchester woman'. There was a large number of wreaths placed on the coffin, including one from the servants at Summerfield.

Elizabeth and Abel were married for almost nineteen years, and all the evidence suggests that they shared many common interests and beliefs. The final six years or so of Abel's life, lived as a widower, though perhaps comforted by the presence in his house of his daughter Elizabeth and her children, must have been marked by this loss. The household in 1891 was tended by three servants all in their twenties, and a coachman and his wife.[31] However Abel had by now apparently also found an anchor in his Unitarian beliefs, which he and Elizabeth had shared, and he was a respected member of the Altrincham congregation until his death, when James Odgers officiated at his funeral.

Religion

In his obituary in the Unitarian magazine *The Inquirer* of 6 January 1894 Abel Heywood's Owenism in his early years was obliquely recalled: 'circumstances compelled him to throw in his lot with a party indifferent to theology, if not antagonistic, for this party only openly declared for the complete freedom which was a necessity of his existence'.[32] But the article went on to explain how eventually he 'found a congenial home among the Unitarians', although even here he was considered 'a kind of free-lance'.

He was tolerant of all religious groups. When the council voted to support equal rights for Jews in Britain, Abel personally proposed a petition that if elected to Parliament they should not be subject to taking the Christian oath, so that this obstacle to their participation in the political process should be removed.

The term 'free-lance' also reflected the way that Abel Heywood had a relaxed relationship with the Church of England. Not only was he a baptised member, but he also married twice in the Anglican church, and his eldest child was baptised in the same church in 1834. The Unitarians were more liberal and relaxed about beliefs than some of their fellow non-conformists and it was possible even to be a regular attender of another body and yet see oneself, and be seen by others, as a Unitarian. None of this prevented Abel from avowing a belief in disestablishmentarianism, made particularly plain in his speeches during the 1865 election campaign. He argued that he was not hostile to the Church of England, but that tithes were so unpopular that to disestablish it would have the effect of liberating it from the ill-feeling that was engendered. But the established Church was probably much too closely associated with the Tory elite for Abel to feel truly at ease within it.

From the 1840s, Abel was increasingly associated with the Unitarians, in particular with the chapel on Cross Street, spiritual home of many of Manchester's reforming middle class. Unitarianism was a form of Christianity which was regarded by many as extreme. In 1885 Joseph Chamberlain, MP for Birmingham, was denounced as a hater of Christianity because of his adherence. Nevertheless, in Manchester the Unitarians included many of the great city families, such as the

Potters, merchants in cotton, the Heywood bankers and John Edward Taylor of the *Manchester Guardian*.

The focus of the sect on educational and social improvement and political reform would have immediately appealed to Abel. Bebbington in his study also refers to the predilection of Unitarian MPs for retrenchment, free trade, peace abroad, the emancipation of slaves, support for persecuted minorities abroad and disestablishment. Temperance was increasingly favoured. Apart from a rejection of Trinitarianism, what particularly singled them out from other Christian groups was their commitment to removing restrictions on Sunday recreations. Abel's battles over bands and museums in the parks found much support in the Unitarian community; 'They drew the line that marked off the sacred from the secular much less narrowly than many of their contemporaries.'[33]

In 1850, in the company of the Cross Street ministers John Gooch Robberds and William Gaskell, Abel attended a meeting in the schoolroom under the Unitarian chapel in New Bridge Street, Strangeways where Dr Beard, the minister there, was presented with a testimonial. Abel was sufficiently 'well in' that he delivered one of the addresses supporting the presentation. During his time as mayor Abel took a great interest in the opening of a new Unitarian chapel for the poor in Miles Platting, presiding over the soiree which celebrated its inauguration on 15 June 1863. He was also apparently active in the Unitarian ministry to the poor and attended a meeting chaired by William Gaskell in May 1868. Meanwhile, two of his children were married in Unitarian chapels; in 1864 Elizabeth married John Charlesworth in the new Upper Brook Street chapel, with William Gaskell officiating, and in 1868 Abel junior married Catharine Johns Woolley in Strangeways chapel.

Abel must have begun his attendance at Cross Street as a non-member of the chapel, and this would have been at the evening service when the pews were open to all. However, from 1860 he paid a pew rent of six guineas a year, as well as giving subscriptions such as that of £5 on 30 June 1867, which may be presumed to be connected to the obsequies of his wife, Ann. As a pew-renter he could attend in the mornings when the pews were designated, and where he would use his own prayer and chant book stored in his pew, number eighty-four. The last recorded payment he made was in March 1871, and it seems that when he moved to Bowdon he ceased to rent a Cross Street pew.

It seems likely that he began to worship at the newly opened Altrincham Unitarian chapel, and indeed a seating plan of the chapel from 1881 shows that part of pew six and all of pew seven were designated 'Heywood'. This was a thriving time for the chapel, and during Abel's period there a schoolroom and chapel-keeper's house were constructed. It was not a large congregation, at seventy-four in 1897, but income in 1893 was £593 a year, of which half came from subscriptions by generous and wealthy members. A committee ran the chapel, made up of those who attended morning services, rented pews and gave donations. It is not certain whether Abel was on this body, but it seems likely as he was designated to chair the annual meeting of the Manchester District Unitarian Association in March 1887 when it met at the Dunham Road chapel; in the event he was ill and Mr Odgers stepped in. In 1882 James Edwin Odgers had been appointed minister; he was a distinguished scholar, and went on later to lecture in ecclesiastical history at Manchester College, Oxford. He stayed in Altrincham until October 1893, just long enough to be able to conduct Abel's funeral in August.

Abel's acceptance into Unitarianism marked another stage in his evolution into a middle-class Liberal radical; Unitarians in Manchester had a tradition of influence way beyond their numbers and as such gained a sort of respect from the rest of the community. Thus, when Abel was chosen by the council to be mayor of the city in 1862, and even more so in 1876, he was already part of a group which had become significant in city government, and it seems likely that his religious commitment may even have helped to smooth his path into the higher echelons of municipal power.

11

The Building of the New Town Hall

Give credit where credit is due.

The author of a great reformation is always unpopular in his own age. He generally passes his life in disquiet and danger. It is, therefore, for the interest of the human race that the memory of such men should be had in reverence, and that they should be supported against the scorn and hatred of their contemporaries by the hope of leaving a great and imperishable name. To go on the forlorn hope of truth is a service of peril – who will undertake it, if it be not also a service of honour? It is easy enough after the ramparts are carried to find men to plant the flag on the highest tower. The difficulty is to find men who are ready to go first into the breach.

Lord Macaulay
(Poster of 1877, signed J. Ashworth)[1]

At around £1m, Manchester's Town Hall turned out to be the world's most expensive building, being accounted 'unequalled for size, completeness and adaptability for its purpose among the municipal buildings of Europe'.[2] It is significant that Macaulay's words were chosen for a poster produced for the inauguration, and certainly true that in pushing forward the project Abel Heywood offended some and inconvenienced others, while also creating many friends among his contemporaries and admirers in posterity.

The idea

The germ of an idea for a new Town Hall had been taking root in the council for many years before it came to fruition, and from the 1850s Abel's voice had been prominent. As early as 1852, he had complained about the poor state of the council chamber in the old Town Hall, and at a dinner in New Cross ward in 1854 he spoke openly about a new Town Hall.

There can be little doubt that during his time as mayor in 1862–63 Abel used his position to push forward the Town Hall project. Initially the project to develop the Bancroft Street, Town Yard site into a fine 'Albert Square' was promoted by Abel and the Improvement Committee as a suitable setting for Thomas Goadsby's Prince Albert statue.[3] It was opposed by some because it was at the time 'an uncultivated city wilderness'. But Alderman Willert pointed out that it 'would also be very convenient for a new Town Hall'.

Abel presided over further discussion in the council in March 1863. Alderman Curtis, concerned about cost, also worried about the distance of the site from the main buildings of the city, centred as they were around the cathedral. On the other hand, Alderman Goadsby said he would be happy for the memorial to be in the new square if it were the prelude to the erection of 'a commodious town hall' in the vicinity. When it came to a vote, Abel as mayor used his casting vote to break a deadlock in favour of the Town Yard development.[4]

In September 1863 he was on record in the council stating that 'a new town hall had become an absolute necessity, not only for the due transaction of business, but to sustain the character of the city. (Hear.) The municipal accommodation was, for the size of the city, perhaps the most inferior of any in the kingdom.' His ally, Thomas Goadsby, backed him up in claiming that a suitable city hall would save the council about £2,000 a year in rent, though he put his finger on the fears of many councillors that the ratepayers were already 'excessively burdened'. Abel blithely 'believed that a plan could be devised that would raise the funds without seriously taxing the inhabitants. (Hear.)'[5]

As soon as he had completed his mayoral year, on 25 November 1863 Abel proposed that a sub-committee of the General Purposes Committee be established with an initial remit to consider the whole proposal. He himself would chair it, and it also included an impressive eight aldermen and two councillors.

The site

The project was contentious from the start and, with city land at a premium, the exact choice of site was predictably the next area of debate. Although Albert was to be placed in Bancroft Street on the promise of a grand square, matters did not move quickly; even the paving of Albert Square did not begin until April 1867. In August 1864 Abel proposed that Albert Square be adopted as the site for the new Town Hall. However, he was accused of having interests in a company formed to build warehouses near Albert Square, probably the Manchester Shipping Offices and Packing Company Limited. He claimed ignorance of this and passed over it quickly, a response which may have been somewhat lacking in honesty. The contention that councillors would vote for the site nearest to their own premises was likewise dismissed in his case, as his business was nearer to another suggested site, Piccadilly, than to Albert Square. As was his wont in such discussions, he had done his homework and produced figures comparing the sizes of the sites and the distances from premises such as banks and other public institutions that would need to do business at the Town Hall. He pointed out that it was not a good idea for all public buildings to be in the same place, and that to put the new building next to the classical facade of the Infirmary would produce a clash of architectural styles. Moreover, it would be inexpedient to place it on the busiest thoroughfare. He acknowledged that Princess Street would have to be widened, but made a virtue of this opening up of the surrounding area. Having 'one great square and one great building' would, he argued, create 'an additional lung for the great city'.

The contention by Alderman Curtis, speaking for an hour and a half in even greater detail, was that a Piccadilly site was preferable because it was nearer to most places of business. He also inadvertently caused amusement when he added that most of those committed in the police courts, which were expected to be in the new Town Hall, lived near to Piccadilly. Alderman Grundy responded: 'Alderman Curtis had argued in favour of placing the hall in the most accessible place for the criminal population, as if their convenience should be specially consulted in order that they might have as short a walk as possible. (Laughter.).' Abel won by one vote the power to continue with the Bancroft Street site through an Act of Parliament. The meeting had lasted a gruelling five hours.[6]

Another sub-committee of the General Purposes Committee was set up specifically to oversee the Town Hall project; its chairman was Abel Heywood and it included ex-officio the mayor, five further aldermen and eight councillors, a high-powered body indeed. Its report was presented at the council meeting of 6 February 1867. They had been asked to consider a suggestion by Alderman King for an extension of the site, and also whether the new building should provide for courts and the transaction of 'police business'. The sub-committee rejected both, in the case of the latter due to the 'nuisance' which these courts occasioned wherever they were held.[7]

Relations between the sub-committee and some on the council were soured over the issue of whether the site should be extended. In his speech to move the adoption of the report, Abel complained that there had been memorials and public meetings on the subject which had been 'worked by the agency of Councillor King'. At one meeting which Abel had attended, he saw that the latter 'stood behind the chairman like a prompter behind the scenes of a theatre. (Laughter.)' He also claimed that many present 'who rarely took part in the public proceedings of the town … seemed to have been resuscitated by the galvanic battery of Mr. King'. Councillor King defended his position and argued that he only wanted to improve the shape of the building from its current 'flat-iron' delineations and ensure that its approaches were fitting so that the council might be encouraged 'to make a Town-hall worthy of the city be the cost what it may'.[8]

The discussions became heated, and at one point the mayor, refusing to adjourn the vote, 'begged that gentlemen would take their seats, and allow the debate to proceed'. Finally, with misgivings on the part of many as to the size of the site and the adequacy of provision for the future, the council voted by thirty-seven to eighteen to accept the sub-committee's report. Abel had won the battle, for now.[9] The following month the council began the process of inviting architects to enter a competition for the honour of designing the municipal palace. Even then the question of the site was not allowed to rest. It was raised again in April 1868 when, in a vituperative debate, Alderman King lost his temper, claiming that the mayor was attempting to 'dictate to and overrule the Council'. He was forced to withdraw his comments and his proposal was soundly defeated by thirty-four to fourteen.[10] The site would be triangular.

The competition

It having been resolved as early as December 1866 that the design of the new Town Hall would be decided by an open competition, in March 1867 the council approved the specifications presented by the General Purposes Committee and drawn up by Abel Heywood and his committee for architects entering the competition. The first stage competition required the preparation of plans for the elevations to Albert Square, Princess Street and Cooper Street and for the ground floor and the principal (first) floor of the building. The whole was to have a basement and four storeys above. The grand main entrance would be on Albert Square. The council would select between six and twelve plans to go forward; the chosen architects would prepare complete drawings and costings and from them one would be employed as the architect of the building. All the architects in the second stage were to receive £300 for their work.

On 12 March 1867 the town clerk issued a set of detailed specifications to the architects with a deadline for submission of plans on 1 July, which was later altered to 5 August on the request of some competitors. The architects were instructed to make full provision for a large hall for meetings, mayoral accommodation in terms of reception rooms and private quarters, a council chamber, committee rooms, provision for the Town Clerk's, Treasurer's, City Surveyor's and Chief Constable's departments, and offices for the city's administrative departments plus lavatories, muniment rooms and accommodation for the head porter. Requests for space for a free reference library were not included. There was a suggested limit of £250,000 for the cost of the building but it was not rigid. Each architect chose a nickname or symbol by which they would be known to the judges, so that there could be no accusations of bias. The competition was fierce and 137 designs were submitted by 123 competitors from Manchester and elsewhere, including London. The sub-committee acquired the services of Mr Godwin, editor of *The Builder* magazine, to help with the adjudication.

On 17 September the town clerk issued further instructions to those eight architects who had made it through to the second round. They included local architect Thomas Worthington, who had designed the Albert Memorial and the

Unitarian Memorial Hall built in Albert Square in 1866. Also among their number were Speakman and Charlesworth (who submitted two designs, one Gothic and one Italian); John Charlesworth was Abel's son-in-law, married to his daughter Elizabeth. The architects were allowed to ask questions for further information, which Joseph Heron, the town clerk, recorded. Their deadline was 14 February 1868, and the designs were put on public display in the old Town Hall. To facilitate comparison of the designs Heron created a chart showing what allotment of space each architect had made for each department.

The final judgement was informed by the advice of a classicist, Professor Donaldson, and a leading expert on the Gothic style, George Edmund Street. Four entries were favoured: those of Speakman and Charlesworth, J. O. Scott (son of the architect George Gilbert Scott), Thomas Worthington and the London architect Alfred Waterhouse, who was already responsible for the design of the Manchester Assize Courts. Worthington and Waterhouse had met the cost limits, and the judges thought the latter's plan superior, although there were voices in the Manchester press who preferred local man Worthington. On 1 April 1868 it was announced that 'St Valentine', Alfred Waterhouse, had won the competition and would be building the Town Hall in his splendid Gothic design. However, Abel did remind the council that they had the right to take ideas from other plans 'without being under any obligation to the unsuccessful architect'.[11] Indeed the modification of plans for the tower was heavily influenced by the work of Waterhouse's rival, Thomas Worthington.

Construction

The newspapers contained minute descriptions of the proposed accommodation and features of the building, and this was clearly a project which excited the municipal pride of the middle classes who read them. The *Manchester Courier* believed it would 'probably prove the most important municipal building in the kingdom'. It would cover over 80,000 square yards of land, and contain over 250 rooms, of which forty-seven would be allotted to the mayor, the council committees and the public, 136 would be occupied by departments of the Corporation, and about seventy would be undesignated.

The main builders of the new Town Hall were Messrs George Smith and Co. of London, who had already been responsible for the construction of the new Houses of Parliament. Mayor Robert Neill laid the foundation stone at the base of the great tower on Albert Square on 26 October 1868. The event began with a procession from the old Town Hall, in which the great and the good of both the city and the county, led by the police band, participated. It was watched by a large number of ordinary citizens and also better off ticket-holders in reserved spaces, including covered enclosures for 1,000 ladies. The *Manchester Guardian* provided a more critical account than the other papers, being somewhat disappointed that the preparations were 'not very extensive' with 'a few flags' flying, but generally 'little attempt at decoration'. On arriving in Albert Square, 'The order of the procession was not well observed, and there was some confusion around the chief centre of attraction before the proceedings began.' For the *Manchester Courier* the mayor was the star of the show but Abel Heywood also had his moment as chair of the sub-committee, and spoke of his hope that the building they were about to erect would 'at least be a monument to the greatness of Manchester for all time to come'. He went on to assure his hearers that the Corporation was mindful of the cost to the ratepayers, and that they would not 'recklessly spend the money of the people'. The sub-committee had prepared a bottle (which must have been very large) which was placed by Mr Lynde, the city surveyor, in the cavity under the foundation stone. It contained copies of Manchester and London newspapers, current coins of the realm, an account of the day's proceedings, a list of the Corporation officers, and a copy of the Corporation Manual, presumably in the hope that if in some distant time it were rediscovered, the future citizens of Manchester might enjoy reading about the splendours of Victorian municipal government. The cavity was covered with an engraved plaque recording the occasion and the names of Mayor Robert Neill, chairman of the new Town Hall sub-committee Abel Heywood, town clerk Joseph Heron and architect Alfred Waterhouse.

Abel next produced a special trowel designed by Waterhouse, made of silver and engraved with a view of the Town Hall, and presented it to Robert Neill on behalf of the Corporation. The mayor laid the stone, hit it twice on each corner with a mallet, and was given three cheers led by Abel for his efforts. He then spoke truer than he knew: 'When the future historian came to write the history of this city he would not omit to mention the transaction in which they were engaged that morning.'

The ceremony was followed by a lunch for 170 gentlemen at the old Town Hall, where there were further speeches, including one in which Abel responded to the toast of banker Oliver Heywood with 'an elaborate history of the progress of the work' which was understandably not recorded in detail by the weary reporters.[12]

The Town Hall Committee, also overseeing the construction of the new Police Court, faced numerous tribulations. Dealing with building workers proved to be quite a challenge. In April 1869 a general stonemasons strike broke out when the employers refused to accede to a request for a reduction in summer of six working hours a week and 1s pay, of which they had been given six months' notice. A few of the masters had agreed, and they were unaffected by the strike. But for the Town Hall it meant that construction was slower than hoped, and the works were short of men. The masons were soon joined by the bricklayers and the plasterers, and as a result of the disruption to work many employers had put joiners on short time as well.

When Alfred Waterhouse reported to the New Town Hall Committee on 26 August, he made the best of the situation, stating that the foundations of the Town Hall, in the hands of Messrs Clay & Sons, were 'progressing in as satisfactory a manner as considering the strike of the masons, could be expected'. There were about eighty masons employed at that time on the works, and they were increasing that number, using blackleg labour.[13] On Saturday 7 August a great demonstration of about 4,000 trades unionists was organised in Manchester in support of the strikers. But by the end of September there were 114 men and boys employed and it was anticipated that the work would speed up.

During October a memorial was presented to the mayor by several trade unions about 'the conduct of the public works of the city' and the reasons for the slow pace of the work. It was also reported in the local press. They believed that only about ten employers were holding out against the terms offered by the strikers, but chief among these were the contractors for the public works in the city 'immediately under the control of the city council'. Claiming that most masons in Manchester and elsewhere were now working under the new terms, they implied that the public contractors were out on a limb. They therefore appealed to the council to put pressure on the contractors to settle with the unions.[14]

The impact of the masons' discontent emerged more clearly at the council meeting of 1 December. At that meeting, Abel claimed that recruitment was so successful that in the last two or three weeks there had been so many applicants for work on site that they had turned many away. He now also felt it his 'duty' to present a memorial given to him six weeks earlier in October by the workers to take to the council. He stated that the memorial had been presented by 'working men, or the friends of working men' (he had not checked the names), and he appealed to the workers to exercise an influence to stop the strike as a matter of public duty.

In his explanation to the council, Abel showed a remarkable hostility towards those who had taken industrial action, and although he had previously on occasion doubted the validity and the effectiveness of trade unions, his handling of the matter is surprisingly harsh for one who claimed identity with the working classes; his attitude can perhaps be explained by his passionate concern for the progress of the Town Hall. He thought that those masons who had gone on strike 'were not at work, and he believed also that they would have to leave Manchester in order to get work... Probably they would have to emigrate to distant lands in order to find employment.' He believed that they had sacrificed their own interests and those of their families by taking on a fight they could not win. He said that the main aim of the memorial was to persuade the council to employ 'a class of men [presumably agitators] whom the contractors did not consider it their duty to employ'. Had they complied, the employers throughout the country would have looked on them with 'thorough disgust'. The council moved no resolution on this memorial, accepting Abel's statement that the case had been dealt with.[15]

But the matter was not allowed to die. The workers reiterated their case in a letter from the masons' committee to the *Manchester Courier* three days later. They were very critical of how Abel had handled the issue, saying that 'evidently he is not fond of much trouble, for he did not scrutinise the names of the parties who signed the memorial...' Complaining that he implied they should 'submit tamely to every innovation that greed, avarice, and a desire for self-aggrandisement on the part of our employers could suggest', they expressed their own abhorrence of strikes, but said that this had been the only way to escape from 'bondage and serfdom' and gain the privileges they now enjoyed, 'and if Mr. Alderman Heywood can point even to the smallest of those privileges as being the spontaneous gift of the employers, and not the result of a strike, or the dread of incurring one, we will not only cease the practice but for ever ignore the strike law'.

The letter went on to assert that Abel was wrong to say the strikers were not at work, and that in fact over 300 of them were employed 'on the terms we demand' and they would continue to prosecute the claims of those still on strike when the spring came.[16] In the event, relations settled down, but there was further trouble with strikers during the final stages of construction. The plumbers and other workers came out in April 1876, as did the joiners in May 1877, but these disputes were relatively easily resolved.

Industrial strife was not the only headache for the committee; there was at least one serious accident on the site. On 25 January 1872 a certain Veevers, the driver of a travelling crane on one of the lower tiers of rails at the Mount Street end of the Town Hall site, was lifting a block of stone with the engine. The structure collapsed and heavy metal and woodwork fell on him. He suffered a fractured leg and had to be cut out. He was taken to the Infirmary, and it is not known whether he recovered. However, such occurrences were not considered to be the responsibility of the employer, and were usually found to be unfortunate accidents, so that the repercussions of such an event were not a serious problem for the Town Hall sub-committee.

A further issue concerned contracts. In June 1872 Waterhouse recommended that Smith and Co. be asked to give prices for the completion of the Town Hall, and that their quote should be accepted without requesting estimates from other companies, as long as the prices were reasonable. The aim was to save time, perhaps as much as a year. The eventual response of the committee was to take his advice and ask Smiths for a quotation. Almost a week later, at a meeting of the council, Councillor Stewart put up a forceful challenge to the decision to use Smith's for the rest of the contract. He estimated that they might charge an extra £40,000 or £50,000 to the council for the work.

Abel defended the decision of the committee to go along with the views of Waterhouse, particularly arguing that the difference in tender suggested by Councillor Stewart (which he questioned) would be offset by the cost of time lost in waiting for another tender. However, he was defeated by thirty votes to twenty and the council voted for a competitive tender. This victory was exploited by Councillor Stewart in seeking re-election to the council, stating to his constituents that he had saved Manchester £30,000. Abel took exception to this as reflecting on the honour of the General Purposes committee, arguing that it had frustrated the progress of the works at the Town Hall; a delay which meant paying out more interest on loans. This time the council supported the committee.

But Alderman Bennett on 5 February 1873 attacked Waterhouse for treating the council with 'contempt', and suggesting that if he could not prepare the information for the tenders then he should resign and they could get another architect. Abel wearily repeated his point about saving time, and said that, 'The council if they passed that amendment, must take the responsibility upon themselves, and off the shoulders of the Sub-committee.' They passed the amendment.[17]

What underlay all this angst in the council was the spiralling cost of the new Town Hall. The architect had originally submitted plans which were within a budget of £350,000, but by 1873 Abel was stating that, with the land added on, it would now be £750,000, due to interest payable and greatly increased labour and materials' costs, attributable to inflation. Councillor Thompson added that the design had been modified by the selectors, such as that the tower was to be higher and of a different character, and Waterhouse himself had said that these changes would raise the cost to £300,000. Ultimately, when Smiths completed their work in August 1875, they were looking at a loss because of inflation; labourers' wages had risen by 17.5 per cent since 1870, the cost of timber by 25 per cent and coke by 350 per cent, for example. Therefore, it was agreed by the sub-committee and confirmed by the council (against the objections of Councillor Stewart) that the company would be paid an extra £38,000 for work carried out which had not been in the original contract, plus 28 per cent on that amount to take account of the inflation in the prices of labour and materials since the original quotations were drawn up.

Not surprisingly, Abel and his committee were beginning to feel under siege over the issue of contracts and costs. In July he complained to the council that there had been attempts to damage the committee in the eyes of the ratepayers when it was claimed that by opening the next contracts up to tender, a saving of £50,000 had been made by 'certain gentlemen' who 'had no lack of trumpeters of their praise'. The new contracts had been awarded, not to Smith's, but to Messrs Clay & Sons. Abel conceded that £21,000 was the difference between the contracts. But he contended that 'The Committee... had acted fairly and honourably throughout; and it was most unfair to try to destroy the confidence the Council had in it by making representations which the facts did not bear out.' The proponents of competition do not appear to have been impressed, and Alderman Curtis hoped that in future the council would insist on it for every contract.[18]

In 1873 the issue of library accommodation was re-opened. In response to requests for somewhere to put the free reference library, Waterhouse had found rooms at the very top of the Town Hall, accessed by 120 steps! The writer and poet Councillor Ben Brierley related in May 1876 how a group of councillors had undertaken an 'expedition' to explore the 'mysterious regions of the carillons' of the new Town Hall, in an attempt to reach the rooms suggested for the library. 'The whole party commenced the ascent of the stairs at the same time, but, like amateur mountaineers climbing Ben Lomond, they gradually became separated – some hanging on here and there by a balustrade, and others trying to emulate the pranks of their boyish days by a grotesque attempt to look nimble. (Laughter.)'[19] The library discussions continued and were not settled till the state of the Campfield building became so precarious in 1877 that Abel Heywood as mayor gave the library the use of the old Town Hall, and the matter was settled for over thirty years.

Moreover, in April 1873 the General Purposes Committee was asked to look into the possibility of putting an art gallery in the unappropriated spaces in the new Town Hall. It seemed as though it was hoped to remedy every perceived lack in the city at minimal expense by provision in the new building. Abel voiced his opposition to this; he was of the view that 'a building which was intended and required for municipal purposes was not adapted to the purposes of an art gallery'. The change was voted down, probably much to Abel's relief.[20]

By April 1874, the external building was almost complete, with only the towers on Albert Square and Cooper Street to be finished. Over 1,000 men had been employed on the work at any one time. The *Manchester Courier* published a detailed description of the whole building inside and out. It also added the critical comment that the main entrance was 'low and wanting in dignity', though this was not a view shared by other observers. However, the stone groining in the ground floor corridors was said 'by contrast of colour' to 'produce a very pleasing effect'. The description was liberally sprinkled with words like 'handsome' and 'magnificent'. The article also included a list of the materials used with the cubic feet of each, and described the machinery and plant used in the construction; notably, eight steam saw frames were worked day and night for over two years.[21]

At the General Purposes Committee meeting of 1 July 1875 Abel was no doubt pleased to announce that the Waterworks Committee's rooms would be ready on the 10th, and the Gas Committee's a very short time afterwards. He showed exemplary patience when Councillor Batty urged they should use even 'greater expedition' in preparing the latter, and asked how the new suites of rooms were to be approached; Abel (probably gritting his teeth) said 'the question of a proper approach had not escaped the attention of the committee, and they had made the necessary arrangements'.[22]

The bells and the clock

Late in April 1875 the sub-committee had asked the architect to get estimates for a clock, dial and bells. Abel and his colleagues had visited Bradford Town Hall and Worcester Cathedral to see their bells, and helped by Sir Becket Dennison they had selected those of the best quality from Messrs Taylor & Sons of Loughborough. After the visit to Worcester and its twelve bells, they began to consider increasing the Town Hall peal from eight to ten. Abel was convinced that such a peal could be used 'on many occasions in the future history of Manchester'. A wit suggested 'At elections', and Abel added 'on her Majesty's birthday'. With an eye to posterity the committee decided to increase the number to sixteen for a carillon to play twenty-five tunes: 'in a building which was to last for centuries… they should make the best arrangements for the occupation of the tower'. In the end, to complete the bells for the carillon, the sub-committee ordered four more, to reach a grand total, including the striking bell, of twenty-one bells weighing over thirty-one tons.[23] On Waterhouse's suggestion, lines selected from Tennyson's *In Memoriam*, along with the initials of a member of the Corporation, were inscribed on each of the bells. They were detailed in W.E.A. Axon's *Architectural and General Description of the Town Hall, Manchester*, published by Abel Heywood in 1878. The quotations were apparently selected by Joseph Thompson, but it is hard to imagine that Abel did not at least concur with the evocative inscription on his own bell, Great Abel: 'Ring out the false, ring in the true.'

The objections, which Abel tried to forestall by a careful and lengthy explanation, were not slow in coming. Councillor Stewart 'objected to the introduction of what was practically a huge barrel organ in the New Town Hall tower'. He argued that 'In the bustle of the day the chimes would never be heard in Manchester.' In Gradgrindian manner he opined that music was foreign to the purposes of the Town Hall, which was a place of business. Then he raised the question of the cost.

Some of the council enjoyed the comedy in the idea of a carillon. Councillor Bright wanted to know what sort of tunes would be played: 'what would Mr. Alderman Heywood suggest as those to which business men would be the better for listening – "Poor Old Joe" and similar stirring melodies? (Laughter).' Councillor Walker suggested 'Champagne Charlie' and 'Not for Joseph?' The atmosphere was, for once, lightened by the introduction of these music hall hits; the vote went in favour of the carillon.[24]

Even after the Town Hall had been officially opened in September 1877, there were aspects which were incomplete, and of these the carillon and the clock caused the most comment, being perhaps most obvious to the voting public. By the new year of 1878, although the clock was still awaiting completion, the carillon was finally working. Crowds gathered to hear it play, although at times the noise of traffic drowned it out. When snow deadened the latter, 'the music was exquisitely sweet and wonderfully clear over a wide area'. The hour bell, 'Big [later Great] Abel' was heard as far away as Withington, due to its great elevation, though less well in the city itself.[25]

The final stages of construction

The *Manchester Guardian* of 21 July 1875 was fulsome in its praise of Waterhouse's achievement so far; the exterior 'makes up a picture on which the eye dwells with delight'. Inside 'one is amazed and charmed with the simplicity of a design which is combined with such elaborate richness of ornamentation'. This report was full of praise for the entrance, which was achieved with 'eminent success'. Considerable interest was shown in the bells, and it was reported that the largest at seven tons would peal the hour and the carillon would play thirty-one tunes on seventeen bells, with a fresh tune every day of the month. It would have barrels for changes, similar to ringing a peal, and an ivory keyboard so that the carillon could be played. The view from the top of the tower was assessed, particularly with regard to the overview it lent of the city's layout. Among the coats of arms carved around the building, the report noted that Abel Heywood (typically) had sited his own over the servants' entrance on Princess Street.

The interior was described in full detail, and many features caused wonder, notably the mosaic floors, created by workmen brought from Italy 'of whom a small colony has been established in the building'. The building was also functional and never more so than in the rooms for the Chief of Police, Captain Palin, who in addition to his offices was provided with 'a number of cells… for the safe detention of prisoners'. The public hall was not as yet decorated and had empty niches for statues and an apse for an organ. The council chamber would be reminiscent of the House of Commons, with the mayor's chair on a dais at the north end and a gallery for reporters above, though there was some concern about the room's acoustic properties.

By October the building work was drawing to a close and most tradesmen were engaged in the 'finishing operations'. The tower was reaching its top storey, and on 4 December Abel, as chair of the sub-committee, was invited to place the top stone of the tower, at a height of 285 feet 6 inches. Despite now being 65 years old, he gamely agreed and climbed up the scaffolding to the top. Although the papers in general did not make a great deal of this, it gave the satirical journal the *City Jackdaw* the opportunity for some fun and a poem, 'Alderman Heywood: Excelsior', which concluded:

> About the time when dinner-ward
> The folks in the surrounding ward
> Were hurrying for the mid-day meal,
> There on the summit reached at last,
> He proudly cried, all perils past,
> With joy he tried not to conceal-
> Excelsior![26]

Not to be outdone, just after Christmas Mayor Curtis climbed to the top to place on its pinnacle a golden ball topped with a spike serving as a lightning conductor. While sitting up there, he apparently wrote a telegram. He and Abel were joshed for their exploits in the council, and their agility was compared favourably to that of the fat old councillors who made the expedition to the proposed library the following May.

Artistic decoration

The committee got a rough ride in March 1876 with regard to the decoration in the building. At the council meeting of 1 March they were taken to task for not offering the decorative work on the ceilings in open competition in Manchester. Alderman Grave defended the use of 'special men to do special work', and in response to a complaint by Councillor Stewart, Joseph Thompson had to justify fees paid to Waterhouse as a commission on the special work, on the grounds that he 'would engage the best men to do the work required in the best manner'.[27] Then Abel waded in to support his colleagues, and added pointedly that 'while the sub-committee had entire confidence in the architect, he thought the council should have confidence in the committee'. He added that 'the remark made by Mr. Stewart was most ungenerous'. The critics were again silenced, for now.[28]

However, the wider public took an interest in this issue, and took exception to the idea that Manchester artisans were not up to the job of special decorations. On 7 March the *Manchester Courier* published a letter from 'A Practical Man' in support of Councillor Stewart and the other detractors, and describing the decision about the ceilings as 'the squandering of the ratepayers' money'. He argued that it was not special work and that there were tradesmen in the city who were well capable of doing it. Indeed, he made the cogent point that he had seen 'one or two of the worthy aldermen on the platform advocating scientific and technical instruction to our youth, and yet they show their inconsistency in what they advocate by sending work out of Manchester which could be executed as well by an apprentice or an art student under the guidance of an experienced architect or designer'. It was indeed true that Abel himself had been a keen proponent of local skills, and did not seem to be putting his ideals into practice. The Practical Man ended with a strongly worded reminder that the electors would have their say about such 'incompetence' and 'wasteful expenditure' at the next municipal elections.[29]

Likewise, the murals continued to excite discussion. It had been explained in January 1876 that paintings on the wall panels in the public hall would be commissioned, and the suggested theme at this point was 'the pastimes of England'. They were to be painted at a very reasonable price of £150 per panel by Henry Stacy Marks, then painting murals at Eaton Hall. However, Marks withdrew when his work was not definitely accepted. Frederic Shields and Ford Madox Brown, one of the great Pre-Raphaelite painters of the day, by June 1877 had agreed to undertake the work. In August a deputation from the Manchester Academy of Fine Arts pressed that the murals, apart from those in the public hall, should be done by Lancashire artists and that the artist J.D. Watson should oversee the work. Waterhouse considered their intervention 'rude and uncalled for', and Brown's reaction was even more hostile and offensive: 'It was one thing for us to work in company with some of the finest artists in the country, and another to form part of the group of nobodies such as there was talk of giving the rest to... Waterhouse agreed to state to the committee that should they insist on giving the other rooms to these Manchester beginners it was likely I would refuse to co-operate.'[30]

The public hall murals were not begun until April 1879. Shields withdrew and Brown carried on the work until 1893; the twelve panels of the public hall became the most famous of the wall-paintings. The work in some other rooms was never achieved, despite Waterhouse's dogged campaigning almost to the end of his professional career; he was still writing to the mayor about it as late as 1895.

Brown agreed to do all twelve panels in the public hall at an initial cost of £275 each, which was raised to £375 by the council in 1884, when Abel argued that his work, considered to be very good indeed, had been undervalued, and that there were difficulties created by the usage of the building and the inconvenience of the public peeping in. An attempt was made to give the artist some privacy by the erection of a canvas booth around him which he said he found 'very comfortable'.[31]

The subjects were supposedly celebrating Manchester's proud history, but in some cases the 'history' was more mythological than factual, as W.E.A. Axon was at pains to point out. Brown, a radical sympathiser, had hoped that Peterloo would form the climax of the series, but this was quashed by the Decorations and Furnishings Sub-committee and the opening of the Bridgewater Canal was substituted. It is not recorded how Abel and his allies felt about the omission of one of the fundamental events of radical Manchester. Even Brown's handling of the new topic did not please some of the council, because as a populist he focused overmuch on the bargee's wife and children. Some panels were not related directly to Manchester's history – the baptism of Edwin took place in York, but it was used to show the Christian heritage of the city. The council were unaware, according to Joseph Thompson who played a big part in overseeing the work, that the last panel painted, Bradshaw's Civil War defence of Manchester, was executed after Brown had suffered a stroke and lost the use of his right hand. The work lasted in total fourteen years; it was Brown's last big commission and he died soon after completing it in 1893, much affected by criticisms of the murals. He was not to know that his murals 'may have established the city fathers as "admired leaders of public art patronage" [Balshaw]'.

The organ

By late summer 1874 it was being mooted that the building should have an organ. The original plan for the Town Hall had not included this, and the decision to accommodate one in the public hall posed some issues. The physicist James Prescott Joule was of the opinion that the recess Waterhouse had created was too small for even the smallest organ, and the architect was obliged to revise his plans. Even so, the organ although complete, could not be very large. The stops were carefully considered to allow of the greatest variety by the builder from Paris, Monsieur Cavaillé-Coll. It was finished before the rest of the hall, and even its platform was 'in a very rough state' just before it was given its first hearing on 18 July 1877. It was played on this occasion by noted organist William Thomas Best in a concert attended by an invited audience of councillors, their friends, musicians and the press. The verdict was that the organ, shown off through a variety of music including Bach,

Sterndale-Bennett, Smart and of course the national anthem, was on the whole very fine and powerful with some 'specially pure and effective' softer stops.

The question of appointing a permanent organist became a focus of debate and in October 1877 Abel was keen to take on James Kendrick Pyne, organist of Manchester Cathedral for at least a temporary contract of six months. He would be expected in that time to give around forty performances and would be remunerated at £100. By the end of March 1878, the six-month tenure of Mr Pyne as Town Hall organist was coming to an end and there was a lively debate as to whether there should be a change of musician for this post. Abel chaired the General Purposes Committee on 28 March when the discussion became heated. Some councillors wanted to offer it to Mr Best; it seems that Abel had prevented his appointment in the first place saying his salary, at £300, would be prohibitively expensive. Joseph Thompson implied that he had not been above board in this, as the sum was based on Mr Best's salary at Liverpool for three concerts a week, whereas he was only expected to perform one in Manchester. Abel got his way; it was agreed that Mr Pyne should continue in post, but Mr Best had agreed to give one recital, and other luminaries of the organ were to be invited from around the country to perform from time to time.

By 1880 it seems that Sabbatarianism, so successful in preventing bands in the parks on Sundays in the 1850s, was being questioned in the council, and it was strongly argued that there should be weekly Town Hall organ recitals of sacred music on Sunday afternoons for the edification of the working classes. Abel spoke up in favour of the proposal. 'He contended that this would be another means of increasing the musical tendencies of the working population of Manchester, and that the performances of sacred music on a Sunday within the walls of the Town hall was no greater evil against society than having music at home or in church.' But he added that since the large room only held up to 1,000 persons, admission would have to be by ticket, and it might be necessary to adopt a minimum age for the admission of Sunday scholars. When it came to a vote there was a draw; the mayor decided to use his casting vote against, to maintain the status quo.[32] Sabbatarianism was still a force to be reckoned with.

The first council meeting

Towards the end of 1876, at the beginning of Abel's second tenure as mayor, the contractors were close to finishing the town clerk's rooms, had completed the mayor's room and begun the 'fitting-up' of the council chamber. There was some comment in the General Purposes Committee that the wallpapers used were 'so dark that they could scarcely see anything in the rooms'. Abel promised tersely that he would talk to the architect.[33]

The council met in its new chamber for the first time on 7 February 1877 when 'aldermen and councillors alike comfortably and without ceremony settled down in their splendidly cushioned seats'. It seems that Abel was not in the best of health at this time as the report states that it was feared that he 'left his home to attend the meeting at some risk to his health', but he was not going to miss this occasion and accompanied by his wife Elizabeth, who sat in the ladies' gallery, he was well received. A large number of ratepayers also gained tickets to attend in the strangers' gallery. Perhaps aware of earlier news comments, Alfred Waterhouse was present 'anxious, no doubt, to test the acoustic properties of the council chamber'; presumably there was no issue, as he was reported to have been complimented on all hands on 'what must be regarded as the handsomest municipal council chamber in the kingdom'.[34]

Despite his indisposition, Abel did not miss the chance to make a speech, and reminded the council of how far they had come since 1842 when the Commissioners of Police had controlled the use of the old Town Hall. He also discussed the growth of the Corporation; in 1842 it had seventy-seven employees (excluding the gas company) and now, in 1877, it had nearly 3,000, carrying out a vastly extended municipal role. He referred to the heavy duties to which the councillors had shown dedication over the years, and particularly to the work throughout of the town clerk, Joseph Heron.

Naming the 'municipal palace'

One question which took up a large amount of council time as the new building neared completion was what it should be called. It seems that to begin with it was taken for granted that it would be called the 'Town Hall' as had the old one on King Street, but in the 1870s voices were raised arguing that the centre of government of a great city like Manchester should have a grander name. In any case, the thinking was that 'town' had referred to the township of Manchester, but now it was a city which included a number of townships.

Joseph Heron seems to have started the ball rolling at the beginning of July 1874 when he asked the General Purposes Committee to consider calling the building the Guild Hall. Nothing further was said until 1876 when the departments were planning to move into their offices and Alfred Waterhouse recommended that it be called the City Hall, and this was moved on behalf of the New Town Hall Committee in the General Purposes Committee by Abel Heywood, in a manner which the *Manchester Courier* described as 'half-hearted'. He said:

> he had no particular liking for one name over another. He had been long accustomed to town-halls, and, as a matter of taste, he should have preferred town-hall to city-hall. But… Manchester now became better known as a city than as a town, and it was on that account that he proposed that the new hall should be called the City-hall, as preferable to the Town-hall.

There were long and impassioned speeches for and against, citing historic prec-edence and linguistic origins, as well as a letter from the Bishop of Manchester.[35] When the council reconvened, Joseph Thompson introduced yet another possibil-ity – Corporation Hall – but this was treated as a joke and provoked 'great laughter'. The decision was still not taken when they met on 5 July and the speeches were even longer than before. There was a lot of interest in what was denoted by a 'guild' and Abel commented that the discussion was 'more fitted for a debating club than for the Manchester City Council'.[36] At the start of August, the council, having already rejected Guild Hall, chose the title of City Hall on the casting vote of the mayor, and indeed this was the designation used in the press for a while.

The question was re-opened for the last time at the first council meeting held in the new Town Hall on 7 February 1877. Alderman Willert moved that the decision to name the building as the City Hall be rescinded, but some councillors were unwilling to discuss this as it could engender ill-feeling and they were about to have lunch together. Mayor Abel Heywood said that he 'had been made acquainted with the fact that there was a decided majority in favour of retaining the old name of Town Hall'. He therefore seconded the resolution. As had been feared, the discussion became acrimonious, and councillors ended up saying that they were so disgusted that they would not vote at all, that a poll of citizens should be taken, that they were ashamed of the matter being raised again, and that the council was making itself ridiculous. The resolution at last found a majority of thirty-five to twenty-three and Manchester finally and incontrovertibly had a 'Town Hall'.

12

Mayor of Manchester and the Inauguration of the Town Hall (1876–77)

On 19 October 1876, a requisition signed by fifty councillors was presented to Abel Heywood requesting him to agree to nomination for mayor for 1876–77. It was fully expected that this year would see the completion and opening of the new Town Hall, and considered only fitting that the presiding mayor for that occasion should be the man who had chaired the New Town Hall Committee and overseen the development at every stage. The opening of the Town Hall on 13 September 1877 was the culmination of a decade's dedication by Abel Heywood, and in many ways it was the pinnacle of his career.

Certainly, it was hoped that Abel would receive a knighthood, and his supporters wanted to ensure his prominence at the opening ceremony, which they expected the Queen to attend:

> And if it should happen that Royalty was present at the opening of the new Town hall, and that Her Majesty should be graciously pleased to bestow her favour upon the Mayor at that time, he [Alderman Willert] did not know that there was any man who was so deserving of such favour as Mr. Alderman Heywood… the man who had had the full charge and superintendence of the erection of the building.

In his reply Abel explained that he had concerns about again taking on the heavy office of mayor. The first was the state of his health, as he appears to have been suffering from some form of depression. He had 'visited another part of the country for the purpose of ascertaining whether the depressing influences which he felt at that time could be removed'. On his return, he had talked to 'those whom it was his duty to consult', presumably his wife and family, and perhaps colleagues, and decided that he could take on the burden of office if it was not too onerous. A second consideration was 'the distance which he lived from Manchester' now that he was settled in Bowdon, but discussion with his wife had settled this and the train service from Altrincham probably helped meet this objection. Therefore, he consented to the nomination with thanks 'from the bottom of his heart'.[1]

On the day of the election the public gallery in the chamber was unusually crowded, 'and there was one lady present' – who is likely to have been Elizabeth Heywood. Abel was proposed by Alderman Willert, nicknamed by the mayor the 'Father of the Council', and Alderman Nicholls, 'the Father of the Mayors'. The election was unanimous. In his response, Abel included details of his early career, saying that he felt sure that the position offered to him was not because of his work on the New Town Hall Committee but because of his dedication to the work of the Corporation. He summarised this by citing his attendances, of which he must have kept a record; over thirty-three years he had only missed 113 committee meetings and sixty-one council meetings. To introduce his priorities, he predicted that if his ideas were adopted there would be tramways to serve the city outskirts, and he averred that the pollution of rivers should be addressed. He also mentioned the baths and washhouses, set up to benefit the working people of Manchester. He rounded off with a quotation from Pope which reflected his wide reading and also his aspiration and its cost: 'Who pants for glory finds but short repose.' The meeting ended with a proposal that the Queen be invited by the mayor on behalf of the Corporation to come to Manchester to open the new 'municipal palace'. There was no discussion as to whether the Queen would accept.[2]

Mayoral duties

The duties of the mayor were as wide-ranging as ever, and although the new Town Hall and its completion were very high profile, much was expected of Abel in many other areas of activity. He began with a burst of hospitality, on 5 and 6 December with dinners at his home in Bowdon for aldermen, councillors, clergymen, academics, the town clerk and city surveyor, the mayor of Salford, and his own two sons, Abel junior and George Washington. The following week he repeated this for other aldermen and councillors, and included on the guest list the Unitarian William Gaskell with the Catholic Bishop of Salford, Herbert Vaughan, plus military and legal gentlemen.

One of the guests at the Summerfield dinner on 12 December was Professor Gamgee, who had invented a process for creating sheet ice, and the following January saw Abel in his official capacity as mayor, accompanied by Elizabeth, opening the Rusholme Ice Rink, grandiosely named later 'the Manchester Glaciarium'. Abel's speech reflected his scientific interest in the process as well as his appreciation of the opportunity for city-dwellers to experience 'healthy recreation'. Abel continued to make similar official appearances throughout his mayoralty; later the same month he and Elizabeth attended the Manchester Police soiree, where again a brief address was expected. This was followed up in April by the annual inspection of the city police, which Abel had first attended in 1863.

In 1877 the city welcomed a very prestigious guest from the United States, with which country cordial relations were assiduously maintained by a city dependent on American cotton and the American market. When General Ulysses Grant, Unionist commander, close ally of Abraham Lincoln and ex-president, undertook a grand tour of the world, Manchester was delighted to receive him and did him proud. Throughout the visit the theme was the special relationship of Britain, and especially of Manchester, with the United States.

In the company of his wife and other important American dignitaries, the general arrived on 30 May from Liverpool by special train to London Road Station, where Abel, his wife 'the Mayoress' and members of the Corporation met him. While the ladies drove directly to the new Town Hall where they had a guided tour from the city surveyor, the gentlemen proceeded by carriage to visit Whitworth's machinery and gun factory in Chorlton Street, Watts and Company's warehouse on Portland Street, the Assize Courts, where a band played 'Yankee Doodle', and the Royal Exchange, by which time the ladies had rejoined the party. As the Exchange was generally quiet on a Wednesday, it had been opened up to all-comers and a decent crowd had gathered, including a lot of ladies in the gallery 'who do not as a rule grace the Exchange with their presence'.

The tour of the sites ended at the new Town Hall, which was nearly complete. In a dedicated council meeting held to approve an address to be presented to the general, Abel spoke of the special commercial relationship between Manchester and the US. When they entered the grand reception room, the mayor led Mrs Grant, and the general escorted the mayoress, and they all sat on the dais together. The address, read by an ailing Joseph Heron, expressed the hope that the visit might 'ultimately tend to the change of ideas pointing to the abolition of restrictions on trade, and to the establishment by common consent of free commercial intercourse between England and America'. Abel reminded the listeners of his earlier mayoralty and the reception of the captain of the *George Griswold*, which had brought supplies from the US to help relieve the victims of the cotton famine, and went on to detail all the other expressions there had been of friendship with the US, including the working men's memorial to President Lincoln.[3]

Abel's position allowed him to influence the council in other matters which were important to him. One of the first events of the new mayoralty was a visit organised by the Health Committee for the council to see the sanitary works in Oldham Road and Water Street and examine two methods of disposing of human waste. They also visited houses where the two methods were in operation; in Gledhill's Court, off Livesey Street, they saw closets used by three families each, where they were subjected to 'loud complaints' by some women. It was clear that more needed to be done to deal effectively with the huge quantities of 'nightsoil' generated by the city. At the dinner provided afterwards by the Health Committee, Abel congratulated them on the progress made in finding uses for nightsoil (as manure, fuel and mortar) and reducing the terrible stenches previously endured. The chairman of the committee, Mr Schofield, knowing he had the ear of a sympathetic listener, took the opportunity to put in a plea for work yet to be done on river pollution, sewage treatment, housing and open spaces for the people.[4]

This was the age of 'gas and water socialism' and Manchester was not immune to the movement. In July, in response to a requisition, Abel held a public meeting to authorise the Corporation to initiate a bill in Parliament to obtain water from Lake Thirlmere in Cumberland; the needs of the growing city were to be met by extending the sources of clean water to the Lake District. This was not the only large-scale project initiated in this year. In October, in the final weeks of his mayoralty, the council attended the laying of the cornerstone of a new gasworks in Bradford, planned to meet rising demand in the following years by producing twenty million cubic feet of gas per day to add to over ten million produced elsewhere in the city. Abel's speech acknowledged disquiet in some quarters about the deleterious effects of the works on the nearby Philips Park and the people living in the vicinity, and he had earlier been heckled when he claimed that opposition had subsided. The ceremony was followed by a dinner in the Town Hall at which Abel provided a retrospect from his encyclopaedic knowledge of council activity, in this case with regard to gas over the previous forty years. A week later, Abel was invited as mayor to the annual dinner of the Manchester Statistical Society, whose work increasingly underpinned the social policies of the council.

Abel also pushed his enthusiasm for the tramways scheme which his Highways and Paving Committee had taken under its wing in preceding years. In February 1877 he took the town clerk and the Tramways Committee to see one of the proposed 'cars' to be used, which would carry forty passengers, though twenty of them would be 'outside'. It was noted that there would be red plush velvet seats, and sufficient lighting to read by, and the usual straw on the floor would be replaced by a wooden and rubber mat. The outside seats would be, quaintly, 'after the style of garden chairs'. It was proposed to run 'workmen's cars' morning and evening at a reduced fare of ½d per mile. The service began on 17 May when a procession of thirteen cars travelled along three miles of double track between Pendlebury and Broughton carrying the mayors of Manchester and Salford and other dignitaries and officials. In October the Tramways Committee's plans for further tramway construction into Manchester city centre were approved by the council; the system was now underway.[5]

All the excitement about trams did not divert interest from railway development and organisation. Abel chaired meetings on unfair railway taxes and the need for government action to prevent accidents. While there was clearly thought about how to run and improve the railway system, new lines were still being opened. One such was that from the 'temporary' Manchester Central Station on Windmill Street to Ranelagh Street Station in Liverpool, opened by Abel's former sparring partner, now Sir Edward Watkin of the Manchester, Sheffield and Lincolnshire Railway. Abel and the rest of the Corporation took the opportunity to travel the new line, which would compete with the London and North-Western Railway Company, the MSL's rival for Manchester trade. As usual there was a crowd to cheer the train's progress and the day ended with a slap-up dinner in the Queen's

Hotel; Watkin took the chair, and Abel Heywood sat on his right. It is to be hoped that they had resolved their earlier differences.

Social and political campaigns

It must have been very gratifying for Abel, with his interest in science, public health and hospitals, as well as a connection which he and his wife were developing with Owens College and its medical school, that in August the British Medical Association decided to hold its forty-fifth annual meeting in Manchester. On the evening of the first day, he attended a reception for the conference at Owens College, where 'a large and fashionable gathering of ladies and gentlemen' thronged the building. This would have been very much to Abel's taste as there was a collection of 'philosophical instruments' in the natural philosophy room, and drawings and diagrams 'illustrating the antiquity of man' were on display in the engineering drawing room. A lecture by Dr Ransome on 'The present position of State medicine in England' proved popular, and gave an account of cutting-edge developments in preventive medicine, stressing the importance of 'the education of the people in sanitary knowledge' and the need to support medical officers of health. This must have been music to Abel's ears.[6]

His interest in other forms of health care provision continued, particularly those which were most used by the poor, the dispensaries, which benefited from the Mayor's Hospital Sunday fund. The Hospital and Dispensary for Sick Children commanded his attention in January 1877 when he presided at its annual meeting. Well over 4,000 children had been treated in the preceding year, and there were building extensions afoot to accommodate more as the numbers were projected to grow. For in-patients there was a hospital in the countryside at Pendlebury, which had admitted 563 patients in the past year and was currently under expansion. Robert Needham Philips MP took the opportunity of having the ear of the mayor at the meeting to ask Abel whether the Corporations of Manchester and Salford, which already contributed to the funds, might raise their contributions, and portentously for the future he ended, 'it seemed that in some way or other they would soon have to apply to the rates to help voluntary movements with regard to these charities'. Abel forbore to reply; the rates were always a contentious issue which a wily politician needed to handle with circumspection, whatever his personal inclinations.[7]

The Medlock Street dispensary also saw Abel take the chair at its annual 'tea meeting' in March. His radical comrade Dr John Watts related how the 5,000 members' contributions had allowed them to be as well provided for in sickness 'as if they moved in the higher ranks of society'. Abel showed continuing interest in the Manchester Southern Hospital for women and children, another dispensary. In October there was an appeal for higher subscriptions, as the hospital was only managing because of special donations and a legacy, and patients were being asked to contribute, which 'tended to pauperise the poor'. They had treated 3,490 patients in 1876. Abel as chairman appealed for more uniformity in the management of funds for dispensaries across the city, and expressed interest in a proposed scheme to gain contributions from those working classes who could afford it.[8]

Similarly as mayor, Abel was enabled and expected to play a role in many of the educational endeavours in the city. Only a few days after his election he presided at the prize-giving of the Lancashire and Cheshire Union of Mechanics' Institutes, which by this time was developing links for its best students with Owens College, in the form of scholarships. Abel was increasingly connected with the latter, perhaps influenced by his wife's considerable interest in the college, and just after the end of his mayoralty he attended the annual dinner of the Owens College (Manchester Royal) Medical School, making the toast to the college, at a time when it had just applied to the government for university status.

Moreover, Abel continued with his usual educational interests in schools and training centres. The annual meeting of the Boys' Refuge and Industrial Homes, Strangeways, of which he was president, proved unusually controversial. He expressed the opinion that such institutions should not be dependent on subscriptions from private sources, but that they 'had a claim on the community and the central government'. But the seconder, Hugh Mason, objected to the 'red-tapism' seen in institutions where local or central government interfered (which he nicknamed 'bumbledom', causing amusement). Abel, perhaps stung by this, in the reply to the vote of thanks revealed that he had thought to offer £200 or £300 a year from the Corporation, but now he would not even hint at it.[9]

Library provision continued to attract Abel's support too, and it was in his mayoralty that moves were commenced towards the establishment of a new, central reference library. A requisition in February occasioned a meeting to propose the use of the old Town Hall in King Street as a central free public library, in particular for reference. There had been a suggestion that the new Town Hall might house such a library, but this had not borne fruit. A major argument in favour of new provision was that Manchester was behind other great cities at home and abroad in its reference provision, and in particular the arch-rival city of Liverpool 'had not only a free library but a noble art institution, just erected'. Mr J. W. Maclure 'looked upon it as a happy omen that this matter should have been brought forward during the mayoralty of Mr. Heywood, who was one of the earliest pioneers of a cheap press, and who had been identified with the issue of cheap literature for schools'.

Abel, who had been included on the council's Free Library Committee in its early years, expressed his pleasure at being able to relay the views of this meeting to the council.[10] When the Campfield Library was examined in March, the appalling state of 'the tottering building' was manifest and it was ordered that the books be moved to the old Court of Record in Cross Street and rooms in the old Town Hall, which had been immediately offered by the mayor. So bad was the state of the library, that there were fears that removing the 76,000 books and shelving would cause a collapse. Thus, a crisis forced the issue, and indeed a Central Free Library was established in the old Town Hall, which continued to house the collections until 1912.

Abel was still a keen patron of lectures, and presided at the talk by Professor Williamson to the Scientific Students Association on the topic of Insectivorous Plants, much of which focused on an explanation of observations carried out by Charles Darwin. He also attended a lecture in January 1877 in the Athenaeum on the expedition to the Arctic Regions by Captain Markham, whose men carried out experiments and observations under difficult conditions. The Bishop of Manchester extolled the virtues of British seamen and rejoiced that they had 'not deteriorated since the day they fell by the side of Nelson at Trafalgar…' They had managed to plant the flag within 400 miles of the Pole, which was the closest to date. Abel seemed more alive than many to the scientific angle, and proposed a vote of thanks that mentioned his admiration for 'the courage which prompted them for a scientific object to undergo the dangers and toils of the Arctic Expedition'.[11]

As mayor, Abel finally demonstrated his support for women's suffrage unequivocally when he chaired the ninth annual meeting of the Manchester National Society for Women's Suffrage in the old Town Hall on 29 November 1876. Abel's opening speech stressed how this was a cross-party issue, and that all three of the Manchester MPs, two Liberals and a Conservative, as well as the council, were in favour of household suffrage for women. Lydia Becker, the leading Manchester activist for women's rights, read the society's report and spoke alongside Jacob Bright. Elizabeth Heywood also had prominence as the proposer of the committee for the forthcoming year.

On 7 November 1877, just before his term as mayor ended, Abel again presided at the society's tenth annual meeting in the new Town Hall. He opined that 'if this question of woman's suffrage was to be successful it must be made a success by the ladies themselves', thus presaging the policy of the Women's Social and Political Union of 1903.[12] The new committee was appointed and the campaigning went on. Abel's chairmanship likewise continued, and in 1879 he made his views absolutely clear:

He said he failed to see how any objection could be raised to the women suffrage movement. Each party said that they did not believe that their side would be strengthened by the addition of women electors. That, however, was not the way the question ought to be looked at. (Hear, hear.) He never had any doubt in his own mind that women were as much entitled to vote as men. (Applause.)[13]

The Liberal *Manchester Times* focused on the need to review tactics in the agitation:

He [Abel] said that… They wanted larger demonstrations of women. But in order to advance that question, he saw no other way than of attaching it to the great party in the State that had for generations supported the greatest and grandest movements for extending the rights of mankind. (Applause.)[14]

Apart from recommending that suffragists form links with the Liberal party, Abel was demonstrating a perception that more 'militancy' in the sense of public demonstrations by women was required. Emmeline Pankhurst, who later adopted the same line in the Women's Social and Political Union, and her husband Richard were proposed by Abel amongst the names for the executive committee in November 1882. On that occasion he remarked that there had been one step in the right direction because Parliament had given women the right to vote in local government elections. He was very optimistic and believed that this was a kind of pilot, and that if it was successful 'they might depend upon it that 'ere long the right to vote for members of the general Legislature would be given to them'.[15]

The annual general meeting of the National Society for Women's Suffrage on 12 November 1884 was attended for the last time by both Abel and Elizabeth Heywood, alongside such luminaries as Lydia Becker and Richard and Emmeline Pankhurst. Elizabeth sat on the platform and seconded the proposal for the appointment of the executive committee. After this meeting bad weather and perhaps infirmity prevented their planned attendance on 17 February 1885 when the suffragists organised a free public meeting in the Free Trade Hall, and they did not reappear again on the women's suffrage platform.

Women's rights agitation was not confined to the purely political arena. When the Manchester Association for Promoting the Education of Women and the Manchester High School for Girls held their meeting in the mayor's parlour at the end of January 1877, Abel similarly showed his support by presiding. As well as the achievement of the school, it was noted that universities were beginning to open up their classes to women, but according to Reverend Steinthal, 'it was a matter of sincere regret that the authorities of Owens College had not adopted a similar policy... this association would use its influence on behalf of the great principle of equal education for all'. In reply Professor Wilkins of Owens College said that 'it would be a dangerous experiment to make organic a change for a small section of the community'.[16]

It may have been in response to such discussion that Elizabeth Heywood left £10,000 to Owens College in her will with the proviso that they admit women students, or at least spend the money on the education of women. And indeed it was not long before the Victoria University began to make provision for the admission of women to their programmes.

Foreign crises

During Abel's mayoralty there were several crises around the world to which Mancunians felt the need to respond. In the midst of a crisis in the Balkans, Abel chaired a meeting on 4 December 1876 where a resolution was passed that Disraeli's Conservative government should be called upon to join with other European powers (especially Russia) to obtain a release from Ottoman rule for their persecuted Christian provinces in the region. By July the following year,

Abel was again in the chair at a meeting about Bosnian refugees who had fled their homes in terror at Turkish attacks, and large amounts of money had been sent by Manchester to relieve the suffering of both Bosnians and Serbs. Prime Minister Disraeli's policy of neutrality came under vituperative attack from his rival, Liberal leader William Gladstone, who produced a widely read pamphlet which was stocked in Abel's shop, *The Bulgarian Horrors and the Question of the East*. Amid righteous Christian indignation at the treatment of their co-religionists, a relief fund was set up in Manchester for Bulgarians massacred by Turkish troops.

Other funds were raised under Abel's supervision as mayor, notably an appeal in the late summer of 1877 for the victims of a famine which had developed in the southern part of Britain's greatest colony, India. Abel donated £20, which was a substantial amount, but it did not put him in the same league as his treasurer, the banker Oliver Heywood, who gave £250. Abel put the case for generosity not only because the people of India were Manchester's customers, but also for reasons of humanity; half a million people had died, and twenty million were now at risk. By the end of August over £4,500 had been subscribed. Other fundraising efforts were added; at the end of September the mayor and mayoress of Manchester patronised entertainments held at Belle Vue Gardens from which the receipts of £215 were donated to the famine relief fund. The occasion was also fun; there were fireworks, and 'the magnificent device of the facade of the Town Hall excited great admiration'.[17] At the very end of his mayoralty, Abel presided over the closing of the fund, which amounted to the commendable sum of £40,808.

Thus far, Abel's second mayoralty yielded little that was new and remarkable; he was continuing in well-worn pathways. Meanwhile, the construction of the new Town Hall was nearing its completion, and it was this which took up most of his time and was expected to lead to a glorious climax to his career, crowned with a knighthood from Queen Victoria.

The opening of the new Town Hall: the invitation to the Queen

Mayor Matthew Curtis in March 1876 had visited London on Corporation business with Alderman Bennett and Joseph Heron, the town clerk. They had a meeting with Home Secretary Richard Cross (also in the company of the MPs Sir Thomas Bazley and Jacob Bright) 'with reference to an invitation to the Queen to be present at the opening of the New Town Hall'. The mayor avowedly had wanted to ascertain the proper procedure for such an invitation, and he may well have wanted to avoid the disappointment which had occurred in 1867 at the unveiling of the statue of Prince Albert.

In the ensuing council meeting when the mayor reported back, he was taken to task by Alderman Worthington, who believed that the New Town Hall Sub-committee should have been allowed to make all the arrangements for the opening, so that 'no portion of the honour connected with it should be taken from them'. In his defence, the mayor said he had only sought information and that what he had found out would be passed to the sub-committee for a decision on whether and when to invite the Queen.

Abel was offended:

> It did… appear to him strange that he, who had been chairman of the Town Hall sub-committee since its embodiment, who had, indeed, brought forward the resolution for the construction of the Town Hall and carried it in the council – and who, especially during late years, had paid very great attention to the works in connection with the building, devoting, in fact, a great portion of his time to it – it did appear strange to him that the object of the deputation should never have been mentioned to him…

He also saw a bigger issue, in that a precedent had been set whereby councillors in London on one aspect of business might interfere in other aspects; this 'was not to be tolerated in a free and popularly elected assembly'.[18]

Matters rested there until the election of Abel Heywood as mayor on 10 November 1876, when the council immediately passed a resolution that the mayor should send the Corporation's invitation to the Queen. Abel acted in good time for the expected opening later in his mayoralty, and by 29 November 1876 he had sent the invitation to the home secretary to be passed on to the prime minister, Benjamin Disraeli, Lord Beaconsfield, hoping that Her Majesty would not only open the 'Municipal Palace' but also inspect the beautiful statue of the 'much and ever to be lamented Prince Consort'.[19] An acknowledgement was received, but as he told his hearers at the city police soiree on 24 January, as yet there was no reply. Perhaps even now there was doubt in his mind as he continued in words that betrayed some lack of confidence: 'He did think that Her Majesty ought not to refuse to come to Manchester, famed as it was for its manufactures, for its population, and for many other things which went to make up the sum of human greatness…'[20]

There continued to be no response and so in February 1877 the town clerk met one of the premier's private secretaries to try to move matters forward. On 2 March, there was a false dawn; the *Manchester Courier* announced that the Queen had agreed to come and open the Town Hall, but there was a denial from the town clerk, speaking on behalf of Mayor Abel Heywood.[21]

The answer finally arrived on 1 April (which some who felt particularly bitter thought was a carefully chosen date), in the form of a letter from the prime minister, Lord Beaconsfield, on behalf of the Queen. It was fulsome in stating that the Queen had much appreciated her visits to Manchester in 1851 and 1857, but there was a sting in the tail. 'The Queen… expressed her regret that it is out of her power to be present on this interesting occasion.'[22]

The council and the people of Manchester were terribly disappointed; this was perceived to be a massive snub. The *Manchester Times* summed up the reaction on 14 April:

The Queen's refusal to visit Manchester in connection with the opening of the New Town hall is a puzzle to everybody. It seems so ill-natured, so rude, so capricious, so insulting, and, from the loyal point of view, so wantonly mischievous, that I find it hard to reconcile the proceedings with Her Majesty's established reputation for discretion and good taste.

The writer clearly felt some bitterness towards the Queen herself, and veered dangerously close to republican sentiments when he claimed that 'the chief function left to Royalty is that of serving as a rallying point for national sentiment, a brilliant centre round which our affections may gather. If Royalty loses this function its game is played out, and it is on the road to extinction.' He ended by blaming both the prime minister and the Queen, and stated that the sovereign could have accepted the invitation even if pressed not to do so by her minister, 'even if he had thrown the wettest blanket over the invitation, in a matter of this sort… the strictest constitutionalist would have absolved Her Majesty for venturing to have a will of her own'.[23]

There was a growing sense that the refusal was also an insult to Abel Heywood himself. How he felt about this is uncertain, as he was very restrained in his handling of the news and made little comment, but it is hard to imagine that he was not horribly disappointed. He had many times expressed the deepest respect for monarchy. He had accepted the mayoralty with an expectation that the Queen would attend the opening of the new Town Hall, and that by implication as mayor he would be honoured with a knighthood. His supporters in Manchester were extremely indignant on his behalf, but his opponents eagerly seized on the refusal as a way of discrediting him.

When the refusal had sunk in, an explanation was hungrily sought for what seemed an inexplicable decision. History has settled on one of those offered at the time which was pedalled assiduously by the Tory faction in Manchester: the radicalism of Abel Heywood. In the first place, Abel himself as a young man had been so devoted to the radical cause that he had suffered imprisonment for selling illegal newspapers. Then more recently he had become to all appearances the joint donor with his wife, Elizabeth, of the Cromwell statue commemorating a man who was viewed by royalists with opprobrium as a regicide. But it seems unlikely that these features of his past alone would explain the refusal; Victoria herself was said to have viewed the Cromwell statue while it was in the sculptor's studio in London and to have admired it, and Abel's championing of the free press in the 1830s was forty years in the past and by the 1870s the newspaper stamps which he had opposed had long been abolished.

Quite a few voices in the press, both in editorials and letters, believed that Victoria's refusal was part and parcel of her widow's seclusion following the death of Prince Albert. It was suggested that it was for this reason that she also had not attended the 1867 unveiling of the Albert Memorial in Manchester. However, everyone was aware that she had come out to attend the service of thanksgiving for the recovery from typhoid of the Prince of Wales in 1872. Moreover, others pointed out that she had attended public ceremonies in both Edinburgh and Wolverhampton in the summer of 1876, on both occasions to unveil statues of Prince Albert.

One completely different and entertaining interpretation, which did not gain much currency, was suggested by Henry Dunckley, the editor of the *Manchester Times* who contributed regularly in satirical vein under the name of 'Verax'. He related how Disraeli had advised the Queen to refuse under a complete misapprehension as to who Abel Heywood was, thinking he was the brother of Oliver Heywood the banker, whose yacht had been run down by the royal yacht in the Solent in the preceding year, causing a dispute. It is an entertaining story, but unlikely, and indeed the 'JW' whom Verax cited as his source took the trouble to write in the newspaper the next week a denial that this had been the import of his information, as the minister who had mistaken Abel's identity was not Lord Beaconsfield.

What may have carried weight with Victoria was the circulation at this time by Abel's enemies of a 'slander' that he had really been imprisoned for selling 'blasphemous' publications. There were dark but unproven accusations at the time that Conservative elements, even on the council, had written to the government with charges against Abel's good name. W.E.A. Axon's pamphlet *The Mayor of Manchester and his Slanderers* stoutly defended Abel. Although the pamphlet did admit that he had 'been the subject of an impotent prosecution' in 1840, the nature of the publications in question was played down as 'written in a controversial style, then not unfamiliar, and one was considered to contain a passage of irreverence'. Axon also pointed out that by the 1870s such material was 'sold in every book shop in the country'.[24]

The supposed secret Conservative attack on Abel's good name was also linked to current political matters. Party politics were blamed insofar as that in the 1876 by-election to replace the deceased Conservative MP Romaine Callender, Manchester had rejected the Conservative candidate, Powell, and returned 'Advanced' Liberal Jacob Bright. Moreover, the Manchester Conservatives had wanted Matthew Curtis to continue as Mayor of Manchester in 1876 but had been defeated by Liberals who selected Abel Heywood. In the reported words of the Salford Liberal Mr Briggs, 'The highest Tory authority in Manchester had publicly declared his determination that as far as his influence went the Queen should not visit Manchester to open the Town hall.'

However, no evidence was ever produced to verify these claims, and the story of communication between Manchester Tories and Westminster, which was retailed most prominently in the council meeting of 11 April by Joseph Thompson, was said by Conservatives to have been fabricated by Dr John Watts. At the end of that council meeting, a telegram was received by the mayor from the Lord Chamberlain's office, claiming that there had been no communication from parties in Manchester, and likewise Mr J.W. Maclure, one of the Conservative Salford candidates in a by-election, stated that he had met with 'leading members of the government who informed him that they knew nothing of any letter having been sent to London'. But the rumours were so rife that they may have had some foundation.[25] The *City Jackdaw*, perhaps not the most reliable source, certainly believed so and on 21 September published a spoof letter supposedly from the Queen, in which she apologised for her absence and claimed to have been misled by 'Captain James Watson and The Great Maclure'. The paper commented that the Queen had been 'the dupe of Watson, Maclure, and the local Tories generally, my Lord of Beaconsfield being their go-between'.[26]

In any case, the Queen and her prime minister may well have been especially disgruntled with Manchester at this time because of opposition to a bill very close to the royal heart. Liberals, some of them members of the council, had held a rowdy meeting and agreed to petition Parliament against the Conservative government's Royal Titles Bill which bestowed on Victoria a title she strongly coveted, 'Empress of India'. Questioning her right to it was not going to endear Manchester to her. Abel himself had not been present at the meeting – but the city itself may have been in bad odour with both the Queen and prime minister over this opposition.

Perhaps then the Queen's own inclinations and the premier's prejudices converged to agree that she would refrain from visiting Manchester, despite the ill-feeling which this was likely to engender in the city. They may have foreseen that Victoria would not personally be blamed for this, but that it would be Disraeli who would bear the brunt of the resulting hostility of the Manchester Liberals. However, if so it was a risky strategy, and Verax expressed a radical perspective on the significance of the Queen's refusal:

> No doubt we shall manage to get our New Town Hall opened without the assistance of Royalty. The operation will cost us less, and it will be seasoned with the quiet assurance that we are able on a pinch to help ourselves. Perhaps, too, we shall be all the better hereafter for this shock of the Windsor shower bath. It will help to brace up our political nerves, and serve as a tonic to our civic virtues; in short, it will make us less like flunkies, and more like men.[27]

Manchester was nothing if not resilient, and immediately after the refusal was made public numerous suggestions were made as to who might replace the Queen in the ceremonies surrounding the Town Hall inauguration. Thoughts turned inevitably to other members of the royal family. The Tory peer Lord Derby as the most prominent local magnate, and the Bishop of Manchester also found favour. Moving across the political spectrum, William Gladstone, Jacob Bright and Dr John Watts were put forward. The *Manchester Guardian*, which reported a large mailbag on the subject, received a suggestion that the mayoress, Elizabeth Heywood, should do the honours. However, it was the opinion of many Liberals, and indeed one shared by some Conservatives, that Abel Heywood himself should open the municipal palace. This was the view presented very forcefully to the council by his ally and colleague on the Town Hall Committee, Joseph Thompson, on 11 April. He stated 'as the building had been erected from the ratepayers money, the Mayor, as the representative of the ratepayers, should be asked to open it'. Alderman Lamb was among those who agreed, though from a different motive. He advocated that they 'let the honour of opening the Town hall be conferred upon the Mayor, and let His Worship be made to feel that, whatever others might think, he had about him those who knew and could appreciate his personal worth and public services.- (Hear, hear.)' The resolution was unanimously supported.[28]

Once the decision was made, Mancunians began with gusto to make preparations for a great show. The suggestions were copious, as evidenced again in the letters pages of the newspapers. The opening was delayed to allow time for the completion of the bells, which would be an important feature of the ceremonies, and the great day was fixed for 13 September 1877.

The opening ceremonies

Abel Heywood, in his capacity as mayor, was the lynchpin in co-ordinating the ceremonies. It was agreed that the inauguration would take place in the middle of the day on 13 September, and a banquet would follow in the evening. On the evening of the following day, the mayor and mayoress would hold a reception and afterwards a ball. On Saturday 15 September, there would be a huge procession of trades and friendly societies. Not everyone was enchanted with the scale of the celebrations, however; there was criticism from some quarters that the project had been so expensive that further lavish spending was unjustifiable, especially when some inhabitants of the city were living in poverty. *Free Lance* described the three-day event as 'a great furore about nothing'.[29]

The auspicious day dawned, and the ceremony passed off without incident, despite appalling weather. The council assembled at 1 p.m. in the old Town Hall, almost all of them in evening dress as agreed earlier, a matter of mild disappointment to the *Manchester Courier* reporter who regretted 'that there was not even so much as an alderman's robe to give picturesqueness to the scene'. They each wore a 'fancy silver tassel' with a tiny scroll as a distinctive badge. The council were to process in order of seniority, symbolically from the old to the new centre of municipal government. They were joined by Mayor Abel Heywood in his chain of office shortly before 1.30 p.m., when the procession was formed for the route to Albert Square. Abel was at its head, with Joseph Heron and Alfred Waterhouse on either side of him.

They set off led by contingents of the fire brigade and the police and accompanied by 100 members of the Dragoon Guards and 200 from the 106th Regiment of the Line, both cavalry and infantry, plus their bands. The walk from King Street to Albert Square was lined with large crowds, controlled by a huge contingent of police; ladies, for whom it would have been unseemly to stand in the pushing and shoving throng, filled the windows in all the buildings along the route. Flags had been hung from the public buildings, principal warehouses and consulates, though the *Manchester Guardian* reporter felt (as usual) that 'the street decorations hardly came up to general expectation' and that the new Town Hall itself 'was externally almost destitute of decoration'. However, the bells more than made up for this in an aural display which was highly praised.

On arrival at the Town Hall they proceeded without delay to the opening ceremony, no doubt eager to get inside out of the weather. Luckily, it did not take long; the town clerk made a short speech to present a large golden key to the mayor with which to open the main door, ending:

> The key, Mr. Mayor, which I have the honour to present may not be intrinsically of great value; but I think it will be of value to you as a pleasing memorial of one of the most interesting and important events which have occurred during the course of your long, your useful, and your truly honourable life.

Abel's reply showed that he too perceived this as a significant personal achievement: 'He felt very strongly that that was an event in his own history, as well as in the history of Manchester.' He unlocked the door 'amidst a flourish of trumpets', and the council proceeded up the main staircase to its new chamber while the Dragoons' band played the national anthem.[30]

Abel and his wife Elizabeth were occupied for a short time in the tower anteroom receiving visitors who had travelled to Manchester. They then took their seats on a dais in the banqueting hall. Meanwhile, the council held a special meeting under the ex-mayor, Matthew Curtis, with the purpose of approving a prepared address to be given to the mayor, thanking him especially for his efforts over the past nine years as chair of the New Town Hall Sub-committee, as well as for his trouble in arranging the festivities for its opening. It was passed unanimously, despite a joking call from Mr Brown for a division. This was a special meeting in more ways than one; among the visitors, who included the mayors of other towns, there were also quite a number of ladies who were seated in the places normally occupied by councillors. The town clerk, Joseph Heron, commented light-heartedly on this in a way which would excite outrage today when he protested that 'if anything like regularity and order is to be maintained in the proceedings of the Council, the ladies must certainly be in the gallery. – (laughter)'. He went on to say that this was because even the ex-mayor 'cannot resist temptation' and could not perform his duties 'so long as he is under the influence of the ladies'. He added a quip about women's suffrage, as the ex-mayor had effectively asked the ladies to vote in support of the address: 'He has proposed to do so irregular a thing as to give you, without the authority of Parliament, votes. (Laughter.)'

In the banqueting hall the address was presented by Joseph Heron, who had recently returned from a rest cure but who, having played such a key part in the development of the project, was certainly not going to miss his moment in the limelight. He executed his commission 'with even more than his usual distinctness, but it was a matter of regret to all present to observe that the exertion caused him evident distress'. The address referred to the illustrious development of the city of Manchester and praised Abel's role in it, as well as the achievements of Richard Cobden, William Neild, Thomas Potter and George Wilson. It extolled the virtues of local self-government and of political economy, and it ended with 'sincere wishes for the long-continued happiness of yourself, Mrs. Heywood, and your family'. Abel responded with a prepared speech which followed the pattern of most of his orations by this time, a recap of his earlier career in Manchester's government and the struggle for Incorporation, praise for those city greats mentioned in the address, for Joseph Heron, for the late Alderman Nicholls, who had been on the sub-committee, and for the architect, Alfred Waterhouse, the achievements of Manchester, and the genesis of the new Town Hall. This marked the end of the formal proceedings, and after offering their congratulations to the mayor and mayoress, the guests occupied themselves in the interval before the banquet at 4 p.m. in looking around the building.[31]

The evening banquet was held in the public hall, with Abel presiding. The *Manchester Times* was fulsome in its praise of the scene, 'which presented a most brilliant and luxurious appearance, the gorgeous decorations of the room being almost eclipsed in splendour by the magnificent floral, silver, and gold ornamentation of the table... the whole of the many-light candelabra were in use, in addition to the richly-gilt gasaliers with which the architect has furnished the room'.[32]

Many of the diners were invited by Manchester's councillors, each of whom had been given three tickets to distribute. In the end the 300 or 400 guests included many big names, such as John Bright, Lord Chief Justice Cockburn, the Lord Mayor of York and the Lord Provost of Edinburgh, but Conservative ministers Northcote, Cross and Derby, earlier rumoured to have been invited, were conspicuous by their absence. They missed the chance to dine on specially made crockery produced by Messrs J. Rose and Company of King Street; it consisted of over 1,000 pieces of Salopian ware of a Gothic design from Waterhouse's drawings, ornamented with the city motto *Concilio et Labore*.

After the meal, Abel gamely proposed the toast to the Queen, admitting that he should have been delighted to receive her on this occasion, but that 'we none the less duly esteem her, and love her for her constitutional rule'. Bishop Fraser of Manchester responded to his toast to the bishop and clergy of the diocese, and was frank in referring to the absence of the Queen as a matter for 'profound regret'. He, as others had before him, warned that loyalty and enthusiasm for royalty may have been damaged, but not to end on a sour note, he did concede that 'if she came tomorrow she would find in their welcome no trace of their present disappointment'. John Bright was the star speaker, and he displayed his usual loquacity on the current state of Parliament, the growth and importance of Manchester and its wealth, and the Indian Empire. In between Mr Pyne played on the 'grand organ' and the listeners were also treated to the strains of Mr J.L. Goodwin's string band. It must have been an exhausting day for Abel and Elizabeth Heywood, who were the centre of attention at what was then considered an advanced age. But, by all accounts, they both bore up remarkably well, and presumably retired to their spacious modern apartments in the Town Hall, and rested until the next marathon event the following evening, the reception at 7 p.m. and ball from 9.30 p.m.

The *City Jackdaw* nailed its colours to the mast on the morning of 14 September in an article entitled simply 'His Worship the Mayor.' The writer was, for once, not mocking but praising his subject but the article affords a snapshot of Abel the man, at this time of arguably his greatest triumph. The author reminded readers that Abel 'always trusted and he still trusts the people. To them he remains very much the man he always was. Honours and dignities have erected no barriers between the two.' The article went on to give interesting and rare insights from a personal observer into Abel's character, stating that he was very 'undemonstrative', which sometimes drew accusations that he was indifferent to the dignity of his office. He was the same with everyone with whom he had to deal, be it 'squire or artisan'. In private, he was said to be not at all loquacious, although his public speeches were sometimes lacking in brevity. He was also physically very youthful and vigorous, if not very well groomed!

> In person Mr. Heywood is, for his years, by far the youngest-looking man in the Council… If the Mayor cared about his toilet at all, or if he could enlist any other member of his family in that interest, he might put back the apparent hand of time a dozen years without any difficulty. Some mayors – like some horses – are 'bad at grooming,' but they have plenty of 'go in' them for all that; and no amount of work seems to daunt our Mayor, who has been twice married.

The article referred to the absence of royalty, but turned that to good effect in that as a result the mayor would be 'monarch of all he surveys, and lord of the fowl and the brute'.[33]

Apart from official guests of the mayor, and a relatively small number invited by a sub-committee from a cross-section of public institutions, each member of the council had been given twenty tickets to distribute for the ball, each of which would admit a lady and a gentleman. Although it was agreed that tickets could be given to 'a respectable mechanic', it became clear that this was not to be an occasion where the working classes, however respectable, were welcome, unless they could find themselves evening dress. Abel was apparently acquiescent on this point. The *City Jackdaw* relished the opportunity to poke fun and published a poem on the sad story of the mechanic Bill and his wife Betsy, who were forced to buy a second-hand suit, but were so shaken in the cab on the way that Bill's suit fell to pieces and they had to go home again. The appearance of social democracy was in reality a sham.

When the guests arrived, they were impeccably attired in evening dress. Despite bad weather, large crowds of those without invitations (or evening dress) gathered in the square to watch their arrival. Mr Goodwin's band provided the music for dancing, which was 'kept up with great spirit until an early hour this morning'.[34]

Finally, on the third day of celebrations the working classes got their opportunity to join in, in a manner which they themselves had suggested. As it was a Saturday, which by then was a half-day for many workers, the employers had been asked to close their works all day to allow a full attendance at a grand trades' procession. Abel himself had taken a particular lead in the planning of this event. On 3 July the representatives of trade and benefit societies had agreed that a committee would be set up under his chairmanship to organise the great procession on 15 September. They were expecting approximately 43,000 participants, representing eighty-six societies. It was estimated that if the workers were seven abreast, and took only a yard per row, the procession might be three and a half miles long. In the event it was almost five miles long and it took three hours to pass by.

There was some suggestion that Captain Palin, chief of police, was concerned about safety and public order. So a decision was made to gather the procession at three points, instead of one: Piccadilly at 11 a.m., Stevenson Square at 11.30 a.m. and New Cross at 12 p.m., from where it would proceed towards the Town Hall. Bands entertained those waiting in Stevenson Square, although sometimes three played at once, so that 'the effect was not particularly harmonious'. When the procession moved off the way ahead of it was cleared by a hundred Dragoons. Abel explained that there would be too many marchers to be accommodated in Albert Square, so it was decided that the procession would approach it from John Dalton Street, march and counter-march in six lines in the square, then leave by Princess Street.[35] Music was to be a key feature of the whole event, and as well as the extensive use of the Town Hall bells as many as fifty bands were engaged to accompany the marchers along their route.[36]

The sympathetic *Manchester Times* covered the event in detail; the workers showed their approval for the new Town Hall, and 'expressed emphatically and unmistakably their admiration and esteem for the personal character and public life of the head of the municipality', as well as acquitting themselves with 'lasting honour'. The whole event was deemed a 'magnificent success' and for a change the weather was kind, and was described as 'real Queen's weather'. The paper attributed the success of the day to the excellent relationship between Abel and the working men: 'for working men account Mr. Alderman Heywood as one of themselves, so closely has he been allied with them, so long and zealously and faithfully has he laboured for them'.

As noon approached, with every window in Albert Square, including those of the Town Hall itself, filled with watchers and crowds standing around the edge of the square, the mayor and mayoress, several other ladies, and many of the council took up their places in front of the main entrance to the Town Hall. Abel wore his chain of office, and then agreeing with Alderman Bennett's suggestion he put on his scarlet robe. When the procession reached Albert Square, the leading band played a specially composed 'Corporation March' and into the empty centre of the square the marchers 'took a serpentine course' until it was filled. Passing the mayor, the workers doffed their hats and cheered, 'the Mayor smilingly bowing his acknowledgements'. The reporter believed this was really Abel's day: 'there must have been 50,000 or 60,000 people within the view of the Mayor, who might well feel proud when he looked around, and reflected that he, officially and privately, was the object of the immense demonstration'.

The first six bands joined the Police Band to play 'God Save the Queen'. After stopping for about fifteen minutes, the procession moved on along Princess Street as planned. A few weeks later, Abel described his own powerful emotions:

> I think those who stood in the position that I did and watched the gradual increase of that mighty mass of men coming from Cross-street, headed by the band which was playing, will agree with me when I say that to my mind they appeared to come forth as though on some grand triumphal march, returning from a conflict in which they were the conquerors. (Cheers.) Steadily they marched, foot by foot, in such a manner as to give you the idea that you were not looking at a procession, but at some mighty creature which had been called forth by some tremendous power - (applause)…[37]

Many societies carried their banners, colourful and richly decorated, bearing coats of arms, illustrations and mottoes of their craft; the dyers' was a pun – 'We dye to live, and live to die.' But some were more political: 'Our only hope is in unity' and especially to Abel's taste 'Capital and labour go hand in hand.' Some also bore the religious sentiments that were closely bound up with unions and societies, such as 'In God is our strength'.

The trades bore emblems and examples of their work. The tin-plate workers included a man dressed in full armour, and one of the pipemakers 'was very quaintly adorned with a string of pipes of various colours, his appearance being strangely suggestive of a medicine man of the North American Indians or an African fetishman with a singlet of horrible charms'. But the reporter 'gave the palm' to the 3,000 strong contingent from the Society of Engineers who 'without much display' bore one model – a locomotive – and were accompanied by three bands. Huge examples of their crafts were favoured by some. The bookbinders carried an enormous book called 'The History of Manchester.' There were a few surprising appearances, such as 800 Druids, and 1,480 shepherds bearing gilded crooks, toy lambs and sheaves of corn. To be fully expected was a contingent of cotton spinners carrying imitation cotton trees and cotton banners bearing a message for their employers: 'We labour to live; we live not to labour.' The final body in the whole procession was the 5,000 members of temperance organisations who 'made an extremely brilliant show of banners, streamers, flags, sashes and rosettes'.

The local Tories seem to have used the opportunity to demonstrate their disapprobation of this jamboree in honour of Abel Heywood, and it was reported that the Conservative Club in St Ann's Street 'was in fact the most barren of spectators of any public building'. But they were very much in the minority. Along the route many of the buildings had put out bunting and 'numberless flags' and there were dense crowds to watch the great spectacle, but 'not the slightest tendency to disorder was manifested'. To gain a better view some more intrepid souls had even climbed onto the roof of Oxford Road station.

At the junction of Upper Jackson Street and Great Jackson Street the procession met 'Mr. Sam Hague's troupe of minstrels in fantastic attire' and divided into groups, some societies going to Pomona Gardens, some to Belle Vue Gardens, some to Manley Park, and a few temperance societies to Alexandra Park. At each venue the huge numbers were admitted with free tickets at the behest of the mayor. It is interesting to note that the fairground entertainments at Pomona, including the launching of a hot air balloon, appealed to the shepherds; the more sedate pleasures of ferneries and gardens at Manley were more to the taste of the Druids. On the whole, the crowds were well-behaved in the evening, with the exception of a few youths at Manley Park who started a full-blown grass fight which stopped the orchestra. At Belle Vue there was open-air dancing, and towards 9 p.m. 'the scenic and pyrotechnic spectacle of the war in Servia was given; and at the close an admirable imitation of the front of the new Town hall was exhibited. The device measured about 100 feet across, and all the lines of the windows, tower, turrets, entrance, &c., were set forth in red and blue fire.'

The Alexandra Park contingent drank tea, heard speeches on temperance matters, and worthily passed unanimously a resolution approving the decision not to go to Manley Park, after the granting of a licence for alcohol there, in which decision they had been supported by the mayor.

The final act of the day was the issue of an address by Abel Heywood thanking the societies who had organised the very successful procession 'which will make the proceedings connected with the formal opening of the Town Hall ever memorable in the history of Manchester'. He also extended his gratitude to the police and the military, and finally to the 'good-humoured and hearty co-operation and support of the assembled masses in the maintenance of order...'[38]

The *Manchester Guardian* summed up the wider purpose of the three days' celebrations in proclaiming the gospel of local, municipal power:

> because our ideas of the duties and functions of local government are indeed widely different from what they were two generations ago... The building that is declared open today stands visibly reminding every citizen of the labours and responsibilities of the community to which he belongs, visibly appealing to men of every rank and station, each in their own way, to unite in helping forward the common interests of all.[39]

The end of the mayoralty

In 1877 Abel reached the good old age of 67. Very soon after the Town Hall opening it was public knowledge that he would not stand again for mayor. The events of the preceding months must have put a tremendous strain on him as both mayor and chairman of the New Town Hall Committee.

But there were honours too. As an original member (since 1871) of the Manchester Reform Club on King Street he was given a dinner on 3 October; the Liberal establishment was eager to show that he had done them proud.[40] The chairman, Robert Leake, recalled how Abel was seen from day to day to enter the club and go to his favourite corner, where he liked to join in a rowdy debate: 'They had beheld him the centre of many a conversational whirlwind which even his calm presence and the majesty of his office had not been able to subdue…' He explained that the Reform Club members' respect for Abel had grown, and that 'it had only needed one flash of glorious sunlight, such as was given in those recent three days, to make their hidden esteem for him bloom forth into full efflorescence. (Cheers.)' Mr Leake exonerated the Queen from all blame for her absence at the opening ceremonies, but 'her Majesty's ministers' were thought culpable. His assessment was that at the reception and ball 'every rank and class of this community were assembled in one great civic society for the first time'. In recalling the trades' procession, Leake related how his little daughter might have viewed it:

> She would remember that great scene when her sunny locks were grown silverwhite, and she would perhaps recount on some future day how she saw their guest of that evening stand in his scarlet robes under the porch of his palace and receive the congratulations of thousands of his fellow men. (Cheers.) She would never forget that the day was a people's day… That day was the crowning triumph of our Mayor's career, municipal and social, and the sun shone splendidly down upon it.

When Abel stood up to respond, he received a standing ovation from the whole company. He spoke in what was by now his usual vein; about his early career, his work with Cobden and Wilson to gain a Charter of Incorporation for Manchester, his support of 'sons of labour, for whom on many occasions I have almost risked everything', notably in the years of Chartist agitation. He then moved on to his work on the Highways and Paving Committee, and claimed 'I have visited every street, every passage, almost every back yard that there is in the township of Manchester'. He also hinted that his municipal service had cost him dear financially and commercially, saying that he had sacrificed a fortune in the service of the city because of the amount of time it had taken him away from his business.

Finally, he discussed the new Town Hall, a project with which he had been perhaps somewhat obsessed; he confided that he had sketched the scheme for the inauguration of the Town Hall to Robert Leake in a railway carriage. Nor was he shy of putting forward his entitlement to be invited to open it in the absence of 'a greater personage':

They asked the man who had for twelve or thirteen years worked in connection with the designing and erecting of the new Town hall – the man who suggested the Town Hall – (hear, hear), the man who during the last twelve years, besides attending the committee with which he has now been connected thirty-four years, has never missed a meeting of the Town Hall committee, excepting through illness, and who has always been at his post…

Abel was sometimes noted for his modesty, but it clearly deserted him on this occasion!

He ended his mayoralty as he had begun; he held a series of dinners, this time in the new mayoral apartments. Guests eclectically included aldermen and coun- cillors, Conservative MP Hugh Birley, Abel Heywood junior, Dr Pankhurst and Captain Palin of the Manchester police. On 9 November Abel chaired his last council meeting as mayor and oversaw the election of Charles Grundy to the post. In his address, Abel particularly praised the work of the town clerk, Joseph Heron, who had after long service retired. He went on to detail the projects with which the council would have to be concerned in the coming year: the Thirlmere water supply scheme, which was about to become a battle; the tramways and the regulation of traffic in the streets; the sewage system; the reference library building; the construction of the new gasworks. But he made it clear that this was not the end of his own public service and he asserted his intention of continuing on the council 'as long as he was thought worthy of a seat'.[41]

13

Swansong (1878–93)

My grandfather, as I remember him, was a handsome old man of whom I was rather afraid.[1]

George Basil, son of Abel Heywood junior, was born in 1874 and included this comment in his history of the family business written almost forty years after Abel senior's death. It reflected his impression of his grandfather in his final years; he was somewhat forbidding and was perceived in the family as more devoted to his work for Manchester than to his business.

The years following the opening of the Town Hall were in some ways not markedly different from those preceding it. Abel continued his work on the council and its committees, though in general (with some exceptions) he spoke less in the meetings. He pursued his longstanding interests in the co-operative movement, education, charities and other methods of improving the lives of the poor. To these he added more recently adopted causes, such as the School of Art and women's suffrage, and became more prominent in the Manchester Liberal Reform Club. His interest in foreign policy was unabated and he was active in campaigns about government policy in the Balkans.

But there were reminders of his mortality; though surviving bouts of illness himself, he attended a large number of funerals of men who were his contemporaries, or even his juniors, such as that of Alderman Matthew Curtis, his fellow tower-climber. Even closer to home, his own wife, Elizabeth, died in January 1887. Aware that his years were numbered, and perhaps with some sense that Abel had not received the national recognition he deserved in 1877, the Liberal establishment were keen to recognise his public service by bestowing honours on him. There was an increasing sense that his life was winding down, but in fact he still had almost sixteen years to live after the Town Hall was opened, which was just as well, as his work on that edifice was not finished in 1877; some of the most significant aspects of the building were completed in the 1880s and Abel continued to chair the Town Hall Committee.

Council role

While Abel's contributions to council meetings may not have been as frequent or as sharp as in earlier years, he was clearly eager to play as full a part as possible in municipal life and he continued to attend them assiduously. As the 'Father of the Council' he was entrusted with representing the Corporation in a wider forum, both in Manchester and London, adding weight and seniority rather than detailed argument. On 27 January 1880 he appeared as deputy chairman of a Town Hall special committee before an inspector from the Local Government Board at the Town Hall, to help explain the Corporation's need to borrow a sum of £200,000 to complete and furnish the new building. Two years later, Abel went with other aldermen to London to represent Manchester at the annual meeting of the Association of Municipal Corporations. This role was broadened in January 1888 when he was appointed to a group led by the mayor, formed to 'watch the measures to be introduced by the Government with regard to local government'.[2] Accordingly, he again went to London in 1888 to attend the meeting of the Association, this time focusing on the effects on local power of the Local Government Bill, which was to set up county councils. The council was keen to resist attempts at centralisation from Westminster, an aim with which Abel fully concurred.

The municipality was expanding considerably in this period to include the out-townships; a sub-committee was appointed to investigate the inclusion of Harpurhey and Newton Heath, and Abel's name was first on the list. Two years later the council was discussing a report by the sub-committee and in a slightly wandering speech (he strayed into the thorny and longstanding issue of a Salford–Manchester amalgamation, for instance), Abel warned that it must not be forgotten that some out-townships were saddled with problems which had been neglected. Having listened to the speech, Alderman Worthington expressed what others probably also felt: a mystification as to Abel's position on the out-townships. Nevertheless, when a settlement with the County of Lancashire had to be reached in 1886 because of loss of rates from areas incorporated into Manchester, namely Rusholme, Bradford and Harpurhey, it was the mayor and Abel Heywood who successfully negotiated the settlement at a lower price than the county demanded, and it seems that Abel was still a useful and effective part of the two-man team.

Taking his usual interest in the health of the working classes, Abel continued to promote the expanding work of the Health Committee, of which he himself had been a member from 1868. In 1885 he became officially involved in attempts to improve Manchester's housing, when as chair of the Highways and Paving Committee he was deputy chairman of a special committee to report on 'the dilapidated or unsanitary dwelling-houses within the city… with a view to their improvement or removal, and also to recommend the purchase, on economical terms, of such as would provide sites for open spaces and play grounds, in densely populated neighbourhoods'.[3] In October the committee reported back, having met eleven times and personally inspected dwellings reported as unfit for human habitation. However, nothing much improved with regard to housing and the committee came in for criticism for its inactivity in December. Local vested interests proved more than a match for the Corporation.

Abel was still active in the Baths and Laundries Company, and in January 1878 presided over the meeting which agreed, as he had long advocated, the sale of the company's properties at Mayfield (Ardwick) and Leaf Street (Stretford Road) to Manchester Corporation. His faith was rewarded, as the council began almost immediately to add to the number of baths, and in 1880 opened a new facility at New Islington. He apparently enjoyed the opening ceremony, in which the audience of ladies and gentlemen were treated to a rare demonstration of swimming in the second-class plunge pool. As well as the dubious pleasures of eating underwater, the programme included 'diving and swimming with the clothes on, the removal of the clothes on the surface and underneath the water, imitations of the chest stroke of Captain Webb, and the double leg stroke of Mr. E. T. Jones, the champion fast swimmer of the world...'[4]

Despite intimating that he was intending to step down from the chairmanship in October 1878, Abel continued to lead the Highways and Paving Committee and to speak in its defence as necessary. There was agitation from the Royal Infirmary in Piccadilly that the stone paving sets in the adjoining streets were too noisy, especially as the new tram system had reduced the width of the pavements by six feet, and that therefore the stone should be replaced with wooden paving. Abel and the committee visited the hospital and went into the wards, but judged that the noise was not unreasonable; they suggested double-glazing instead. Abel's role also brought him into contact with technological developments in communications – telephone and telegraph wires. It was typical of his lifelong interest in new inventions that he believed these forms of technology 'marked an era in the progress of civilisation such as they could scarcely refer to in the previous history of the country'. In 1881 he joined a council committee to co-ordinate the growing profusion of wires above the streets, and investigate the cost of putting them underground.[5]

Transport continued to figure large. Railway bills before Parliament which the council opposed required active campaigning and in 1881 Abel was included in a deputation to London charged with such action against the Cheshire Lines. However, it was the developing tram system which occupied much of Abel's time as the newest branch of the Highways and Paving Committee's activities.

A special meeting of the council was convened on 21 November 1877 at which a proposal was made for the extension of tramways throughout the city. Abel introduced it with a detailed speech, in which he claimed during the preceding twelve months to have inspected 'nearly every other tramway that existed in our large towns'. He also pointed out that tramways were being constructed by the out-townships and presciently predicted that this means of transport would be a way of carrying the poor to the edge of the city 'where they might be able to breathe much purer air than in Manchester'. He accordingly advocated a system of charging 1*d* to make trams affordable. Despite some opposition and discussion, a resolution was passed to apply to the government for authority to proceed.[6] The Board of Trade on 20 February 1878 convened an enquiry in the Town Hall. Abel, assisted by the deputy town clerk and the city surveyor, responded confidently to all objections and acquitted himself with great aplomb. Authorisation duly arrived, and the system was put out to tender; in July 1879 the council confirmed acceptance of the Manchester Carriage Company's proposal and construction could begin. In his inimitable way, Abel treated the council to a detailed and highly complicated explanation of the costs of construction and maintenance; indeed he prefaced his exposition by saying that 'he trusted that the Council would be able to follow him in the explanation he was about to give'. Whether they understood it all is a moot point, but they were sufficiently impressed by Mr Goldschmidt's calculation that the cost of construction could be recouped in under eleven years, and thereafter there would be a profit of £14,000 a year, that they voted to adopt the report.[7]

Despite a sad accident in which a carter was killed on the City Road in Hulme on the day the Stretford line was opened, in November 1880 Abel successfully proposed a second tranche of tramway construction, which was to include Market Street. In an attempt to allay the criticism that trams were dangerous, he exhibited a stoicism which would be censured today when he opined that 'gentlemen who had watched the progress of great enterprises would have learned that in many of those enterprises somebody had to be sacrificed in the beginning... but it did appear to him that if ordinary care had been taken there would have been no necessity for the sacrifice of life'.[8] In fact, Abel and his committee seem to have been more upset about deputations, letters to the press and memorials about a lack of trams in Market Street, and his response was a letter to the *Manchester Guardian* defending 'the best abused committee of the City Council'.[9] Despite the gripes, the tram system became the everyday means of transport for ordinary Mancunians until well into the twentieth century. Their utility has been recognised again in the last twenty-five years by the advent of their modern incarnation, the Metrolink, which has proved anew the popularity of trams.

In 1882, the council had decided to support a new venture in transport, the Manchester Ship Canal. Abel was less enthusiastic about this; in the meeting of 6 December 1882 he voted against a resolution to put £1 million of city money into the project on the grounds that Manchester would gain nothing and would only see a rise in the rates, which he expected to be around 6*d* in the pound, to pay for the investment. Nevertheless, he characteristically took the trouble to inform himself, and in July 1890 attended the International Congress on Inland Navigation. The project was overwhelmingly supported by the council but Abel did not live to see the canal eventually opened in January 1894, by Queen Victoria.

He was also, perhaps surprisingly, hostile to an attempt by Councillor Birch to get the council to approve a memorial to the Home Secretary asking for attention to the plight of young children selling newspapers, matches, etc. on the street 'at unseasonable hours'. He expressed the somewhat idiosyncratic view that such children were of huge value in 'the circulation of news' and as such they were 'messengers of mercy'. His motive seems also to have been that he did not want to see the children imprisoned for selling papers.[10] The following October Abel appeared on the executive committee appointed at a public meeting to express an opinion on the state of the law on children in common gaols. It was also suggested in the council discussions that the answer to the issue of street children might be found in the industrial schools, and Abel was supportive of such bodies. When the Nicholls Hospital was set up 'for the education and maintenance of 100 poor boys' aged between 7 and 10 in Hyde Road, Ardwick, Abel was one of the trustees. However, according to the will of the founder, the boys had to be born legitimately and to have parents who were 'honest, industrious, and in needy circumstances', as well as being church or chapel-goers (unless the children were orphans). In other words, they must be 'deserving' poor.[11]

It may be remarked that as time wore on there was sometimes a slight sense that Abel was not quite on the ball in terms of his contributions to discussions in the council. On occasion, he was still chosen to chair meetings and carried out his duties competently, but this did not prevent his launching into long speeches which delved into the history of the council. There was a lot of discussion on market tolls in 1882–84 and on 9 August 1882 Abel was loquacious about the history of Manchester markets, starting even before Incorporation, in which he seemed to be attempting to show that restrictions and tolls imposed by the Markets Committee were irksome for market users. However, his argument was obscured by the historical detail, as Alderman Worthington put it, 'it would be difficult for him to follow Mr. Heywood in the historical portion of his remarks, and he failed to see its bearing on the question now under consideration. They did not want to know the history of the market.'[12] The following month Abel presented a memorial from the people doing business in the Smithfield Market with regard to the payments to which they were subject. He was prevented by the mayor's intervention from launching into a further long explanation, so instead he made a 'speech of some length' on the history of the General Purposes Committee but so many councillors walked out as he was speaking that there was no longer a quorum and the meeting was precipitately ended.[13]

It may have been in response to this apparent decline, combined with his clear interest in the early years of Manchester's government, that the council chose to give him a role in the preservation of the records of the old Court Leet, which extended from 1552 to 1846. Now as 'Father of the Council' it also became Abel's role annually to move the resolution for the election of the new mayor in November and to chair the meetings which were usually held earlier to decide on a nominee, avoiding a painful election process. When Mayor Matthew Curtis died in office in June 1887, it was Abel who presided at the meeting to select a replacement.

This increasingly honorific role was nowhere more marked than in the reception of important visitors to the city. Abel was appointed to deputations to receive such personages, some of whom came to examine Manchester's advanced systems, such as the London Corporation in 1878 who focused on the efficiency of Manchester's fire brigade and their use of new technology, in the form of water hydrants, to quench fires. When the following year Princess Mary of Cambridge and the Duke of Teck, accompanied by the Danish Minister to the Court of St James and others, drove over from Heaton Park, they got the full Town Hall treatment. They were met by a deputation which included Abel; the bells played the national anthem, they undertook a guided tour, had lunch in the banqueting hall, and attended an organ recital by Mr Pyne in the public hall. As well as foreign deputations, there were also celebrated individuals whom Abel was detailed to entertain: Ferdinand de Lesseps, builder of the Suez Canal; Henry Stanley, the African explorer; Lord Rosebery, leading Liberal; George Goschen, Chancellor of the Exchequer; Lord Arthur Balfour, Chief Secretary for Ireland; the Duke of Edinburgh, the Duke of Albany, and Prince Albert, eldest grandson of the Queen; not to mention the Lord Mayor of London. All of these dignitaries were received with varying degrees of pomp, depending on their eminence, their importance to Manchester, and the length of time for which they would require entertaining, and Abel was frequently at the heart of the planning as well as the actual event.

His role was particularly fulfilled in 1887, the year of Queen Victoria's Jubilee, which was marked in Manchester by a special exhibition, and a visit by the Prince and Princess of Wales at the start of May to open it. Appointed to chair the jubilee committee, Abel spoke in praise of the Queen's reign, choosing to focus on the freedom of the press, abolition of taxes on corn, and the establishing of the penny post. He then tagged on a reference to the 'political liberty' which had been granted to 'the great masses of the people in this country'.[14] The royal couple were shown around the state apartments in the Town Hall by the mayor, deputy-mayor and Alderman Abel Heywood.

On the day of the jubilee itself, 22 June, in the absence in London of the mayor, Abel acted as his deputy. In true Liberal manner, he contrasted the hymn at the jubilee of George III about the fire-power of the British navy with the line sung on this day 'And Briton's rights depend on war no more', showing the new emphasis on peace. He stood in the doorway of the Town Hall to receive a procession of 75,000 children from ragged schools around Manchester who had previously been given a hearty breakfast at municipal expense. From four in the afternoon in the Free Trade Hall Abel presided at a tea for about 3,000 people of the same or a greater age than the Queen, that is sixty-eight years. At some point before the end of proceedings, Abel was 'compelled to leave'. Before he departed, though, a vote of thanks was carried with enthusiasm.[15]

Right into the 1890s Abel continued to attend the council and even joined the new Sanitary Committee set up in 1890 as chairman of the Highways, Paving and Sewering Committee, which he continued actively to chair until November 1892. He was also re-appointed as deputy chairman of the Town Hall Committee. Abel's response was grateful and proud. 'It might be said that he was not only the father of the Council, but the father of the Town hall also. For some 12 years, whilst that building was being brought into the state in which it was now, he visited it every day except Sundays…'[16]

In general Abel confined his contributions in council meetings to voting. However, in April 1892 he was roused to indignation on a characteristic topic of interest, temperance. He opposed the granting of a theatrical licence to a music hall, the Palace of Varieties, because it would have allowed the sale of alcohol, which Abel had already voted down in the licensing sessions. To the last, he was committed to the great campaigns of his heyday.

Social, cultural and political campaigns

Nowhere was this clearer than in Abel's support of working men. In 1883 he led the executive committee for the establishment of a new exhibition for the building trades. He was keen to smooth the path of industrial relations, and performed the role of arbiter apparently successfully in the painters' dispute in 1880. When the novel idea of a labour bureau to help men find work was mooted by a certain Joseph Waddington in 1884, Abel donated 5s to his efforts, in keeping with the idea of local efforts to improve the lot of the working man.

Another aspect of self-help, the co-operative movement, continued to receive Abel's backing. The members of the Manchester Society, to thank Abel for a visit to the Town Hall on the occasion of its opening, presented him as chairman with an address in the form of a book. This evoked memories for Abel of his early days, and he talked about how he sold the unstamped papers in Oldham Street. As often, he had his eye on posterity when he said that 'if the reporters took that down… it would be mentioned in history'.[17]

When all else failed, Abel was as keen as the next Victorian to see the poor properly buried, and therefore was the treasurer of the national Rational Sick and Burial Society by the end of the 1870s. Representatives from all over England met in Hulme Town Hall on 3 June 1879 and listened to his address in which he praised the work and the success of the organisation in providing for sickness and death. He went on to advocate 'a system of superannuation' which would provide also for 'a period when a man was no longer able to work' and thus prevent him 'from resorting to the poor rate and the workhouses'. Effectively, he was advocating, ahead of his time, the provision of an old age pension. He continued to attend the meetings and took the chair as late as 1891.[18]

Another continuing interest was, of course in education, but he had ceased to be a mover and shaker, and rarely spoke out, confining his participation to voting in council and appearing on platforms. Abel supported the Mechanics' Institution by presiding in 1878 at a talk by Dr Pankhurst on political economy. He also made an unusual appearance at the speech day of Manchester Grammar School in 1880.

Finally, when in 1892 Earl Spencer was installed in the Town Hall as Chancellor of the new Victoria University of Manchester, Abel was in attendance in the audience.

He also continued to support the Manchester School of Art, temporary exhibitions and the art gallery at the Royal Institution. On 27 April 1881 the new School of Art was opened at All Saints by the Earl of Derby. Abel took a prominent place on the platform to the right of the chairman. In February 1882 at the next prize-giving, Abel was appointed a member of the committee for the school for the next year. He continued to attend meetings until as late as 1889.

In the autumn of 1882, Manchester hosted a 'Grand Fine Art and Industrial Exhibition', patronised by a high-powered coterie of local aristocrats, joined also by municipal dignitaries, headed by 'Mr. Alderman Heywood, J.P.' as chair of the executive committee. The exhibition was opened by the Earl of Wilton, and another celebrated visitor with whom Abel lunched at the opening was William Morris, whose company had sent in exhibits, and who spoke about his views on the decorative arts. Continuing the theme, Abel pushed the idea that the Royal Institution should be transferred to the council to host a public art gallery and museum. The matter became urgent in December when John Slagg MP wrote to ask whether Manchester would like reproductions of works of art and other objects from the London museums. At the end of August 1882 the council was ready to appoint its representatives on the Art Gallery committee; Abel was on the list. Finally, a year later, the new Manchester Art Gallery was opened with an autumn exhibition. The occasion was marked by a procession from the Town Hall to the Art Gallery, and in the evening a soiree at which Abel took his place on the platform. As part of his lifelong desire to improve the moral and educational standards of the people, Abel had ever been a supporter of art galleries which were accessible to all, and he must have felt a great satisfaction that at last the city had achieved a worthy institution.

Abel also continued to show a lively interest in foreign affairs. By 1878 the country was in the grip of war-fever over Russian activity in the Balkans. As the danger of war continued, in February an estimated 18,000 to 20,000 Conservatives in Manchester rallied in Pomona Gardens to back Disraeli's government in its support for Turkey against Russian incursions. In reply, the Liberals, with Abel as president, held a meeting for working men in Stevenson Square, protesting against a vote in Parliament of £6 million credit for the army and navy in preparation for a possible war. The meeting, 'orderly, enthusiastic, and unanimous', voted to support Abel's motion against the war credits. Dr Pankhurst proposed a resolution of no confidence in the government, which was carried 'with acclamation', and the meeting ended with cheers for Mr Gladstone, Sir Thomas Bazley and Jacob Bright, followed by the inevitable groans for the prime minister.

Nevertheless, on 12 February, the latter ordered the fleet to Constantinople, in pursuit of the traditional policy of the British; that is to support the Turkish Empire in the face of Russian threat in the Balkans. On 30 March the Russians imposed the punishing Treaty of San Stefano on the Turks; it was unacceptable to the British government, which pushed for a new treaty. On 3 April deputations from Liberal organisations in towns all over England and Scotland travelled to London to meet Liberal Lords Granville and Hartington, and put the case against calling out the reserves and in favour of the government's attending a proposed congress. Abel was present as a representative of the Manchester Liberal Association. The group was led by several MPs, and most prominent were John Bright, A.J. Mundella and the Birmingham MP Joseph Chamberlain, supported as he was by the National Liberal Federation and the National Reform Union. Ultimately, of course, Disraeli and his foreign secretary, Lord Salisbury, achieved what they wanted at the Congress of Berlin in June, without having to resort to war, and the premier came home to a hero's welcome from his supporters, proclaiming 'Peace for our time.' This appears to have been the last time that Abel involved himself in agitations about foreign policy, and although he was now in his late sixties, the reason may be because the settlement reached at Berlin did indeed patch things up in the Balkans until after his death, and the threat of a major war in Europe receded for the following thirty years.

Manchester Liberal

Abel had presented himself very much as a mainstream Liberal during the anti-war campaign, and indeed after 1867 he seems to have been taken gladly into the bosom of the Manchester Liberals, delighted no doubt that he was no longer determined to stand as a Radical Liberal candidate for Manchester, thereby splitting the Liberal vote. This was all the more important in these years because the Conservatives, for so long in the wilderness in Manchester and the country at large, were enjoying a renaissance under their dazzling, if enigmatic, leader Benjamin Disraeli, Earl of Beaconsfield. In 1871 the Manchester Liberals had opened a splendid new Reform Club on King Street, and Abel as a founder member of the institution was listed in their records as one of the original guarantors. He does not seem to have been very active in the club until the end of the 1870s, but thereafter appeared frequently at their lectures and meetings.

When in 1880 the Liberal council met to choose a replacement for the ailing MP Sir Thomas Bazley, Abel's name was thrown into the ring by the radical Richard Pankhurst.[19] The Liberal council fully recognised Abel's 'distinguished services for the town and life long devotion to his principles', but it was another candidate, John Slagg, who was selected; he had the right background to attract the votes of Liberals of all complexions. It may also have been the hope that vacillating Conservatives might be won over by such a candidate.

Abel's radical past told against him, and even his recent role in the campaigns with regard to the Balkans may have made him suspect in some quarters, as the *Manchester Courier* eagerly pointed out. It seems likely that his age and declining powers did not help his suit. He accepted the decision (at least publicly) with equanimity. Perhaps it was as a thank-you and a compensation that he was elected vice-president of the Reform Club in February 1880 and without opposition on 22 February 1881 as president.

Abel presided when the Collegiate Ward Liberal Association held a social evening in March 1880. He enjoined unity so that they might return a majority of candidates pledged to support Mr Gladstone and Lord Hartington. He condemned the warlike policies of the Conservative government, referring presumably not only to the threat of war against Russia, but also to the colonial wars fought in South Africa and Afghanistan, so strongly attacked by his hero, William Gladstone. For his own part, 'With regard to the contest in Manchester, he urged the importance of sinking minor differences in order to support the general Liberal opinion throughout the country.' Jacob Bright and John Slagg called in briefly to address the meeting. Slagg expressed the hope that Abel would support him and went on to give an address which Abel apparently chose to see in a positive light, but which also undermined Abel's suitability as a representative of respectable Liberalism. Referring to the royal snub of 1877, Slagg offered, 'it seemed strange when a large and important constituency like Manchester made the very natural request that Her Majesty should come down and honour it by her presence that that occasion was made the opportunity of administering a deliberate and, he said, an unforgivable affront to their esteemed chairman.- (Loud cheers.)'

Abel's feelings on hearing these words were not recorded, but the meeting went on to carry enthusiastically his suggestion that Slagg's candidature be approved and support pledged on and before the polling day.[20] John Slagg topped the poll, with Jacob Bright a close second, and Hugh Birley the Conservative being the third MP. This reflected a national trend which signalled the triumphant return of Gladstone to the premiership for his second ministry. It was the first time a Liberal had come top in Manchester since 1867.[21] The Reform Club celebrated in style with a dinner for candidates which Abel chaired; of the thirty-one members who had stood across the Manchester region, only three had not been successful.

Although the Liberal majority had been the largest ever, it became clear in Manchester Council discussions that a large number of working-class men who were registered had not voted. The Liberal government introduced a bill to lengthen the hours of voting, for both general and municipal elections, from 8 a.m. to 8 p.m.; currently polling ended at 4 p.m. Some on the council had taken exception to this interference in Manchester's affairs. To justify it, Abel added up the votes, and showed that out of a potential 60,000 voters, only 45,000 had voted, and pointed out that it was Benjamin Disraeli, the Conservative Earl of Beaconsfield, author of the 1867 Reform Act, who was 'godfather' for the greater number of electors who had to be fitted into the limited time available. He also ridiculed suggestions that an extension of polling hours would lead to 'disturbances'. Since the bill had recently been modified to make it permissive, probably in view of such debates in councils up and down the country, Manchester Council agreed that they would petition for the decision to be left to the local authorities, and this was carried.[22]

With the possibility of another election in 1883 due to the death of the Conservative MP Hugh Birley, the Liberal Association after some debate decided not to contest the seat. Despite this, a few days later Dr Richard Pankhurst put himself forward. There was talk of Abel Heywood as a 'Radical' also standing. The meeting at which Pankhurst formally declared his hand on 20 September was chaired by Abel junior. In his introduction, the latter stated that his man was the candidate for the working class, and scotched the rumour about his father. 'There was a reported rumour in one of the papers that morning that his father, Mr. Alderman Heywood, was about to offer himself as a candidate. He had mentioned the matter to his father [who] had told him in order to at once settle the matter to put his name down on Dr. Pankhurst's election committee. – (Cheers.)'

This was accordingly carried into effect. Some of Pankhurst's views accorded well with what we know of Abel's own; he laid out principles of peace and cheap and local government, as well as the disestablishment of the Anglican Church. In other respects Pankhurst was much more radical than Heywood; he was by now a republican, who advocated the abolition of the monarchy and the House of Lords. He also filled his speeches with 'violent rhetoric and bloody metaphors', despite his gentle demeanour and slight stature.[23] In defiance of the Liberal Council Pankhurst continued to press his candidature with prominent support from Abel Heywood junior, but in the end the Conservative candidate W.H. Houldsworth was elected. The response of the rebels to the attitude of the Liberal Association was to set up a breakaway Radical and Liberal Association; Pankhurst's censure of the Liberal Association for its dictatorial methods was reminiscent of Abel Heywood senior's criticism of the same body in 1859 and 1865. Indeed, the latter lent some support to the new body, and was scheduled to appear with Pankhurst at its Hulme branch in January 1884, being prevented from doing so by 'indisposition', which may have been expedient.

Indeed, Abel senior continued to back the main Liberal Association. In 1884, as part of the agitation for the impending Franchise Bill, the Liberals organised a demonstration at Pomona which would be addressed by John Bright and Lord Hartington and Abel took his place on the platform amongst the leaders of the Manchester Liberals. The result of the Third Reform Act of 1884 was to extend the franchise to agricultural workers, with the effect that around two-thirds of men could now vote. It was accompanied by a Redistribution Act in which the principle of single-member and equal constituencies was at last established; Manchester was divided into six new constituencies, which meant that both Liberals and Conservatives had to re-think their electoral strategies. The divisions among Manchester Liberals were set aside in February 1885, when a bust of Dr John Watts was presented to the Reform Club at a dinner in his honour. Eulogies were given by his particular supporters, among whom was Abel Heywood senior. The Tory *Manchester Courier* enjoyed the opportunity to poke barbed fun at the diversity within the Liberal party:

The advanced Liberal regards the moderate Liberal as a slow coach, and the Radical, who is also a Liberal, regards them both as standing in need of the application of a powerful galvanic battery. The Republican-Liberal looks upon all other forms of Liberalism as partaking very much of the character of a sham, and the Socialist-Liberal regards all the other divisions of the army as being on the wrong scent... And yet, here in Manchester... the leading members of the Manchester Reform Club, including Mr. Jacob Bright, M.P., Mr. Alderman Heywood, the Rev. Mr. Steinthal, and Mr. B. Armitage, M.P., assembled to do honour to the leading Socialist in Lancashire – Dr. John Watts.[24]

Attempts to heal divisions were thwarted, however. By 1887, with the Liberal party split in Westminster over the issue of Home Rule, for which Gladstone had declared his support in 1886, Ireland had become a burning issue for the Manchester Liberals. One positive effect of the adoption of the Home Rule policy, and opposition to Tory coercion measures, was a marked increase in support from the large Irish population, which may well help explain the fact that the Manchester Liberals' showing improved dramatically in the election of 1886, from only one MP out of a possible six in 1885 to three in 1886.

As the Liberal split over Ireland became wider and more permanent, in 1890 Abel was active in the Reform Club in countering the threat from Liberal Unionism. It became acute in the Manchester Liberal party when a member of the club, Alfred Hopkinson, accepted the Conservative nomination as a candidate for South-West Manchester in opposition to Jacob Bright, that year president of the club. At a special meeting condemning the renegade's actions as inconsistent with membership of the club, feelings ran high and Hopkinson was greeted with calls of 'Traitor.'

It was Abel who was to propose the resolution of condemnation, but his speech reflected his advancing years and was somewhat rambling; he reflected on how Hopkinson's position was similar to his own in 1859 in that both of them challenged Jacob Bright, except that in his case he represented the working classes, and the vote in 1859 vindicated his standing again in 1865. In the same way that his candidacy was not an attack on Bright, but an offer of his own merits, this speech was not an attack on Mr Hopkinson, but a defence of the Reform Club. Abel then went off into a discussion of whether the candidate was independent of the Conservatives, as he had apparently promised them nothing, and got side-tracked into the position of the Church of England. The bell for time had been rung twice and there were cries of 'Time' so he ended his speech, but in a personal moment, he confided in the time-honoured way of elderly people, 'he would move the resolution, but before he did so he would just tell them something, which he dare say they did not know; it was this, he would be 80 years of age on Tuesday next. (Cheers, and a voice, "Another grand old man.")' After lively discussion the resolution was carried with a large majority.

The *Manchester Courier* reflected on these proceedings with predictable hostility, and commented particularly on Abel's contribution as 'in the last degree infelicitous'. It stated that he was neither an intelligible nor an intelligent speaker, and that his point about how he differed from Mr Hopkinson was incomprehensible. What no one could deny, however, was that Abel's position was staunchly and markedly Gladstonian.[25]

By 1889 Abel was fully ensconced in the Reform Club. He had been a widower for two years and perhaps the club provided the company he missed at home. One account describes him surrounded by his friends among the Liberal aldermen:

> For many years there had been what was known in the Club as the "Corporation Table"… Here, waited on by one of the oldest waiters, foregathered some of the senior Liberals of the City Council. Chief amongst them were Alderman Abel Heywood, the Father of the Council and Mayor of the City at the time of the opening of the new Town hall; Alderman Joseph Thompson, Alderman Harry Rawson… and Alderman J.F. Roberts.[26]

Nevertheless, Abel had not forgotten his radical roots. Indeed, it could be said that he was more concerned about the commemoration of past working-class heroes than were the working classes. The monument to Henry Hunt, erected in 1842 in Ancoats, had been removed and sold off for a mere £3. Abel was eager to launch a crusade to find and restore it. When he visited New Islington and the Ancoats Recreation Committee in October 1888 he appealed for something to be done to restore the monument and the audience applauded. But the Hunt monument had gone for good, the stone was sold off, and a scheme the following year failed to raise sufficient funds to erect a new monument. Abel was seeing the end of his era. Perhaps more to the taste of both working- and middle-class Liberals was the monument to John Bright, who died in 1889. After consideration of other sites, Abel proposed the Highways and Paving Committee's suggestion, which the council accepted, that it should be placed in Albert Square.

The Reform Club was keen to honour the ageing member with a presentation for his eightieth birthday in February 1890 of a silver casket, 'richly gilt and engraved with bold bas-reliefs'. The cost of the gift was £15. It was formally presented at a crowded meeting in the private dining room on 26 March. Thomas Bazley, in the chair, recalled that he had looked to Abel as his guide in the council. Mr Prestwich made the presentation, and reminded the audience that Abel had been a 'maker of history' and said that he was still 'in perfect health of mind and body'.[27]

Indeed, this may well be true, despite spells of illness; even as late as January 1893 Abel was re-elected to represent the Collegiate ward on the general council of the North-West Manchester Liberal Association. Yet his continuation in office was more a recognition of his past achievements than an expectation for the future, and so far as is known Abel showed no awareness of developments in the party which would become 'New Liberalism', nor of the potential political threat from the Labour movement. He was certainly a respected elder statesman of the party, but his Gladstonian brand of Liberalism with his pretensions to radicalism were now dated.

Bereavements

Abel, generally still active and in good health apart from spells of illness in 1883 and 1888, and a trip to Malvern in 1885 which may have been a rest cure, must have felt increasingly the isolation of outliving many of his contemporaries. He attended the funerals of Corporation colleagues such as that of Alderman Curtis. He was also present at the obsequies of William Gaskell, Minister of the Cross Street chapel, and of the famous philanthropist John Rylands. His old radical comrade, Dr John Watts, died in 1887, being buried just near Abel's home at Bowdon Church. At the end of the decade, 1889 saw the deaths of two other major figures in Abel's life: John Bright and Joseph Heron, the retired town clerk.

But of course, the greatest loss of all must have been that of his wife, Elizabeth, who died on 11 January 1887 at their home in Bowdon. Abel planned a dignified funeral for her on 14 January. She was to be buried with Ann Heywood in Philips Park Cemetery, Bradford-cum-Beswick.[28] Abel's colleagues on the council were sympathetic to his loss, and in particular the Highways and Paving Committee recorded in their minutes on 12 January in one long, unpunctuated sentence:

> That this Committee desire to express their most sincere and heartfelt sympathy with their esteemed Chairman Alderman Heywood in the overwhelming and irreparable loss which he has sustained by the death of Mrs. Heywood and although they are aware how utterly inadequate to lessen his grievous sorrow any expression of theirs may be yet they venture to forward to him this resolution in the hope that it may in some degree be a solace to him to know how deeply and how earnestly from their affection and regard for him the feelings of each individual member have been touched by the severity of his affliction.[29]

The feelings thus expressed are so strong as to perhaps reflect the impact which Elizabeth's death had on Abel, and may provide a glimpse into the depth of his relationship with, and dependence on, his second wife.

Honours and recognition

It was in these later years that Abel reaped the rewards of recognition from his fellow Mancunians, many of whom still keenly felt that he had not received his due from royalty. In October 1880 the council accepted a bust of him which was to be placed in the Town Hall. The letter which accompanied it revealed that it was the gift of Dr John Watts and Mr H. Slatter, although the fact that they said they were 'authorised' to offer it suggests there were others behind it who were unnamed. 'From hereditary nobles the nation is right in expecting high services… But, Mr. Mayor, there are nobles amongst us who have to struggle against adverse circumstances for recognition…'[30]

In 1888 there even seems to have been some contemplation in certain quarters of erecting a statue to Abel Heywood as the Father of the Council; his name in this regard was uncharacteristically coupled with that of Lord Beaconsfield by the *Manchester Courier*, but in neither case was this ever achieved in Manchester. The suggestion was likely to have been linked to the fact that this year marked Abel's fifty-year jubilee on the Manchester council, for which other celebrations were forthcoming. The council discussed the idea of a banquet and address for September. There were some who felt that it should not be a closed affair, and Ben Brierley, now no longer a member, wrote to the *Manchester Guardian* supporting this viewpoint, and offering to pay for himself so that the ratepayers were not burdened: 'I am not a rich man, but I could manage to scrape up a guinea for such a purpose.'[31] A touching appeal was made in the letter pages of the paper when a 'Handloom Weaver' referred to the case of his eighty-year-old friend who had always been a supporter of Abel Heywood, following his progress and his work for the city. 'This old man has known and watched and admired the career of Alderman Heywood from his youth up, and can tell some thrilling stories of those bygone days…'[32] The date was fixed for 26 September, and in the end Ben Brierley somehow managed to gain entrance; whether the veteran supporter was also invited is unclear. Abel's two sons were present, but it was claimed 'that such was the esteem in which he was held by the public that had this banquet been thrown open to the public the Town hall would not have sufficed to accommodate those who desired in this way to do honour to Mr. Alderman Heywood'.

Abel was presented with a framed and illustrated address, bearing a colour portrait of himself in mayoral robe and chain seated in the council chamber, and scrollwork inscribed 'The dawn of truth, long overcast, shall kindly kindle into day at last.' His coat of arms, which he had at some point acquired, also appeared with its motto, appropriate in view of Abel's philosophy of life: 'Help yourself.' Among other illustrations was a view of the Town Hall with a text from Shakespeare: 'The very stones shall prate of me.'

In presenting this document, the mayor, Sir John Harwood, referred to Abel's 'deep and unwavering faith in the goodness of your fellow men', and his part in the crusade for personal, civil and religious freedom and social prosperity with cultivated intelligence, won with struggle and at a personal cost. In reply, Abel called this 'the crowning moment of my life'. In case the listeners were afraid they were in for a very long speech, and aware of his own tendencies in that direction, Abel reassured them 'do not fear that I am going to give you a fifty years' history of Manchester. I have studied how best within becoming limits of time I might refer to some few points which may be of interest to my colleagues and the public.'

What Abel chose to say had been considered carefully and reflected his judgement of what he thought most notable in his own career. He started with the campaign against newspaper taxes, then went on to the changes in Manchester's system of government and his support for Incorporation. Having spent too long on this section despite all his good intentions, he then decided to pick out only a few salient points for the rest which included the purchase of the manorial rights from Sir Oswald Mosley and of the waterworks, and his work on the Highways, Paving and Sewering and the Improvement Committees. He stressed that in both areas his main concern had been 'as far as I could [to make] the lives of the very poor worth living'. In recounting the building of the Town Hall he waxed lyrical:

> Time may have darkened the outside purity of those walls, but the graceful, tapering towers and noble archways are still full of beauty as when the sounds of the last hammer and chisel ceased; while the long cathedral aisles of the interior, this magnificent banqueting hall, the splendid central hall with the mural paintings on which Mr. Madox Brown has bestowed so much artistic care – these are the admiration of every stranger who visits our city.

He ended with his thanks, and expressed the belief that Manchester's future was great and in good hands: 'Those who unselfishly give themselves to the great work will find, as I in a full measure have found tonight, that Manchester is far from being ungrateful.'[33]

In early September Alderman Windsor had suggested that further to these honours, a portrait should be commissioned. A special committee was set up in December to oversee this project and later in that month it was agreed that, to supplement the large amount already publicly subscribed, the city would pay up to £250 for the commission, which would be carried out by Henry Turner Munns. It was completed by the following June and it was planned to exhibit it in the City Art Gallery for public perusal.

By the end of the 1880s Abel was in his eightieth year, and although now more subject to periodic illness, he still participated in the life of the city and the Corporation to a remarkable degree. He soldiered on into the 1890s and the honours continued, but it must have been anticipated that each accolade would be his last. The greatest was perhaps the Freedom of Manchester, which was bestowed in 1891. There were two public figures who had already been thus honoured, but both were from a very different background from that of Abel Heywood. The first was Oliver Heywood, the banker and philanthropist, of impeccable upper middle-class origins. The second was the American explorer Henry Stanley who had visited Manchester to lecture about his adventures in darkest Africa.

Abel Heywood was the first man of working-class origin and radical politics who was thus honoured by the city fathers. He had been very ill earlier in 1891; he missed all the council meetings in May and June. There were daily bulletins in the newspapers updating the public on his illness, which it was clearly feared would be his last. Indeed, Abel himself later said he had not expected to recover. However, by mid-May it was reported that he was much better; after a rest at Malvern, he was welcomed back in the council on 15 July 'looking as well as ever'. The idea of bestowing on him the Freedom of Manchester, the city's greatest honour, was introduced in the General Purposes Committee by Mayor Mark in October 1891, who described Abel as 'a very nice old man… and he is a very careful and wise counsellor, not only to the Mayor but to others'.[34] The council, having been informed by the mayor that Abel regarded the honour as of 'priceless worth', ratified the decision a few days later. Alderman Harwood probably expressed the sentiments of many when he said:

> It was a very desirable thing, when a man had rendered such signal services during a long life as Mr. Alderman Heywood had given to this city, that they should not leave recognition of them till he died, but should break the alabaster box of ointment over him while he was living, and should give a liberal interpretation of their admiration for his mind and character. – (Hear, hear.)[35]

On the day, the council chamber was filled. There were many distinguished guests such as Earl Spencer, several MPs, prominent citizens like Oliver Heywood and C.P. Scott, and members of Abel's family; his sons, Judge George Washington Heywood and Abel Heywood junior, and his grandsons, Abel and George Basil. Also in attendance, just in case, was Abel's physician, Dr Mules.

As Abel was conducted into the chamber by Alderman Mark, ex-mayor, and Sir John Harwood, the whole assembly stood and applauded loudly. It must have been a great moment for someone who still liked to describe himself as 'a working man'. The town clerk read the resolution conferring the Freedom of Manchester, whereupon Abel signed the Roll of Freemen. Mayor Bosdin Leech presented the resolution to Abel on a scroll placed in a silver-gilt casket made by Elkingtons. On the centre panel it bore the initials AH encircled by oak and laurel leaves in enamel. The other panels contained civic emblems in relief: the mace, the mural crown, the civic sword and the lamp of learning. On the top were the city arms.

The mayor accompanied the presentation, which he said was 'better late than never', with words of his own about Abel's life and career. In response, Abel's theme was that there had been huge change, mostly for the better, but that there was still work to be done to improve the lot of the poor. He related how, perhaps prompted by his illness to take stock, he had recently made a record of the key features of his public life possibly using the official handbook, as he referred to it a little later. He reflected on the individuals with whom he had worked, in particular Richard Cobden, Corn Law repealer; John Edward Taylor, owner of the *Manchester Guardian*; Archibald Prentice, editor of the *Manchester Times*, 'a burly Scotsman, who somehow seemed rather out of place in our paving deliberations'; Alexander Kay, who purchased the manorial rights for Manchester from Sir Oswald Mosley; Thomas Potter and John Brooks, 'princes among merchants, and leaders in all liberal and progressive movements'; and Joseph Heron, town clerk and 'the wise director of the council almost from the day of its birth'. These were the figures who stood out in his memory as the makers of the city.

The event was followed by a lunch, and notably women were included, the mayoress attended and also Abel's daughter, Elizabeth Charlesworth, and all his seven grandchildren still in England. In reply to the mayor's proposal for his health, Abel gave the Corporation his blessing: 'I am called by the Mayor the father of the Corporation. I wish to say, as your father, that I bless you all.- (Laughter and loud applause.)' When Earl Spencer rose to speak, Abel would have been gratified to hear himself referred to by a member of the aristocracy as one of the city's 'oldest and noblest citizens'. Sir Edward Watkin MP also addressed the gathering and claimed that he had probably known Abel for longer than anyone else present, as their acquaintance went back sixty years. He recalled going as a very small boy to the shop in Oldham Street to purchase the *Poor Man's Guardian*, 'which he considered a most virtuous publication' and he likewise considered Abel, who sold it, 'a most virtuous man'. Similar sentiments were expressed by Oliver Heywood, who also referred to old Manchester.[36]

Abel lived on to attend the funeral of that illustrious Mancunian in March 1892, and he also was to see two more distinguished citizens, manufacturers and philanthropists Thomas Ashton and James Jardine, admitted to Manchester's Honorary Roll of Freemen in October. He would have been gratified to know that his hero, William Gladstone, had been presented at Braemar with a copy of the *Poor Man's Guardian* for 31 December 1831, the very paper for which Abel had gone to prison; Gladstone had demonstrated a thorough knowledge of the campaign to abolish the tax on knowledge 'and said how pleased he was to know that the man who had done and suffered so much was still one of Manchester's most honoured citizens and sons'.[37]

Conclusion

Abel was clearly very frail by New Year 1893; he telegraphed the mayor to inform him that he did not dare leave home to attend the council on 4 January, which the mayor attributed to the weather. Finally, at 7.30 on the morning of Saturday 19 August 1893, at the age of 83, he died of 'Heart disease' at Summerfield, attended by his daughter, Elizabeth Charlesworth.

Manchester mourned him. Even the *Manchester Courier*, so hostile particularly in his earlier, very radical years, was full of respect and praise:

> The deceased was a Manchester man in the fullest and truest sense of the phrase. In other words he was thorough in all his actions, shrewd in his business dealings, candid, and outspoken at all times. Patience and perseverance were qualities which distinguished him throughout his long life, and he was also very energetic, prompt, and painstaking in the discharge of his public duties.

It is a sign of how times had changed that the article then went on to relate sympathetically even his campaigns for a free press and Incorporation.[1] On the following day the magistrates registered their regret at Abel's passing, noting his diligence, and that he 'gave them the benefit of his advice'. He had never been short of opinions. But Alderman Lloyd added a personal thought that 'a more amiable, kind-hearted, and industrious man it would be impossible to know'.[2]

The *Manchester Guardian* included other details:

> The Corporation as it is to-day may be said to have grown up under his wing. He was the sole remaining relic of a generation which has passed away, and a repository of our local traditions for a period far beyond the memory of most people who are now living... he was naturally of a shy and retiring disposition, though when occasion required it he was never wanting in the courage necessary to place himself in the front... He loved regular and systematic work, and was most in his element when something had to be done. His attendance at his own modest place of business in Oldham-street went on with the regularity of

clockwork. He was never too proud for its functions.... For fifty years and more his name has been a household word in the homes of Lancashire.... His shop was a Pharos light, telling innumerable readers where they could get what they wanted and diffusing its beams over the whole country... He had his heart in the cause as well as in the business which hung upon it, and never in after years grudged the endurance of a penalty which had in it something of the merit, if not the splendour, of martyrdom... The ABEL HEYWOOD of those days was 'W. H. SMITH & SON' before their time...

When the council met on 6 September, the Paving Committee recorded a resolution which was infused with a genuine sense of loss. 'This committee feel that they cannot adequately express the loss which they have experienced by the removal from their midst of their dear friend and greatly esteemed colleague... his geniality of manner and his kindness of heart have truly endeared him to each member of the Committee.'[3]

Abel was buried on 22 August with his wives in Philips Park Cemetery, Bradford. In comparison with most ordinary funerals it was a grand affair, though not when compared with the great fuss made for wealthy men like William Neild or Oliver Heywood. The Corporation, including the mayor, aldermen and councillors as well as employees, gathered at the Town Hall ready to join the funeral cortège. Flags were flown at half-mast and Great Abel was tolled. As the hearse and mourning coaches entered Albert Square having travelled from Bowdon, the police band in front of the Albert Memorial struck up the 'Dead March' from Handel's *Saul*. There were thousands of people in the square and lining the streets to the cemetery; the route went through the working-class districts of Ancoats and Bradford; they had not forgotten the poor boy who had made good.

Heavy rain fortunately stopped for the interment. Those present at the burial also included Ben Brierley, alongside representatives of the Bowdon Local Board, the Rational Sick and Burial Association, the Manchester Reform Club, the Typographical Association, the Manchester Typographical Society, and the Queen's Building Society. There were about twenty employees from Abel Heywood & Son. The chief mourners were Abel's two sons, Abel and George Washington.

Mr Odgers officiated: 'We feel that our friend presents to us a type of character that is not easily replaced – that has in it something monumental and specially belonging to a period now fast closing upon us.' He then went on to eulogise Abel: he was abstemious and frugal, never pretended to be something he was not, and always acknowledged his past. However, the implication that he had not employed 'impressive speech or... clamour or emphasising of this or that' belied a knowledge of Abel which excluded the fierce debates of his earlier years.[4] Reflecting Mr Odgers's claim that Abel did not value self-indulgence or ostentation, the grave was marked by a very plain horizontal stone detailing only the names and dates of the three occupants, and Abel's status as 'Alderman and Freeman and twice Mayor of the City of Manchester.'

Abel had made his will three months after Elizabeth, his wife, in 1883. He had not been excessively rich; his personalty was worth under £25,000, which is substantial (around £1,250,000 today), but which pales into insignificance when compared to the over £323,000 left by his namesake Oliver Heywood in 1892. His executors were his wife and his two sons, and he left all his personal goods to his wife who of course had predeceased him. It was typical that he was not sufficiently interested in these goods to detail any of them. Moreover, what became of his casket from the Reform Club, his golden keys of 1877 and 1891, or the addresses with which he was presented in 1888 and when he was made a Freeman of Manchester, is not known. What really occupied his thoughts in 1883 was the 'nitty-gritty' of his business wealth.

This was shared between his five children, although his son and partner Abel Jnr was to be given the option to buy out his share of their business, and his land in Taranaki, New Zealand, was to be part of the share devised to his daughter Jane's family. Abel was mindful of the potential problems of women holding property, and provided for the trustees to pay each of his daughters the income of her share 'for her sole and separate use independently of her husband (if any) for the time being and of his debt control and engagements'.[5] It is clear that Abel wanted to give all his children, male and female, a just (though not necessarily equal) share in his estate.

Right up to his final year of life, Abel Heywood continued to serve the city he loved. His powers were declining, and the frustrations he experienced can only be guessed at. Nevertheless, Manchester had made sure that he felt appreciated and cherished, and his late speeches showed that he died in the knowledge that the 'shock city' had evolved into a great and proud metropolis which could boast modern amenities and a vibrant cultural life. And he could take huge satisfaction from his own role in that transformation. His recognition that there was still work to be done in terms of political rights and the conditions of the poor illustrated his understanding that he had played an important part in a long process, and that others would carry the torch forward into a future which was unknown, but which promised an illustrious destiny for Manchester which is still being fulfilled.

Joseph Johnson in 1860 thought that Abel Heywood was a 'Famous Man'. He was right in terms of his own time, but not in the light of hindsight. But his achievement was to be a man with a passionate vision who never ceased to strive to achieve it, and who, despite personal failings and errors of judgement, made real differences in the development of his city and beyond. He was one of the many who have created the society we inhabit today.

Abel's constant aspiration for Manchester was to improve the lives of the poor, and his work on the council, often unglamorous and hidden, helped to lay the foundations of the modern city by constructing streets, sewers and tramways. His agitation for a free press, universal suffrage, popular education and latterly women's rights contributed to political and social developments which today are taken for granted and are part of the fabric of civil society. The city's pride was enhanced by his support for art galleries, libraries and museums, culminating in the new Town Hall, his most unique and tangible legacy.

As a young man in the 1820s and '30s his aspirations led him inevitably into radicalism and this was a label which he bore proudly throughout his life. The argument that by the last quarter of the nineteenth century the evolution of the political climate meant that Abel was a thoroughgoing Gladstonian Liberal of the establishment, rather than a radical, can be challenged. Although he certainly espoused the rallying call of 'Peace, Retrenchment and Reform', insofar as he still supported such ideals as universal, including female, suffrage and compulsory, free and non-sectarian education, as well as the disestablishment of the Church of England, his radicalism was clear, although admittedly of the old school.

Despite being described as 'a very nice old man', Abel had not been without enemies; particularly in early life his outspoken declarations in public meetings, the council and the press brought him detractors and opposition. This was partly a matter of his radical beliefs, but also linked to his aggressive style in debate. The passion he exhibited in his pronouncements coloured his relations with Manchester political society. The forces that worked against his election to Parliament, and his ennoblement in 1877, were strong testimony to this antipathy. Late in life, however, his reputation for industry and kindness began to predominate and the accolades he received seem to have been widely endorsed.

Perhaps the life of Abel Heywood should be assessed on his own terms. The portrait by Munns, painted at the behest of the council in 1889, reflects his self-image. The full-length portrait shows a tall, lean and bewhiskered gentleman with a full head of thick hair, smartly dressed in honour of the portrait, with highly polished shoes, gazing piercingly but benignly at the viewer. Around his neck is a chain with spectacles, showing a love of reading. He is holding a folded newspaper, significantly a copy of the *Poor Man's Guardian*, and on the table beside him is another newspaper, both representing his lifelong dedication to the free press and political rights for all. The other aspect of his business is represented by two printed books, symbols of education. Behind him is a large painting of Albert Square and the new Manchester Town Hall. Thus did Abel want to be remembered by history; for his radical campaigning for the press, universal suffrage and education, his business, and his role in the construction of Manchester's municipal palace.

His record proves that he was brave and committed enough to risk not only the success of his business, but also his freedom, to achieve political, social and economic justice for ordinary people. Although there were occasional lapses where he allowed personal ambition, vanity or comfort to dictate his actions, he maintained his crusade to the end of his life and his candour and integrity won him widespread respect. His ambitious rise in society from the ranks of the very poor to the wealthy middle class and the accompanying influence was unusual in its degree. He was even more remarkable in that at the same time he maintained his power base in the working classes throughout his life, and never lost their support, whilst gaining the respect and backing of the radical and liberal middle class, and even on occasion the grudging admiration of middle-class conservatives.

The portrait and the record may have been largely forgotten, but Abel Heywood, always aware of posterity, sent a message to the future citizens of Manchester which is still in evidence today. It would surely have delighted him that Great Abel, inscribed with Tennyson's words, still rings out every hour over the city, reminding its citizens of the great ideal to which he aspired; to 'ring out the false, ring in the true'.

Notes

Introduction

1. Martin Hewitt, *The Emergence of Stability in the Industrial City, Manchester, 1832–67* (Cambridge University Press, 1996), p. 240.

1   In the shadow of Peterloo: Genesis of a Radical

1. A. Briggs, *Victorian Cities* (Penguin, 1990), pp. 88–97. Manchester was not officially designated a city until 1853.
2. Cited in Alan Kidd, *Manchester* (Carnegie Publishing, Lancaster, 2006), pp. 31, 89–91.
3. *N[orthern] S[tar]* 9 November 1839 [Newspaper transcript (c) The British Library Board. All rights reserved. With thanks to The British Newspaper Archive www. BritishNewspaperArchive.co.uk].
4. *M[anchester] G[uardian]* 27 March 1890 [courtesy of www.proquest.com].
5. Joseph Johnson, *Clever Boys of Our Time* (London, 1860), pp. 182–4. This is the most informative source on the young Abel, but its purpose was to inculcate in the young ideals such as 'self help', as popularised by Samuel Smiles in his book of 1859. Where Johnson's facts can be checked, other sources bear them out, but his interpretations may be more suspect; Abel himself probably provided much of the material, and therefore the version of events given is what Abel himself wanted to pass on to posterity; B.E. Maidment, 'The Manchester Common Reader – Abel Heywood's "Evidence" and the Early Victorian Reading Public', *Transactions of the Lancashire and Cheshire Antiquarian Society*, vol. 97 (2001), p. 100.
6. *M[anchester] T[imes]* 11 November 1876 [Newspaper transcript (c) The British Library Board. All rights reserved. With thanks to The British Newspaper Archive www. BritishNewspaperArchive.co.uk].
7. J. Hassall, 'The Bennett Street Sunday School, Manchester' (Unpublished PhD thesis, University of Manchester, 1986), pp. 96, 144–5, 109. For further discussion of the school, see Ian Shaw, 'Rev. William Nunn and the Bennett Street Sunday School Manchester, 1817–24', *Manchester Region History Review*, vol. 12, (1998), pp. 27–33.
8. John Heywood, possibly Abel's older brother, who seems to have left Bennett Street around the same time as Abel, shone at both mechanical and architectural drawing, carrying off first prizes in both in 1828, one of the few years in which prizes were recorded; J[ohn] R[ylands] U[niversity] L[ibrary of Manchester],

Special Collections, Mechanics Institution Minute Book, GB133 M1/1/1, pp. 297 and 298 [courtesy of the University of Manchester]. Johnson, *Clever Boys*, p. 184; Hewitt, *Emergence of Stability*, p. 168, citing W.T. Marriott, *Some Real Wants* (1860), pp. 12–13; JRUL, *Mechanics Institution 23rd Annual Report, 25 February 1847*, GB133 M1/2/1. For what follows on the Mechanics' Institutions, see M. Tylecote, *The Mechanics' Institutions of Lancashire and Cheshire before 1851* (Manchester, 1957), pp. 35ff, 129–89.

9. Paul A. Pickering, *Chartism and Chartists in Manchester and Salford* (London, 1995), pp. 4, 108–9, 143, 153–4, 31.
10. The *P[oor] M[an's] G[uardian]*, 31 December 1831 [Newspaper transcript (c) The British Library Board. All rights reserved. With thanks to The British Newspaper Archive www.BritishNewspaperArchive.co.uk].
11. MG 21 August 1893, p. 5; Johnson, *Clever Boys*, p. 187.
12. Abel Heywood junior, *Three Papers on English Printed Almanacs* (Manchester, 1904), pp. 19–20, 24–5.
13. *Select Committee on Newspaper Stamps* (HMSO, 1851), p. 385.
14. Johnson, *Clever Boys*, p. 186.
15. MG 27 March 1890.
16. MG 21 August 1893.
17. MG 21 August 1893.

2   The Chartist: National Notoriety

1. J.F.C. Harrison, quoted in Mick Jenkins, *The General Strike of 1842* (Lawrence and Wishart, 1980), p. 41.
2. The six points of the People's Charter were: a vote for every man over 21; secret ballot; no property qualification for MPs; payment for MPs; equal voting constituencies; annual elections.
3. Maidment, 'Manchester Common Reader', p. 105.
4. Edmund and Ruth Frow, *Manchester and Salford Chartists* (WCML, 1996), p. 97.
5. NS 22 August 1840.
6. NS 23 November 1844.
7. NS 13 November 1841; Pickering, *Chartism and Chartists*, pp. 153–4. There was a radical tradition of selling all sorts of miscellaneous goods to raise money for the cause; in the early 1830s Abel had sold 'Orator Hunt's Matchless Boot Blacking'. See also NS 10 October 1840.
8. NS 10 October 1840.
9. NS 28 May 1842.
10. NS 9 November 1839. Many Chartists espoused teetotalism, in theory at least, as a sign of their moral probity and seriousness. The problem was that many meetings were held in pubs, where the temptation to lapse was very great; Pickering, *Chartism and Chartists*, pp. 127–31.
11. NS 2 November 1839; NS 1 February 1840.
12. See Leonard Williams Levy, *Blasphemy: Verbal Offense Against the Sacred, from Moses to Salman Rushdie* (University of North Carolina Press, 1995), pp. 442–3.
13. The National Archives, HO 44/35/355-6; Charles Shaw to S.M. Phillips, 20 May 1840; See Pickering, *Chartists and Chartism*, pp. 150–1; Hewitt, *The Emergence of Stability*, p. 240. Joseph Johnson is having none of it, though, and he blames the Tory *M[anchester] C[ourier]*, which had 'in a dastardly spirit, actually accused Heywood of being a Government spy!' He goes on to say that the paper withdrew the accusation

under a threat of prosecution; Johnson, *Clever Boys*, p. 189. Nevertheless, his list of
those who supported Abel is headed by Sir Charles Shaw.

14. University College London, Chadwick Papers 1794/30-2, 8 February 1841 [Courtesy of University College London].
15. Maidment, 'Manchester Common Reader', p. 105.
16. NS 13 February 1841; 23 July 1842. The interest in the magic lantern was not confined to Abel. Charles Leslie Heywood recounts how Abel's elder brother, William, who ran an engineering works, in the 1850s gave many lantern lectures at the Mechanics' Institution; M[anchester] C[entral] L[ibrary] MSC 920/H, 'The Wonderful Magic Lantern', pp. 1–2 [Courtesy of Manchester Libraries, Information and Archives, Manchester City Council].
17. Eileen Yeo, 'Robert Owen and Radical Culture', in Sidney Pollard and John Salt, eds, *Robert Owen: Prophet of the Poor* (London, 1971), p. 111 refers to Abel Heywood as a bridge between Owenism and Chartism.
18. Hewitt, *The Emergence of Stability*, p. 240.
19. MG 11 July 1840. Although a man called Thomas Davies was charged with this assault, in the end the evidence was inconclusive and the case failed; MT 11 July 1840.
20. Pickering, *Chartism and Chartists*, pp. 101–3; MT 24 June 1843.
21. NS 12 March 1842.
22. NS 28 May 1842.
23. MT 18 June 1842.
24. L. Faucher, *Manchester in 1844* (published by Abel Heywood, 1844), p. 149.
25. NS 22 August 1840.
26. MG 8 October 1842; NS 8, 15 October 1842.
27. HO 44/38/655-8.
28. MC 6 June 1840 [Newspaper transcript (c) The British Library Board. All rights reserved. With thanks to The British Newspaper Archive www.BritishNewspaperArchive.co.uk].
29. HO 44/35/353-4; NS 6 June 1840; Hetherington and Watson in London were also being prosecuted on the same charge at this time; MC 6 June 1840.

3   The Businessman

1. MT 18 June 1842. The *Manchester Courier* on 4 December 1841 carried a large notice detailing the hardship and unemployment amongst printers and compositors, with over 1,500 unemployed in the town; one of the collection points for the relief fund was Abel Heywood's shop.
2. For Reach's account of Abel's shop, see A.B. Reach, *Manchester and the Textile Districts in 1849*, ed. C. Aspin (Helmshore Local History Society, 1972), pp. 37–40.
3. Maidment, 'Manchester Common Reader', pp. 114–16.
4. MG 8 July 1849, for example.
5. Martin Hewitt and Robert Poole, eds, *The Diaries of Samuel Bamford* (Sutton, 2000), pp. x, xii, xv, xvii, xxx. Quotations from the diaries use Bamford's own spellings and punctuation.
6. Ibid., p. 20.
7. Ibid., pp. 28, 29. Abel did make an effort to sell the new edition of *Passages in the Life of a Radical*, however; it was advertised in the *Manchester Courier* on 22 January 1859, for instance.
8. Ibid., p. 92.

9. Ibid., p. 97. I have been unable to ascertain the exact meaning of the word 'shab-rag', but its general import is clear enough. Bamford was illustrating the widespread antisemitism of the age.
10. Ibid., pp. 223–4.
11. Ibid., pp. 344, 353.
12. Johnson, *Clever Boys*, p. 194.
13. MC 9 April 1859.
14. MT 14 January 1871.
15. MC 16 March 1870.
16. MT 31 March 1866; MT 6 July 1872. Manchester by-laws had made school attendance compulsory for under 13s
17. MG 27 July 1864, 13 August 1864. Abel came in for the criticism that he was promoting his own interests in putting forward Albert Square as the site for the new Town Hall in October 1864.
18. MG 15 May 1858. C[heshire] R[egistry], will of Abel Heywood, dated 1883 and proved 1893, pp. 2–4.
19. George Milner, ed., *Bennett Street Memorials, A Record of Sunday School Work* (Abel Heywood, 1880).
20. G.B. Heywood, *Abel Heywood and Son Ltd., 1832–1932* (Abel Heywood, 1932), p. 6.
21. MT 6 October 1877.
22. MG 28 August 1879.

4   The Radical Liberal (1840–64)

1. NS 25 June 1842.
2. MC 6 August 1842; MC 13 January 1844.
3. MG 6 December 1845.
4. MG 16 January 1847.
5. MC 12 April 1848.
6. MC 26 January 1861; MT 26 January 1861.
7. MC 18 April 1863.
8. MG 31 December 1851. This is but one example of his support for adult education; another was his presiding at a 'Grand Promenade Soiree' to raise support for the formation of a People's College at the Music Hall on Charles Street; MT 2 February 1850.
9. MC 12 March 1859.
10. MT 12 November 1861.
11. MG 11 January 1851; 19 February 1851; 26 February 1851. In the end the workers subscribed something over £800 to the fund. See MG 4 September 1852 for the opening.
12. MC 18 January 1864.
13. MC 14 October 1854. Abel's claims for his Committee were valid, so far as they went, but a letter from 'a working man' published on 21 October in the same newspaper pointed out that although 'stench traps' had been put in the streets they had not been made compulsory in the houses, so that 'we get the full discharge of all the stink from the sewers drawn up into our houses'. Since the theory of miasma was still current in explaining cholera, the writer believed that the spread of disease was the result of 'stink from the sewer'.
14. MC 1 August 1857.
15. MG 21 June 1856.

16. MG 20 March 1852.
17. MC 1 April 1854; MG 5 April 1854.
18. MC 21 November 1863.
19. MT 20 March 1852.
20. MT 7 June 1845.
21. MG 26 September 1846.
22. MT 18 May 1853; MG 28 May 1853.
23. Arthur Redford, *The History of Local Government in Manchester*, vol. II, (London, 1940), p. 127.
24. MC 21 January 1854; MG 24 January 1854.
25. MG 22 October 1853.
26. MC 17 July 1852.
27. MC 2 October 1858.
28. MC 26 September 1864; MT 1 October 1864.
29. MT 4 August 1849; MC 12 July 1851.
30. MT 22 April 1854.
31. MG 22 April 1854; MT 22 April 1854.
32. MG 27 January 1855. A footnote to the war was discussion about whether to site captured Russian guns in the public parks; Abel's belief in peace led him to oppose this move.
33. MT 7 July 1860; MT 14 July 1860.

5   Police Commissioner, Town Councillor and Alderman (1836–62)

1. Pickering, *Chartism and Chartists*, pp. 73, 84; another who joined the Commission at the same time was Revd James Scholefield.
2. Derek Fraser, ed., *Municipal Reform and the Industrial City* (London, 1982), pp. 47–8.
3. MC 27 February 1841.
4. MG 24 June 1843.
5. MT 11 November 1876.
6. MT 17 April 1846.
7. MG 18 December 1852.
8. Redford, *Local Government in Manchester*, p. 66. Ironically, the new prison was too small to house all Manchester's prisoners, and some were still sent to the New Bailey.
9. MC 10 October 1846. The *Manchester Courier* had long opposed Abel Heywood as a radical, and on 31 October 1846 Middleton was described in its report as 'a formidable opponent… whose manly and straight forward conduct had won for him golden opinions throughout the ward'. His defeat in the election was predictably explained by the paper by the claim that he and his friends 'were too confident of the victory' and had therefore made insufficient effort in the campaign; MC 4 November 1846.
10. MG 4 November 1846.
11. MG 21 December 1844; 26 February 1848.
12. MC 7 August 1847.
13. MG 13 November 1850; MC 16 November 1850 was less exact: 'only three or four hands being held up against it'.
14. MT 16 November 1850.

15. MC 16 November 1850. The writer also referred to a claim in the *Manchester Guardian* that Abel called the clique 'the tea party'. This may refer to a rather obscure quotation in Abel's speech which talked of one man being controlled by another:
It was positively a fact that –
"What between *dinner* and *tea*,
It's crucified we shall be."
16. MC 25 January 1851.
17. MT 12 October 1853.
18. MC 18 October 1851. He also objected to using ratepayers' money to frame and glaze the council's address to the Queen, even though he feared he was seen as a 'general grumbler'; MT 18 October 1851.
19. MC 1 November 1851.
20. MC 21 February 1852. By this time, Abel was closely associated with the Unitarians, and by 1861 had begun to rent a pew in the Cross Street chapel.
21. MC 29 October 1853.
22. MC 26 November 1853.
23. MC 5 February 1854.
24. MG 20 June 1855.
25. MC 23 February 1856. Abel was seconded by his now frequent ally, Thomas Goadsby.
26. MG 7 August 1856.
27. MG 25 June 1857; MC 19 September 1857.
28. MC 13 March 1852.
29. MG 8 October 1859. The ragged school project was mentioned in the interview and Mackie certainly expressed a desire to see it through, and the council obligingly supported him against Abel and others.
30. MC 29 October 1859. Abel's stance appears to have done him no harm in the council; his term as alderman was up in November 1859, but he was re-elected easily with forty-two votes.
31. MG 19 January 1860; MT 21 January 1860; MC 21 January 1860; MC 28 January 1860. It is significant that all three newspapers reported the discussions in detail, illustrating the importance in the thinking of Victorian society of charitable efforts to relieve poverty.
32. MC 28 January 1860.
33. MG 3 March 1860.
34. MC 11 August 1860; MC 25 August 1860; MG 16 August 1860; MT 18 August 1860.
35. MT 24 November 1860; MC 26 January 1861.
36. MC 4 May 1861.
37. MC 18 March 1854; MT 18 March 1854.
38. MC 10 April 1858.
39. MG 21 March 1861.
40. MC 4 May 1861.
41. MG 10 November 1860.
42. MC 10 November 1860.

6   Political Aspirations: the Would-Be MP (1859)

1. MG 19 December 1846. The Tory *Manchester Courier* and the liberal *Manchester Guardian* claimed he acted as a member of the Reform Association, which had voted seventeen to seven to support Bright's candidacy; MC 19 December 1846, MG 19 December 1846.

2.   MG 7 August 1847.

3.   MG 3 May 1848. The move towards 'incrementalism' with regard to the suffrage here exemplified became much stronger in the 1850s; for a general discussion of the preparedness of radicals to countenance more moderate reforms as an instalment, see Hewitt, *Emergence of Stability*, chapters 8 and 9.

4.   MT 12 December 1849; it is always notable that ladies did not attend any of these kinds of functions. It was also reported in the *Manchester Courier*, but the Tory organ was much more negative, as might be expected, about this gathering of the liberal interest; MC 15 December 1849.

5.   MG 29 September 1851; MC 27 September 1851; Pickering, *Chartists and Chartism*, pp. 178–9; Hewitt, *Emergence of Stability*, pp. 286–9. Abel also sold tickets for the event.

6.   MG 27 January 1855, MT 27 January 1855.

7.   MG 20 March 1857.

8.   MT 28 March 1857.

9.   The Tim Bobbin stories were part of the local Lancashire dialect tradition, embodied in the foundation of the Lancashire Literary Club in 1862, of which Abel Heywood junior was a member. Many of their works were published by Abel Heywood.

10.   MT 19 March 1859; MC 19 March 1859. The Chartists were still holding open-air meetings, such as one in Stevenson Square on the preceding day, but these seem to have had little real impact, though they did decide to present a petition to the Commons.

11.   MG 18 March 1859.

12.   MG 11 April 1859.

13.   MG 16 April 1859. The *Manchester Courier* stated that Abel's candidacy, linked with that of Thomas Bazley, was intended to oust James Aspinall Turner as MP for Manchester; MC 16 April 1859.

14.   MG 12 April 1859.

15.   MC 16 April 1859; MG 13 April 1859.

16.   MG 14 April 1859. The 'League' refers to the middle-class liberals in the LRU meeting in the old Anti-Corn Law League rooms in Newall's Buildings.

17.   MG 16 April 1859; MC 16 April 1859.

18.   MG 19 April 1859.

19.   MC 23 April 1859; MG 21 April 1859.

20.   MG 25 April 1859. He also gained unanimous support in his Newton Heath meeting.

21.   MG 27 April 1859.

22.   'An elector of St George's ward' later in 1865 claimed that when a show of hands was called for Abel Heywood a large placard was shown saying 'Both hands up for Heywood.' This skewed the show of hands, it was stated; MC 11 July 1865; MC 30 April 1859; MG 30 April 1859. The *Manchester Courier* noted also that many spectators thought the show of hands was rather in favour of Denman and Heywood.

23.   MC 3 May 1859.

24.   MC 7 May 1859. In fact, when the case of poor old Mr Wood of Bowdon was discussed in the council, Abel had been against prosecutions for sitting on monuments.

25.   MC 21 May 1859.

26.   MT 7 May 1859.

27.   MT 17 December 1859.

7   Mayor of Manchester (1862–63)

1.   MC 18 October 1862.

2. MT 15 November 1862; MG 11 November 1862. For a detailed study of the period, see W.O. Henderson, *The Lancashire Cotton Famine 1861–5*, 2nd edn (Manchester, 1969).
3. Indeed, when the famine had abated in 1866 the workers were keen to show their appreciation for the help they had received from the Provident Society, in particular the work of James Smith, and Abel spoke at the meeting to raise a subscription for the purpose.
4. Henderson, *Lancashire Cotton Famine*, p. 109, citing *The Times'* account.
5. MC 6 December 1862.
6. MC 2 May 1863.
7. MC 21 November 1863, 5 December 1863.
8. Henderson, *Lancashire Cotton Famine*, p. 90.
9. MT 6 December 1862.
10. MG 1 January 1863.
11. MC 21 February 1863; when the American ship had berthed at Liverpool, the Liverpool Chamber of Commerce presented an address to the captain of the ship at St George's Hall, where Abel as Mayor of Manchester took part in the proceedings.
12. MC 3 January 1863. It is not clear how Abel managed to be in two places on the same evening, but presumably this meeting was earlier than the one in the Free Trade Hall, which continued till 11.20 p.m.
13. MC 29 November 1862, 7 February 1863.
14. MC 28 February 1863, 7 March 1863.
15. MG 17 January 1863; MG 4 June 1863; MC 10 October 1863.
16. MC 21 February 1863; MG 3 March 1863; MC 7 March 1863; MC 14 March 1863.
17. MC 14 March 1863.
18. MC 28 February 1863.
19. Henderson, *Lancashire Cotton Famine*, p. 109, citing *The Times* 14 March 1863.
20. MC 25 April 1863.
21. MG 15 July 1863.
22. MG 21 February 1863; *Hawera and Normanby Star*, vol. XXXXVII, issue 5019, 5 September 1899.
23. MC 6 December 1862.
24. MC 2 May 1863.
25. MC 18 April 1863.
26. MC 20 June 1863.
27. MC 17 October 1863, 24 October 1863.
28. MG 29 August 1863.
29. MG 30 January 1863; MC 31 January 1863.
30. MC 14 November 1863. At the Royal Institution exhibition later in the month, Abel's mayoralty was commemorated by 'a very characteristic portrait' by A. Bottomley; MC 28 November 1863.
31. MG 23 October 1876.

8 Liberal Elder Statesman (1860–76)

1. MG 10 November 1871.
2. MC 18 February 1860.
3. MG 15 March 1866; MC 17 March 1866.
4. MC 2 August 1866; MT 4 August 1866.
5. MG 5 October 1871.

6. MC 7 October 1869; MT 9 October 1869.
7. MG 20 December 1866; MT 22 December 1866.
8. MG 1 September 1871; MT 2 September 1871; MG 29 January 1872.
9. MG 29 January 1875; MT 30 January 1875.
10. MG 19 July 1869; MC 21 July 1869.
11. MT 4 March 1865.
12. MC 5 July 1866; MT 7 July 1866.
13. MC 4 April 1867, 10 April 1867.
14. MG 5 March 1868.
15. MT 13 May 1871.
16. MG 12 May 1868. Significantly, Reverend S. Robinson objected that 'it would be utterly impossible for him to attend to his own duties, and to find time to furnish the Health Committee with information of even a moiety of the houses which were unfit to be inhabited in the Rochdale Road district'.
17. According to the *Manchester Times* he also claimed that medical men no longer advocated the use of Turkish baths; MT 10 February 1866.
18. MT 1 November 1862, 5 November 1864; MC 2 February 1865; *Manchester Evening News* 11 February 1870 [Newspaper transcript (c) The British Library Board. All rights reserved. With thanks to The British Newspaper Archive www.BritishNewspaperArchive.co.uk.]; MT 1 May 1875; MT 24 December 1869; MC 3 June 1869.
19. MC 29 September 1864; MT 1 October 1864.
20. MG 15 February 1865; MT 18 February 1865.
21. MG 22 February 1865.
22. MT 8 April 1871.
23. MG 17 April 1873.
24. MT 2 November 1867, 9 November 1867.
25. MC 26 September 1867.
26. MG 4 July 1872.
27. MC 4 May 1865; MG 4 May 1865.
28. MT 27 January 1866.
29. MG 11 March 1861.
30. MC 6 April 1865; MG 6 April 1865; MT 8 April 1865. For a summary of Cobden's relationship with Manchester, see Simon Morgan, 'Cobden and Manchester' from www.academia.edu, accessed 2015.
31. MC 23 April 1867.

9   'Old Blazes': The 1865 Election

1. MT 21 January 1860; MC 4 February 1860.
2. MG 5 March 1860. According to the *Manchester Times*, Abel was less outspoken; it merely reported that he had said 'it would be a great boon to the working people if the noble lord would repeal the ratepaying clauses'; MT 10 March 1860.
3. MC 9 November 1864.
4. MT 18 February 1865.
5. MT 13 May 1865.
6. MCL, Wilson Papers, Jan.–July 1865, GB127.20/33
7. MC 6 June 1865.
8. MCL, Wilson Papers, GB127.20/33, 13 June 1865.

9. MG 19 June 1865.
10. 'Broadcloth' was a short-hand term for the well-off, who could afford the more expensive cloth for their clothing, whereas the poor man wore 'fustian'. For an analysis of this usage, see Pickering, *Chartism and Chartists*, p. 168. Abel himself elucidated his meaning by adding 'where the influence of working men or shopkeepers was of no avail'.
11. MC 20 June 1865; MG 20 June 1865; MT 24 June 1865.
12. MC 22, 24, 26 June 1865.
13. MCL, Wilson Papers, GB127.20/33, 25 June 1865.
14. The *Manchester Courier*, however, seems to suggest that he challenged Bright, especially as it was known that the latter had joined up with Bazley.
15. MG 27 June 1865; MC 27 June 1865; MT 1 July 1865.
16. MC 28 June 1865. In his St Michael's ward meeting the following evening Abel, answering an attack from Robert Rumney, head of Bright's election committee, said seventeen of his election committee of 1859 had not been informed of the selection meeting; MG 29 June 1865. On 8 July they named twelve of them; MC 8 July 1865. However, in the edition of 10 July one of them, William Bond, distanced himself because he and two of the others no longer lived in Manchester, so that he believed the committee had 'acted with perfect good faith'.
17. MC 29 June 1865; MT 1 July 1865. On 30 June at a meeting in Hulme, Abel added to his list of beliefs that he favoured the establishment of a conciliation court for the settlement of disputes between masters and workmen; MG 1 July 1865.
18. MC 30 June 1865; MG 30 June 1865.
19. MG 4 July 1865.
20. MT 1 July 1865.
21. MCL, Wilson Papers, GB127.20/33, 3 July 1865.
22. MG 4 July 1865.
23. MC 5 July 1865.
24. MG 7 July 1865; MT 8 July 1865; MC 7 July 1865. Callender seemed also to think that Abel would vote against Church disestablishment, and indeed his earlier replies might have encouraged that impression.
25. MC 8 July 1865.
26. MG 8 July 1865.
27. MC 10 July 1865.
28. MC 13 July 1865.
29. MT 28 April 1877.
30. MC 13 July 1865; MT 15 July 1865.
31. MG 13 July 1865.
32. MG 13 July 1865. The sort of control which the Bazley and Bright camp had tried to exert was used by the Liberals to great effect in the 1880s in Birmingham under Joseph Chamberlain, and was equally reviled by opponents. It was nicknamed the 'caucus' system.
33. MC 15 July 1865.
34. MG 14 July 1865. It is interesting to note that Abel did not wear broadcloth but fustian. This was not through lack of funds, but was a symbolic act of solidarity with the working classes, or more cynically a tactic to win popular support. See also MC 14 July 1865, where Abel is reported to have said even more specifically 'which would not allow Manchester to be represented by a man who did not wear broadcloth'.
35. MC 15 July 1865.
36. MT 15 September 1866.
37. MT 29 June 1867.

38. MC 4 April 1867.
39. MC 18 November 1867.
40. MG 8 July 1867; MC 22 July 1867; MT 21 September 1867.
41. MC 14 November 1867.
42. MG 15 November 1867. This was not the only time that Abel stood up for the Jews.
43. MC 27 November 1867.
44. MT 12 February 1876.
45. MG 11 February 1876; MC 16 February 1876.
46. MG 21 August 1893. 'Young England' refers to the group of radical Conservatives in Parliament, led by Benjamin Disraeli.

10 The Respectable Family Man

1. Terry Wyke, 'Publishing and Reading Books in Nineteenth Century Manchester', *Lancashire and Antiquarian Society*, vol. 97 (2001), p. 32; MCL, MSC 920/H, Memoirs of Charles Leslie Heywood, 'The Heywood and Pilkington Families', p. 1. Perhaps Abel invested in John's business as, despite the rift, Abel Heywood & Son still owned shares in John Heywood in the early 1960s: University of Reading, W.H. Smith archives, PA134/4, for instance.

2. Reach, *Manchester and the Textile Districts*, p. 61.

3. *Manchester Official Handbook, 1844–5, 1845–6, 1846–7, 1847–8*; Manchester Rate Books in the Manchester Collection, www.findmypast.com.

4. It is interesting to note that Elizabeth's children seem to have inherited their grandfather Abel's interest in the press, as they produced their own handwritten magazine, *The Literary Aspirant*, from 1881 onwards. Sixteen-year-old Arthur was the editor. I am grateful to Julia Piercy for this information.

5. JRUL, Axon Papers, Item 1245 [courtesy of the University of Manchester]. Manchester Record Office, Death Certificate of Ann Heywood, 26 July 1867 [Courtesy of Greater Manchester County Record Office].

6. *Illustrated London News*, 22 January 1887, p. 89, quoted in Steve Cunniffe and Terry Wyke, 'Memorializing its Hero: Liberal Manchester's Statue of Oliver Cromwell', *Bulletin of the John Rylands Library*, vol. 89, no. 1 (autumn 2012), p. 189.

7. CRO, Will of Elizabeth Heywood, pp. 206–9 [Courtesy of the Cheshire Record Office].

8. MC 14 September 1877; MT 6 October 1877.

9. Derek Brumhead and Terry Wyke, *A Walk Round Manchester Statues* (Walkaround Books, 1990), pp. 24–6; MC 24 January 1867; MG 24 January 1867.

10. MC 24 December 1868, 12 January 1887; MG 12 January 1887. As early as 1857 Elizabeth had loaned two carved ivory statuettes of Venus de Medici and Diana Robing to the Art Treasures Exhibition. In 1868 Abel got in an opportunity to make a short speech about the benefits of the School of Art for the artisans of Manchester.

11. MG 27 November 1876; MT 2 December 1876, 8 December 1877.

12. MG 27 July 1886; MC 5 August 1886.

13. MG 20 July 1868.

14. Census 1871; MC 1 April 1876.

15. MC 9 September 1893.

16. MG 10 February 1881; MC 22 June 1881, 25 June 1881.

17. Cunniffe and Wyke, 'Oliver Cromwell', p. 189; MG 26 November 1875.

18. MG 26 November 1875; MT 27 November 1875.

19. On 25 June 1874, the town clerk said 'It was admitted to be one of the finest statues that Noble had ever executed, and it would be a great ornament to the city'; MG 30 July 1869, 5 August 1869.
20. MC 26 June 1874.
21. MT 27 November 1875.
22. MG 20 November 1875. Cathedral worshippers were also reportedly aggrieved at its juxtaposition to the cathedral.
23. MG 27 November 1875.
24. C[ity] J[ackdaw] 3 December 1875.
25. Cunniffe and Wyke, 'Oliver Cromwell', p. 197.
26. Cunniffe and Wyke, 'Oliver Cromwell', p. 206.
27. MC 22 January 1887.
28. CRO Will of Elizabeth Heywood, pp. 210–11.
29. Will of Elizabeth Heywood, p. 213.
30. The obituary in the Unitarian journal *The Inquirer*, 22 January 1887 was probably written by Mr Odgers.
31. Census 1891. A coachman and his wife also still occupied the lodge.
32. *The Inquirer*, 6 January 1894.
33. Geoffrey Head, 'Cross Street Chapel in the Time of the Gaskells', www.cross-street-chapel.org.uk; D.W. Bebbington, 'Unitarian Members of Parliament' (April 2009), pp. 16–20, http://dspace.stir.ac.uk, accessed 2015. There is a detailed description of the Cross Street chapel in the 1820s in MG 16 April 1881.

11 The Building of the New Town Hall

1. JRUL, R182986.2.56, courtesy of the University of Manchester.
2. Stuart Hylton, *A History of Manchester* (Phillimore, 2010), p. 192.
3. MC 14 February 1863. He had originally proposed that it be sited in Piccadilly, but the Improvement Committee had rejected this idea.
4. MC 7 March 1863.
5. MC 5 September 1863.
6. MC 6 October 1864; MT 8 October 1864.
7. MC 6 December 1866.
8. MT 3 November 1866.
9. MC 7 February 1867; MT 9 February 1867.
10. MG 2 April 1868; MT 4 April 1868.
11. MT 4 April 1868.
12. MC 27 October 1868; MG 27 October 1868; MT 31 October 1868.
13. MC 27 August 1869.
14. MC 26 October 1869. See also MC 28 October 1869; MT 30 October 1869.
15. MG 2 December 1869.
16. MC 4 December 1869.
17. MG 31 January 1873; MG 6 February 1873.
18. MG 3 July 1873.
19. MC 4 May 1876; MT 6 May 1876.
20. MG 17 April 1873.
21. MC 11 April 1874.
22. MT 3 April 1875; MG 2 July 1875.
23. MC 28 January 1876.

24. MT 23 October 1875.

25. In fact, Big Abel developed a crack, the cause of which was unclear, and had to be replaced by another bell, Great Abel, which at eight tons was one and a half tons heavier than the original.

26. CJ 10 December 1875. This poem was a pastiche of one of the same name by Henry Wadsworth Longfellow.

27. In fact, Waterhouse wrote to the sub-committee in July and explained that he had never intended to charge commission on the mural work.

28. MG 2 March 1876; MC 2 March 1876; MT 4 March 1876.

29. MC 7 March 1876.

30. Julian Treuherz, 'Ford Madox Brown and the Manchester Murals', in John H.G. Archer, ed., *Art and Architecture in Victorian Manchester* (Manchester University Press, 1986), pp. 169–71.

31. MC 5 January 1884; Treuherz, 'Ford Madox Brown and the Manchester Murals', p. 177.

32. MG 8 January 1880.

33. MC 28 April 1876, 2 December 1876.

34. MT 10 February 1877.

35. MC 26 May 1876.

36. MT 3 June 1876; MC 6 July 1876.

12 Mayor of Manchester and the Inauguration of the Town Hall (1876–77)

1. MG 20 October 1876, MC 20 October 1876; MT 21 October 1876.

2. MC 11 November 1876; MT 11 November 1876.

3. MG 30 May 1877; MC 31 May 1877; MG 31 May 1877.

4. MG 2 December 1876.

5. MG 17 February 1877; MC 18 May 1877; MT 19 May 1877, 6 October 1877.

6. MG 8 August 1877.

7. MG 25 January 1877.

8. MC 26 October 1877.

9. MT 27 January 1877. At the other end of the social scale, Abel, by virtue of his office also chaired a meeting of the Manchester JPs to select one of their number to sit on the governing body of Manchester Grammar School; MG 29 June 1877.

10. MC 22 February 1877.

11. MG 25 November 1876, 20 January 1877.

12. MC 8 November 1877.

13. MC 13 November 1879, 14 November 1879.

14. MT 15 November 1879.

15. MG 8 November 1882.

16. MT 27 January 1877.

17. MC 29 September 1877; MT 29 September 1877.

18. MG 16 March 1876; MT 18 March 1876.

19. MC 12 April 1877.

20. MG 25 January 1877.

21. There were clear grounds for hope, it seems, as at some point Abel informed the public about a claim by Princess Louise that the Queen intended to visit Manchester; MC 30 April 1877.

22. MT 14 April 1877; MC 4 April 1877; W.E.A. Axon, *The Mayor of Manchester and His Slanderers* (Manchester, 1877), p. 4.
23. MT 14 April 1877.
24. Axon, *The Mayor of Manchester*, pp. 11, 14.
25. MT 14 April 1877; MG 12 April 1877; MC 12 April 1877; MC 16 April 1877.
26. CJ 21 September 1877.
27. MT 14 April 1877.
28. MC 4 April 1877; MG 12 April 1877, 9 April 1877.
29. *Free Lance* 14 September 1877.
30. MG 14 September 1877.
31. MG 14 September 1877.
32. MT 15 September 1877.
33. CJ 14 September 1877.
34. MC 15 September 1877, which includes an extensive list of the principal male guests.
35. MG 31 August 1877, MC 31 August 1877; MT 1 September 1877.
36. MG 8 September 1877.
37. MT 6 October 1877. See Figure 11.
38. MT 22 September 1877. The report recorded the procession in minute detail.
39. MG 12 September 1927.
40. MT 6 October 1877.
41. MT 10 November 1877.

13 Swansong (1878–93)

1. George Basil Heywood, *Abel Heywood and Son Limited, 1832–1932*, p. 6.
2. MC 6 January 1888.
3. MC 2 January 1885.
4. MC 1 May 1880; MG 1 May 1880.
5. MC 8 January 1880, 1 April 1881.
6. MC 22 November 1877.
7. MG 3 July 1879.
8. MC 18 November 1880.
9. MC 15 October 1881; MG 27 October 1881, 9 February 1882.
10. MC 5 February 1880; MC 4 March 1880.
11. MT 26 April 1879; MC 19 July 1880.
12. MG 10 August 1882.
13. MG 14 September 1882.
14. MG 3 May 1887; MC 4 May 1887.
15. MC 22 June 1887.
16. MC 4 December 1890.
17. MC 17 December 1877.
18. MC 9 June 1879, 1 May 1891. In 1894, the Association noted Abel's death with regret, recalling that he had been a trustee for thirty-seven years.
19. Pankhurst's words in 1883 showed that he was clearly annoyed at how his suggestion had been handled by the Liberal council; MG 5 October 1883.
20. MG 13 March 1880. In the event, Abel seconded his nomination.
21. MC 3 April 1880; MT 3 April 1880.
22. MG 15 June 1880.
23. Edward Vallance, *A Radical History of Britain* (London, 2009), pp. 446–8.

24. MT 21 February 1885; MC 18 February 1885.
25. MC 12 February 1890, 22 February 1890. For a detailed discussion of Manchester Liberalism at this time, see James Moore, 'Manchester Liberalism and the Unionist Secession 1886–95', *Manchester Region History Review*, vol. 15 (2001), pp. 31–40.
26. Arnold Thompson, 'The Liberal–Unionist Secession', in William H. Mills, ed., *The Manchester Reform Club, 1871–1921* (Manchester, 1922), p. 80.
27. JRUL, MRC 1/2/1, pp. 2, 8, 12; MG 18 March 1890; MC 27 March 1890.
28. MC 14 January 1887.
29. MCL M901/28625, p. 387. Abel was back in harness on 26 January.
30. MG 21 October 1880.
31. MC 22 August 1888; MG 1 September 1888.
32. MG 10 September 1888.
33. MG 27 September 1888; MC 27 September 1888.
34. MC 7 May 1891, 12 May 1891, 13 May 1891, 15 May 1891, 6 June 1891, 16 July 1891; MG 23 October 1891.
35. MG 29 October 1891, MC 29 October 1891.
36. MC 14 November 1891, 28 November 1891; MG 28 November 1891.
37. MG 23 August 1893.

Conclusion

1. MC 21 August 1893.
2. MC 22 August 1893, MT 25 August 1893.
3. MG 7 September 1893, 4 September 1893.
4. MC 23 August 1893.
5. CRO, Will of Abel Heywood, p. 677.

Bibliography

Published sources

Archer, John H.G., ed., *Art and Architecture in Victorian Manchester*, Manchester University Press, 1986.

Ashton, Owen R., and Pickering, Paul A., *Friends of the People*, Merlin Press, 2003.

Axon, W.E.A., *Architectural and General Description of the Town Hall, Manchester*, Abel Heywood, 1878.

Axon, W.E.A., *The Mayor of Manchester and His Slanderers*, Manchester, 1877.

Banks, Mrs G. Linnaeus, *The Manchester Man*, Abel Heywood, 1896.

Briggs, Asa, *Victorian Cities*, Penguin, 1990.

Brumhead, Derek, and Wyke, Terry, *A Walk Round Manchester Statues*, Walkround Books, 1990.

Busteed, Mervyn, 'The Manchester Martyrs: A Victorian Melodrama', *History Ireland*, vol. 16, no. 6 (Nov–Dec 2008), pp. 35–7.

Cunniffe, Steve, and Wyke, Terry, 'Memorializing its Hero: Liberal Manchester's Statue of Oliver Cromwell', *Bulletin of the John Rylands Library*, vol. 89, no. 1 (autumn 2012), pp. 179–206.

Faucher, Leon, *Manchester in 1844*, Abel Heywood, 1844.

Fraser, D., ed., *Municipal Reform and the Industrial City*, London, 1982.

Fraser, D., *The Evolution of the British Welfare State*, 2nd edn, London, 1984.

Frow, Edmund and Ruth, in *Dictionary of Labour Biography*, vol. 6, London, 1982, pp. 141–4.

Frow, Edmund and Ruth, *Manchester and Salford Chartists*, WCML, 1996.

Henderson, W.O., *The Lancashire Cotton Famine, 1861–5*, 2nd edn, Manchester University Press, 1969.

Hewitt, M., 'Radicalism and the Victorian Working Class: the Case of Samuel Bamford', *Historical Journal*, vol. 34 (1991), pp. 873–92.

Hewitt, Martin, *The Emergence of Stability in the Industrial City, Manchester, 1832–67*, Cambridge University Press, 1996.

Hewitt, Martin, and Poole, Robert, eds, *The Diaries of Samuel Bamford*, Sutton Publishing, 2000.

Heywood, A., *Three Papers on English Printed Almanacs*, Manchester, 1904.

Heywood, G.B., *Abel Heywood and Son Ltd. 1832–1932*, Abel Heywood, 1932.

Hollis, Patricia, *The Pauper Press*, Oxford, 1970.

Hylton, Stuart, *A History of Manchester*, Phillimore, 2010.

Jenkins, Mick, *The General Strike of 1842*, Lawrence and Wishart, 1980.

Johnson, Joseph, *Clever Boys of Our Time*, London, 1860.

Kidd, Alan, *Manchester*, 4th edn, Carnegie Publishing, Lancaster, 2006.

Kirby, R.G., 'An Early Experiment in Workers' Self-Education, the Manchester New Mechanics Institution, 1829–35', in *Artisan to Graduate*, ed. D.S.L. Cardwell, Manchester, 1974.

Levy, Leonard W., *Blasphemy: Verbal Offense Against the Sacred, from Moses to Salman Rushdie*, University of North Carolina, 1995.

Maidment, B.E., 'The Manchester Common Reader – Abel Heywood's "Evidence" and the Early Victorian Reading Public', *Transactions of the Lancashire and Cheshire Antiquarian Society*, vol. 97 (2001), pp. 99–120.

Mansfield, Orlando A., 'W.T. Best, His Life, Character and Works', *The Musical Quarterly*, vol. 4, no. 2 (April 1918), pp. 209–49.

Marshall, L.S., 'The First Parliamentary Election in Manchester', *American Historical Review*, vol. 47, no. 3 (April 1942), pp. 518–38.

Mechanics' Institution 23rd Annual Report, 25 February 1847, JRUL GB133 M1/2/1.

Miliband, Ralph, 'The Politics of Robert Owen', *Journal of the History of Ideas*, vol. 15, no. 2 (April 1954), pp. 233–45.

Mills, William H., ed., *The Manchester Reform Club, 1871–1921*, Manchester, 1922.

Milner, George, ed., *Bennett Street Memorials, A Record of Sunday School Work*, Abel Heywood, 1880.

Moore, James Robert, 'Progressive Pioneers: Manchester Liberalism, the Independent Labour Party, and Local Politics in the 1890s', *The Historical Journal*, vol. 44, no. 4 (Dec. 2001), pp. 989–1013.

Moore, James, 'Manchester Liberalism and the Unionist Secession 1886–95', *Manchester Region History Review*, vol. 15 (2001), pp. 989–1013.

Nicholls, David, 'The Manchester Peace Conference of 1853', *Manchester Region History Review*, vol. 5, no. 1 (1991), pp. 11–21.

Official Catalogue of the Great Exhibition, London, 1851, II.

Pass, Anthony J., *Thomas Worthington*, Manchester, 1988.

Pickering, Paul A., *Chartism and the Chartists in Manchester and Salford*, London, 1995.

Pollard, Sidney, and Salt, John, eds, *Robert Owen: Prophet of the Poor*, London, 1971.

Prentice, Archibald, *Historical Sketches and Personal Recollections of Manchester*, 1851.

Proctor, Richard Wright, *Memorials of Bygone Manchester*, Manchester, 1880.

Reach, A.B., *Manchester and the Textile Districts in 1849*, ed. C. Aspin, Helmshore Local History Society, 1972.

Read, D., *Cobden and Bright*, Hodder and Stoughton, 1967.

Read, D., *The Age of Urban Democracy*, London, 1994.

Redford, Arthur, *The History of Local Government in Manchester*, vol. II, London, 1940.

Select Committee on Newspaper Stamps, London, 1851.

Shaw, Ian, 'Rev. William Nunn and the Bennett Street Sunday School Manchester, 1817–24', *Manchester Region History Review*, vol. 12 (1998), pp. 27–33.

Slugg, J.T., *Manchester Fifty Years Ago*, Manchester, 1881.

Smith, Harold L., *The British Women's Suffrage Campaign 1866–1928*, 2nd edn, Harlow, 2007.

Strange, Julie-Marie, *Death, Grief and Poverty in Britain, 1870–1914*, Cambridge University Press, 2010.

Swindells, T., *Manchester Streets and Manchester Men*, 5th series, Manchester, 1908.

Teagle, Frances, and Midgley, John, eds, *The Unitarian Congregation in Altrincham*, 1997.

Turner, Michaael J., *Reform and Respectability: The Making of Middle Class Liberalism in Early 19th Century Manchester*, Chetham Society, 1995.

Tylecote, M., *The Mechanics Institutions of Lancashire and Cheshire before 1851*, Manchester, 1957.

Vallance, Edward, *A Radical History of Britain*, London, 2009.

Wach, Howard M., 'Unitarian Philanthropy and Cultural Hegemony in Comparative Perspective: Manchester and Boston, 1827–1848', *Journal of Social History*, vol. 26, no. 3 (Spring 1993), pp. 539–57.

Wiener, Joel H., *The War of the Unstamped*, Cornell University Press, 1969.

Wyborn, Theresa, 'Parks for the People: the Development of Public Parks in Victorian Manchester', *Manchester Region History Review*, vol. 9, no. 4 (1995), pp. 3–14.

Wyke, Terry, 'Publishing and Reading Books in Nineteenth Century Manchester', *Lancashire and Cheshire Antiquarian Society*, vol. 97 (2001), pp. 29–49.

Wyke, Terry, *A Hall for All Seasons: A History of the Free Trade Hall*, Charles Halle Foundation, 1996.

Unpublished sources

Allaway, Jill, '"Paper Ghosts": The Almanack and the Year Book, 1790–1860', unpublished PhD thesis, University of Huddersfield, 2004.

Greaves, John Neville, 'The Last of the Railway Kings: the Life and Work of Sir Edward Watkin, 1819–1901', unpublished M.Litt. thesis, Durham University, 2002.

Hassall, J., 'The Bennett Street Sunday School, Manchester', unpublished PhD thesis, University of Manchester, 1986.

Love, Jonathan, 'A Grand Incarnation of Progress: A Study of Cross Street Chapel Unitarians and Their Disproportionate Contribution to Eighteenth and Nineteenth Century Manchester', unpublished BA thesis, Nottingham Trent University, May 2004.

Manuscript sources

CRO, Death Certificate of Abel Heywood, 21 August 1893.
CRO, Death Certificate of Elizabeth Heywood, 13 January 1887.
CRO, Will of Abel Heywood 1883, proved 1893.
CRO, Will of Elizabeth Heywood 1883, proved 1887.
Cross Street chapel, Pew Rent Book, 1860–71.
JRUL, Axon Papers.
JRUL GB133 M1/1/1 Mechanics' Institution Minute Book.
JRUL R182986.2.56 Poster of 1877, signed J. Ashworth.
Manchester Registry ARD47/366 Death Certificate of Ann Heywood.
MCL N228C; 229A Manchester Spectator.
MCL 920/H Papers of Charles Leslie Heywood.
MCL 1868, M296 The Town Hall Competition.
MCL GB127.20/33 George Wilson Papers.
MCL 28610, 28613 Highways Committee Minutes.
MCL GB 127.M79 Thompson Papers.
The National Archives, HO 44/35; HO 44/38.
The National Archives, MH 12/6042
University College London 1794/30-2 Chadwick Papers.
University of Reading PA134/4 WH Smith Archives.

Newspaper sources

City Jackdaw, Manchester Central Library.
Free Lance, Manchester Central Library.
Manchester Courier and Lancashire General Advertiser, www.britishnewspaperarchive.co.uk.
Manchester Evening News, www.britishnewspaperarchive.co.uk.
Manchester Guardian, www.proquest.com.

Manchester Spectator, Manchester Central Library.
Manchester Times, www.britishnewspaperarchive.co.uk.
Northern Star, www.britishnewspaperarchive.co.uk.
Poor Man's Guardian, www.britishnewspaperarchive.co.uk and Manchester Central Library.
The Hawera and Normanby Star, Vol. XXXVII, Issue 5019, 5 September 1899, www.paperspast. natlib.govt.nz.

Websites

http://dspace.stir.ac.uk/bitstream/1893/1647/2, D.W. Bebbington, 'Unitarian Members of Parliament in the Nineteenth Century.'
http://dx.doi.org/10.1080/09612020000200264, Eleanor Gordon and Gwyneth Nair, 'The Economic Role of Middle-Class Women in Victorian Glasgow', *Women's History Review*, vol. 9, no. 4 (2000), pp. 801–4.
http://heritagearchives.rbs.com/companies/list/alliance-bank-ltd-london-and-liverpool.html
www.academia.edu, Simon Morgan, 'Cobden and Manchester.'
www.ancestry.co.uk.
www.banxico.org.mx, Eduardo Turrent, Banco di Mexico, 'A Brief Summary of Banking in Mexico.'
www.branchcollective.org, Janice Carlisle, 'On the Second Reform Act, 1867', in *Britain, Representation and Nineteenth-Century History*, ed. Dino Franco Felluga.
www.britishnewspaperarchive.co.uk.
www.findmypast.com.
www.openlibrary.org.
www.paperspast.natlib.govt.nz.
www.proquest.com.
www.victorianpolicestations.org/sir-charles-shaw-and-the-watch-committee-1839-1845. html (accessed 2015).
www.victorianweb.org, 'The Manchester Murals, by Ford Madox Brown (1821–1893)', Jacqueline Banerjee.
www.victorianweb.org/history/pms/gladston.html.

Index

 LIVING VENTURES

Living Ventures Group are the proud operator of some of the most exciting brands in the UK restaurant and bar market.

Established in Manchester in 1999, we are proud to have helped keep the city's history and heritage alive through the sponsorship of this publication.